龍谷大学アジア仏教文化研究叢書Ⅲ

《編著》
中西 直樹
那須 英勝
嵩 満也

仏教英書伝道のあけぼの

Ryukoku University Research Center
for Buddhist Cultures in Asia Monograph Series,
Number 3
The Dawn of Buddhist Missionary Documents in English
compilation :
Naoki Nakanishi, Eisho Nasu, Mitsuya Dake

法藏館

はしがき

一八八〇年代後半、廃仏毀釈から立ち直りの兆しを見せはじめた仏教界において、若き仏教者たちは海外への仏教雄飛の志を抱いた。そこには、国家権益の拡大に向けた使命感、アジア仏教に対する偏見、教団利益誘導の姿勢がすでに介在していたものの、大きな社会変動に直面して旧態依然たる日本仏教の問題性を強く認識し、これの克服をめざす方向性を有していた。

本学・龍谷大学の前身校の一つ普通教校に、一八八八（明治二一）年八月頃設立された海外宣教会が、日本仏教の国際交流の先駆的役割をにない、翌年七月には英文機関誌『THE BIJOU OF ASIA（亜細亜之宝珠）』を創刊したことは知られている。しかし、これに先立つ一八八三年頃から仏教英書伝道に向けた動きは、すでにはじまっており、海外宣教会の設立以前に、赤松連城・南條文雄・ツループ（James Troup）らにより数種の英文で書かれた仏書（仏教英書）が刊行されている。

これら仏教英書は、神智学協会のオルコット（Henry S. Olcott）の『A BUDDHIST CATECHISM』とその邦訳『仏教問答』の刊行（一八八六年四月）に強い刺激を受けて刊行されたものであった。欧米での仏教への関心の高ま

i

りに呼応して、英語により仏教教義・真宗教義を説明する必要に迫られた結果であった。

しかし、現在、これら仏教英書は忘れられた存在となっており、所蔵している研究機関も、本学大宮図書館を含めわずかに過ぎない。そこで本書は、初期の仏教英書伝道に関する資料を復刻するとともに、これについての解説論文を付した。本書が広く読まれることを通じて、近代仏教が欧米の異文化に対峙して何を伝えようとしたのかが改めて考え直され、ひいては日本仏教の再生の一助になることを願ってやまない。

本書は、二〇一五年からはじまった龍谷大学アジア仏教文化センター（BARC）に所属する研究グループが、個々に調査・研究を進めるなかで生まれた共同研究の成果である。同センターには、九の研究グループがあるが、本書の刊行には、嵩満也先生を中心とする「明治仏教」班（G1・UB・S1）、中西を中心とする「戦時下日本仏教」班（G1・UB・S2）、那須英勝先生を中心とする「多文化共生」班（G2・UB）の三研究グループが関わった。

この三研究グループは、明治期・戦時下・現代と、主たる研究対象とする時代は相違する。しかし、多文化共生社会における日本仏教の課題と可能性を探るという共通の課題を追及するなかで、日本仏教国際化の起点となった初期の仏教英書伝道の調査・研究の必要性を痛感したのであった。今後、他の研究グループとも協力して前記の研究課題を深化させていきたいと考えている。

なお、資料の復刻にあたって、「真宗大意略説」（『興隆雑誌』第三號付録）は東京大学大学院法学政治学研究科附属近代日本法政史料センター（明治新聞雑誌文庫）所蔵本を、その他については個人所蔵の原本を使用した。記して深く感謝申し上げる次第である。

編集代表　中西　直樹

仏教英書伝道のあけぼの＊目次

はしがき……………………………………………………中西直樹 i

第Ⅰ部　解説論文編

仏教英書刊行の濫觴
　——オルコット『仏教問答』の刊行とその影響——……………中西直樹 5

復刻資料の解説……………………………………………那須英勝 33

赤松連城著「A BRIEF ACCOUNT OF "SHINSHIU"」について……嵩 満也 43

第Ⅱ部　復刻資料編

『A BUDDHIST CATECHISM』BY HENRY S. OLCOTT
（『仏教問答』）……………………………………………………… 3 (404)

『A SHORT HISTORY OF THE TWELVE JAPANESE BUDDHIST SECTS』（『仏教十二宗綱要』）………………………………… 79 (328)

『'TRUE SECT' OF BUDDHISTS』（『英文真宗教旨』）……………………………………293（114）

「A BRIEF ACCOUNT OF "SHINSHIU"」（「真宗大意略説」）…………………………345（62）

「龍谷大学アジア仏教文化研究叢書」刊行について………………………楠　淳證　408

編著者紹介　410

仏教英書伝道のあけぼの

第Ⅰ部　解説論文編

仏教英書刊行の濫觴
――オルコット『仏教問答』の刊行とその影響――

中 西 直 樹

はじめに

　一八八八（明治二一）年八月頃、龍谷大学の前身校の一つ普通教校に設立された海外宣教会は、日本仏教の国際交流の先駆的役割を担い、翌年七月には英文機関誌『THE BIJOU OF ASIA（亜細亜之宝珠）』を創刊した。しかし、それに先立つ一八八二年頃から仏教・真宗教義を英語で紹介しようとする動きはすでにはじまっており、海外宣教会の設立以前には、赤松連城・南條文雄・ツループ（James Troup）らにより数種の英文で書かれた仏教書（仏教英書）が刊行されている。

　一八八八年一〇月発行『教学論集』掲載の「英文仏教書」は、数種の仏教英書が日本でも刊行されている事実を踏まえ、インド・中国を経て長らく日本で停滞していた仏教が欧米へと弘通する時機を迎えているとの認識を示している。そして、さらなる仏教英書刊行の必要性を訴えている。この時期の英文仏教書は、神智学協会のオルコット（Henry S. Olcott）の『A BUDDHIST CATECHISM』とその邦訳『仏教問答』の刊行（一八八六年四月）に影響

を受けて刊行されたものであった。

本論では、オルコットの『仏教問答』が日本で刊行された経緯を検証しつつ、赤松連城らが仏教英書を刊行した意図と歴史的意義とを検討する。

一、日本仏教と神智学協会との邂逅

日本人で最初に神智学協会と接触したのは、真宗大谷派の僧侶笠原研寿であろう。笠原は一八八二（明治一五）年一〇月、英国留学の帰路にセイロンに立ち寄り、同地の神智学協会の支部を訪れている。笠原は同地での詳しい状況を書簡に認め、南條文雄に送っている。[4]それによれば、笠原の訪問の主な目的はアヌラーダプラの菩提樹を参拝することにあったようであるが、スマンガラと思われる人物にも会い、大乗・小乗の事について問答し、パーリ語を学ぶ日本人僧侶の現地留学の受け入れなどを要請している。

笠原は、神智学協会支部の訪問を当初から想定していなかったようである。現地のペレラという支部長の勧誘で支部を訪れ、オルコットの著書や協会規則書などを渡されたようだが、現地の仏教徒がオルコットを称賛する様を、「仏教徒ノ此人ヲ信用スルコト無量ナリ、生ガ予テ其名ヲ知ラザリシヲ怪ミタリ、田舎風ハ恕スベシ」と冷ややかに眺めている。また、現地の僧侶に対しても、「隣ニ一仏寺アリ、其僧来リ話ス、オルコットヲ讃嘆スルコト無量ナリ、少々狂気ノ由」といい、オルコットを支持する姿勢に共感を抱かなかったようである。この結果、あと数日でオルコットが来ることを理由に、出発の延期を求めるペレラらの説得も聞かず、「然レドモ生ハオルコットニ逢ハネバナラヌコトモナク、又法事行列ヲ見タクモナキ故ニ断然之ヲ去リタリ」と述べて現地を離れた。

笠原研寿が現地でのオルコットの熱烈な支持と神智学協会の隆盛を見聞しながらも、全く関心を示さなかったのに対し、日本から書簡を送り、神智学協会とのコンタクトを試みたのが水谷涼然であった。水谷は、一八八二年一一月一日にオルコットに書簡を送っており、これに対するオルコットからの返信を含めて、その後も神智学協会関係者から水谷宛に書簡が送られてきた。現時点で筆者が当時の新聞・雑誌から確認できた水谷宛の書簡は、次の四通である。

① 一八八三年一月一四日付、水谷同朋宛、エッチ、エス、オルコット書簡[5]
② 一八八三年一〇月二七日付、水谷君宛、神智学会社ノ書記ダモダル、ケー、マーバランカ書簡[6]
③ 一八八七年七月六日付、水谷涼然君宛、エッチ、エス、オルコット書簡[7]
④ 一八八七年一二月一四日付、水谷涼然君宛、神智協会書記エッチ、ドン、ダビット書簡[8]

二、水谷涼然宛書簡の検証

水谷涼然宛の上記四通の書簡から、神智学協会が日本仏教に何を求めたのかを検証しよう。①の書簡でオルコットは、『A BUDDHIST CATECHISM』（仏教問答）を同封して、その翻訳・出版を水谷に求めている。また、セイロン島でキリスト教布教に対抗して教育・出版事業を推進して仏教興隆に努めていること、そのための資金を必要としている状況が説明されている。そして、セイロン仏教を中心としてアジア諸国の仏教勢力の結集を図り、日本仏教とも提携したいとの希望が述べられている。この書簡を受けた水谷は、一八八三（明治一六）年三月に赤松連城を出張先の熊本に訪ね、書簡と『A BUDDHIST CATECHISM』を示した。赤松は同書の日本語訳を京都中学

校長であった今立吐酔に託し、一八八六年四月に至ってようやく日本語訳『仏教問答』が刊行された。

②の書簡は、①の書簡から約九カ月後に神智学会社書記マーバランカが発送したものであるが、この書簡が『教学論集』に掲載されたのは一八八六年七月のことであった。なぜ三年近く後になって書簡が公表されたのかは不明である。年月の誤植も考えられるが、『仏教問答』刊行が遅れたためや、松方デフレの関係で神智学協会のスリランカでの活動に応えられない経済的事情もあったのかもしれない。マーバランカは、この書簡で神智学協会の要求に応えられない経済的事情もあったのかもしれない。マーバランカは、この書簡で神智学協会の要求に応えられキリスト教進出の抑止に一定の成果を上げていることを強調している。しかし、資金不足に直面しており、「此四十万ルピーノ金額ヲ集ルニハ是非トモ他国ノ同胞ニ向テ協力ヲ仰カサルヲ得サル義ニ御座候」といい、具体的な金額を示して資金援助を申し出ている。さらに緬甸（ビルマ）仏教との提携が進行中であることも語られ、「日本錫蘭緬甸三国ノ仏教徒同盟ノ実功」が提言されている。注目されるのは、その提携に宗派性が障壁となることを次のように指摘している点である。

抑仏教中宗派ノ相異ハ僅ニ教中ノ小異同ニ過キス今日其源頭ト称スヘキ当地ノ教法危急ノ時ニ際シテハ宗派ノ異同ハ且ク御閣キ被下度候」凡人心ノ同シカラサルヨリタトヒ両人ノ間ト雖精細ニ同様ナルコト能ハス故ニ互ニ譲リ合テタ、同様ノ感覚ヲ喚起スルヲ以テ本会ノ基礎ト仕候

また、「所謂宗派ノ相違ト申スコトハ多クハ想像ノ上ニト、マリ候コトモ有之候是等行違ハ思想ノ交換ニ依テ氷釈可仕候其力為ニコロネル、ヲルゴット氏錫蘭所伝ノ説ニヨリ仏教問答ヲ出版被致候」とも述べている。確かに宗派性の克服は、キリスト教に対抗して国内外の仏教勢力を結集する上で重要な要素になったといえようが、宗派の

相違を単に「想像ノ上」や「行違」で片付けてしまうことに、宗派関係者は強い違和感を抱いたに違いない。この辺りに書簡が直ちに公表されなかった理由があったとも推察される。さらにマーバランカは、上述の目的の実現に向けて神智学協会のメンバーを日本へ招請することの必要性を訴えており、水谷に繰り返し「真宗法主」への具申を求めている。しかし、水谷がこの要求の実現のために動いた形跡は認められない。

オルコットらの日本招請は、この書簡の公表後さらに九カ月経過した一八八七年四月、平井金三がオルコットに書簡を送ったことで実現に向かった。③の書簡は、その三カ月後の七月六日にオルコットが水谷涼然に送ったものであり、前年一二月に撮影された印度霊智協会東洋図書館での集会の記念写真が同封されていた(本書カバーに掲載)。しかし、これに対する水谷の反応も不明である。さらに翌日、オルコットは平井にも書簡を出している。

結局、その一カ月後の同年八月には平井と佐野正道とが「米人ヘンリー、エスオルコット氏招聘義捐金募集広告」を発表し、オルコット招聘事務所が開設された。さらに一〇月には平井金三により神智学協会京都支部が設置され、一八八九年二月にオルコットらが来日した。

④の書簡は、平井により神智学協会京都支部が設置された直後に、神智学協会書記のエッチ、ドン、ダビット(後のダルマパーラ)が出したものである。この時期にオルコット招請事業が平井金三らによって進められつつあったことは神智学協会側も承知していたであろうが、文面に「オルコット氏著ノ仏教問答ヲ貴下ニ於テ日本語ニ訳述出版セシメ広ク貴国人民ニ幸福ヲ与ヘラレシハ実ニ我輩ニ於テモ欣喜ノ至ナリ」とあるように、日本語訳『仏教問答』刊行に関わった水谷に、改めて協力を要請したものと考えられる。

総じていえば、神智学協会からの協力要請の内容は、(一)キリスト教勢力への対抗のための協力、(二)アジア仏教勢力の結集、(三)超宗派的協力関係の構築に集約でき、そのための第一歩としてオルコットらの日本招聘が

あったと考えられる。

三、日本仏教の神智学観と対応

それでは日本仏教側は神智学をどのようにみなし、その提携要請にどのように対応したのであろうか。この点を検証する前に、まず水谷涼然の人物像から確認しておこう。

水谷への書簡の内、①②には単に「水谷」と記されるのみである。(12)③④の書簡では「水谷涼然」と明記されている。このため、吉永進一は天台宗の「水谷仁海」であったとしているが、③④の書簡では「水谷涼然」と明記されている。一八八七(明治二〇)年四月発行『令知会雑誌』の記事にも見出すことができる。(13)この記事では、「会員水谷涼然」が英国領事ツループから『真宗教旨』訳述の再訂書を贈られたことが記されている。ここから、水谷涼然が令知会の会員であったこと、本願寺派と関係の深いツループ(後述)とも密接な関係のあったことがわかる。また前述②の書簡で、マーバランカが「真宗法主」への提携具申を繰り返し水谷に求めていること、水谷がオルコットから書簡を赤松連城に見せて相談したことを考えると、水谷涼然が本願寺派の僧侶であった可能性が考えられる。

さらに今立吐酔の日本語訳『仏教問答』が刊行された一八八六年四月に、英語版の『仏教問答』も刊行されており、その奥付に翻刻出版人が「京都府平民 水谷了然」と記されている。日本語訳が仏書出版会から、英語版が仏典協会本局から同時期に別々に刊行されており、日本語訳の奥付に水谷の名はない。その経緯は不明であるが、水谷了然と水谷涼然とは同一人物ではないかと考えられる。このほか、水谷涼然は、一八八六年に『帝王護法録』(14)という本を刊行している。この奥付によれば、水谷は当時東京京橋区松山町に寄留していたようである。さらに一八

八八年九月発行『法之雨』掲載の「法雨協会」の特別会員にも水谷涼然の名前を見出せるが、住所は「兵庫県神戸市」と記載されている。

ところで、京都府内の本願寺派寺院のなかで、水谷姓で代々住職の名に「了」の一字を付するのが京都市上京区の順照寺である。この点から、水谷涼然（了然）は順照寺の出身であった可能性が考えられる。現時点でこれ以上、水谷涼然に関する情報は入手できていないが、おそらく水谷は、本願寺派関係者や令知会会員の協力を得て神智学協会と接触していたと考えられる。

水谷涼然が神智学協会との交流に先鞭をつけ、神智学協会側も水谷を日本仏教との提携の有力な窓口と考えていたのにもかかわらず、交流の当初以降、水谷に目立った行動を確認することはできない。その後、オルコットの日本招請は、一八八七年八月の招聘義捐金募集広告の発表によって平井金三・佐野正道の手に移り、両名は翌年一月『明教新誌』の広告で募集に応じた寄付者の氏名を掲出している。しかし、このなかにも本願寺派関係者の名前をほとんど見出すことはできない。目立つのは、阿部慧行・渥美契縁・江村秀山などの大谷派有力者・菊池秀言・奥村円心・太田祐慶・豊島了寛など同派の中国・朝鮮布教を推進してきた人物らの名前であった。

本願寺派ではその一方で、一八八七年三月に普通教校の教員松山松太郎がニューヨークの神智学協会のジャッジに書簡を送り、これを契機に欧米通信会が結成された。欧米通信会というアジア仏教との連携への関心は薄く、まして従来「小乗仏教」と蔑称してきた南方仏教となるとなおさらであったと考えられる。

おそらくオルコットらが示した提言のうち、キリスト教勢力への対抗については日本仏教各宗派で一致した協力が可能であったろうが、アジア仏教勢力の結集となると、宗派により意見の分かれるところであった。早くからア

ジア布教に着手していた大谷派は比較的、積極的な姿勢を示したが、本願寺派の姿勢は慎重なものがあった。とところが、一見「興亜」と「脱亜」に方向性を異にするかに見える大谷派と本願寺派も、その相違は決定的なものではなく、自宗派の勢力拡大という目的を根底に共有する戦略的相違に過ぎなかった。そして、日清戦争の勝利後に日本仏教の指導的立場を明確に意識してアジア仏教諸勢力と対峙したとき、両派の方向性は同一化していったのである(21)。また根底に自宗派の勢力拡大という強い意識を有している以上、オルコットらの主張する超宗派的結集に関しては、平井金三のような宗派性の希薄な者は別として警戒感が強かったと考えられる。

こうした事情から、特に一八八九年二月発行の三号「反省会雑誌」の論調は、平井金三と佐野正道のオルコット招聘事業に賛同できない旨を宣言した上で、次のように記している。

我々は兼てオルコット氏が印度の仏教を興復するに熱心なるを知り大に感服するところにして又氏の持説を聞き氏の信仰を知り且つ氏が生前運動の結果を見んことを欲するものなり然りも態々数千金を抛ちて氏を日本に聘くせんとまでには思はず我々は現今日本の仏教を以て西漸せしめんことを望み且つは自ら任するものなり思ふに発起者招聘の趣意は仏教は一地方の小教にあらずして将に全世界に伝播せんとする傾向あるものなり思ふに発起者招聘の趣意は仏教は一地方の小教にあらずして将に全世界に伝播せんとする傾向ある事実を示して以て日本仏教の信仰を回復せんと欲するもの、如しその発起諸氏か為法の精神は実に感するに余りあるも其の手段に至りては我々はそもそも(感服し難きものなり我々は発起諸氏が寧ろ自ら海外に渡航して大乗仏教の教義を宣布せんことを望むものにぞある(22)

であり、その際に宣布すべきは「大乗仏教」でなければならないというのである。さらに同年七月発行の二〇号は、横浜の英字新聞『ジャパン・メール』に掲載されたオルコットの『仏教問答』の批評を日本語訳して紹介している。

南條文雄氏ガ、本願寺ニテ教示サレタル仏説ト全ク反対セル箇所如斯多キニモ拘ハラズ、此ノ問答書ニ跋セラレタルハ、実ニ其奇態ナルニ驚カザルヲ得ザルナリ（中略）

問答書九十八ノ二節ニ問フ仏教徒ハ仏陀ノミノ徳ニ依リ吾々各人ヲ罪障ヨリ救済シ得セシメムルト考フル乎、答曰否、全ク然ラザルナリ、如何ナル人モ他人ノミニテハ罪障ヨリ救済セラル、能ハズ彼レハ自ラ其ノ救済ヲ計ラザルヲ得ズト。

此一問一答ニテ忽ニシテ日本仏教々旨ノ基礎トセシ阿弥陀仏観世音及他力中ノ自力ト称スル大旨等ハ概スルニ之ヨリ如何ニ成リ行クヤ、

カーネル雄ルコット氏ハ、寧ロ和合ヲ謀ラント欲シテ合従ヲ危殆ニセシニアラザル乎、抑モ吾人ハ阿弥陀仏ニ依ツテ救済セラル、トモ然ラザルトモ意ニ介スルニ足ラズト為ス乎(23)

この批評の筆者は不明であるが、『仏教問答』の内容が真宗教義と背反する点が多いことは容易に察しのつくことであり、そうした教義の相違を無視した連携が、「和合」ではなく「野合」に過ぎないという指摘には共感するところがあり、この批評を日本語訳して掲載したと考えられる。

四、赤松連城著『英文真宗大意』刊行の経緯

一八八七（明治二〇）年三月頃に発足した欧米通信会は、その直後にニューヨークからの照会に応じて、南條文雄訳『英文仏教十二宗綱要』、ツループ訳『英文真宗教旨』、赤松連城著『英文真宗大意』の三冊を送付した(24)。これら仏教英書は、オルコットの『仏教問答』日本語訳の刊行が進められるのと併行して、急ぎ準備されたものであった。その刊行には、宗派存立の意義を認めない神智学協会に対し、真宗教義と各宗教義を説明する意図がうかがえる。以下にこれら仏教英書刊行の経緯を検証しよう。

赤松連城は、一八八三年三月に水谷涼然からオルコット書簡と『仏教問答』を見せられた。しかし、オルコットと神智学協会の活動にすぐに賛同する気にはなれなかったようであり、そのときの感想を次のように記している。

余取テ之ヲ読ム書簡陳スル所大ニ我教ノ弘通ヲ謀ル者ノ如シ然レトモ同氏ハ何ノ因縁ニ由リ此ニ従事スルヤ将其「セヲソフィカル、ソサエチー」（神智学会社）ハ何ノ目的ヲ以テ之ヲ設立セルヤヲ詳ニセス(25)

その後、一八八三年八月上旬に赤松は、本願寺でフェノロサの訪問を受けた。フェノロサは、京都の寺社の什宝調査の一環として本願寺も訪ね、ビゲローも同席し(26)、その際に話は神智学のことにも及んだようである。赤松は、オルコットのことを報じた同年七月一五日付『ジャパン・メール』新聞の記事を示され、その一部がロンドンの『ポール・モール・ガゼット』紙にも転載されたこと、英国人シネットが『イソテリク、ブヂスム（秘密仏教）』を

著したことを聞いた。イギリス本国にも神智学が一定の広がりを見せているという確かな情報を得た赤松は、八月中旬、『奇日新報』に「仏教の西漸」を発表し、ここにオルコットの水谷宛の書簡と『ポール・モール・ガゼット』紙の記事の抄訳を掲載した。

『ポール・モール・ガゼット』紙の記事には、オルコットが英国政府に対し仏教保護を働きかけていく次のような報道がある。おそらく赤松は、こうした点には大きな期待を抱いたことであろう。

コロネルオルコットハ業已ニ載セシガ如ク現今我国ニ在リテ英領殖民事務局ニ出願シ錫蘭ノ仏教徒ノ保護ヲ政府ニ仰カント欲スルナリ其請願ノ落着ヲ得テ直チニ緬甸ヲ巡回シ国王ヲ説キテ彼国ノ仏教ヲ恢復センコトヲ計ラントス緬甸ノ事業稍緒ニ就クニ及ヒテ暹羅ヲ巡回シ遂ニ支那及ヒ西蔵ニ到ルナルヘシ

しかし、真宗僧侶である赤松が、同紙に延々と記されたオルコットが入信に至った神秘体験に心底から感銘したとは考えにくい。むしろ赤松の真意は、「余仏教西漸ノ縁アルヲ喜ヒ亦東洋弘通ノ人ナキヲ嘆ス」という記述が示すように、神智学の広がりを欧米での仏教興隆の一現象として紹介し、日本仏教への奮起を促す点にあったといえよう。このため赤松は、『仏教問答』の翻訳を本願寺派僧侶で京都中学校長であった今立吐酔に委ね、自身は『英文真宗大意』の刊行事業に当たった。

そもそも『英文真宗大意』は、一八七九年二月に本願寺を訪れた英国議員リードの求めに応じて真宗教義を示すために書かれたものであった。リードは海軍卿川村純義の案内で広島や関西各地を訪問し、二月二七日には本願寺を訪れている。『英文真宗大意』は同年五月発行の『興隆雑誌』の付録として発行され、日本語訳は同誌や一八八

三年一〇月発行の『教学論集』にも掲載された。

欧米での仏教への関心の高まりを知り、赤松連城は、改めて一八八六年二月に『A BRIEF ACCOUNT OF SHINSHIU（英文真宗大意略説）を無外書房から一小冊子として刊行し、広く一般に読まれることを期したようである。それは、今立吐酔訳『仏教問答』刊行の二カ月前のことであった。

『仏教問答』にも赤松は「著言」を寄せている。しかし、次のように欧米での仏教への関心の高まりをヤンスとするものの、必ずしもオルコットの言動に賛意を表しているわけではない。

近来東西ノ交際日ニ親ク西人漸ク東洋ノ事情ニ通シ我教モ亦弘通ノ機ヲ生ス（中略）客年ヲルコット氏ノ英国倫敦ニ至ルヤ英人之ヲ基督教ノ保羅ニ比スト熱心ノ甚キ以テ想フヘシ今ヤ独リ該氏ノミナラス英ニシネット氏アリ米ニアルノルド氏アリ仏ニ独ニ往々奉仏ノ学士ヲ出ス経ノ所説果シテ虚カラズ因テ一言ヲ叙シ其書簡ヲ巻頭ニ掲ケ以テ縁起ヲ示ス卜云爾

『英文真宗大意略説』は、わずか四頁の小冊子であったが、英文で簡潔に真宗教義の説明を試みたもので、五月には普通教校の課業（講義テキスト）に採用され、六月に赤松自身が普通教校の法話で本書のことについて講じた。

こうした一連の動きを経て、翌八七年に結成された欧米通信会も、赤松連城の意向を受けていたと考えられる。

五、佐野正道と南條文雄訳『英訳仏教十二宗綱要』

大谷派関係者はオルコットの招聘に協力的であった一方で、『英訳仏教十二宗綱要』の刊行にも尽力した。日本語版の『仏教十二宗綱要』も同時刊行されており、同書は大谷派の小栗栖香頂を中心に各宗有力者の協力を得て編纂され、「一名東洋哲学及宗教概要」とのサブタイトルが付されていた。各宗の担当執筆者は以下のとおりであった。

総叙　小栗栖香頂
倶舎宗　佐伯　旭雅　成実宗　上田　照遍　律宗　上田　照遍
法相宗　高志　大了　三論宗　上野　相憲　華厳宗　小栗栖香頂　天台宗　上邨　教観
真言宗　小栗栖香頂　浄土宗　福田　行誡　禅宗　辻　顕高　真宗　赤松　連城
日蓮宗　小林　是純
（付録）倶舎宗　江村　秀山　（佐伯旭雅師ノ原稿延着ナルヲ以テ本文ヲ英訳ノ原稿ニ用ユ）華厳宗　卍山　実弁　（本文ハ文章高尚ニ過キ童蒙ニ解シ難キヲ以テ別ニ付録ニ掲ク）[33]

『仏教十二宗綱要』は、日本語版・英訳版（南條文雄訳）ともに一八八六年一二月に仏教書英訳出版舎より刊行された。出版人は佐野正道であり、佐野は一八八四年一二月に南條文雄を訪ね英訳を依頼している。[34] 後に平井金三とともにオルコットの日本招請の中心的役割を果すことになる佐野正道とは、いかなる人物だったのであろうか。佐

野正道は、『仏教十二宗綱要』以外にも、前後して次のような数種の出版物を手がけている。

大内青巒居士題字・佐野正道編輯『英語節用集』明教社　一八八四年十一月
編集兼出版人　大坂府平民　佐野正道　大坂府摂津国西成郡勝間村八十六番地

佐野正道訳『スペリング独稽古（ウエブストル氏）』大阪東洋館　一八八五年八月
訳者　佐野正道　大坂東区高麗橋五丁目一番地寄留

南條文雄著『印度紀行』一八八七年八月
出版人　大阪府平民　佐野正道　京都下京区第廿二組鷲尾町四十番地寄留

エッチ・エス・オルコット編『仏教金規則』東洋堂出版　一八八八年二月
翻訳者兼発行者　大阪府平民　佐野正道（住所同右）
平井金三校

佐野正道は、大坂府摂津国西成郡勝間村（現在の大阪市西成区玉出西）の大谷派長源寺に同寺住職藤枝正雲の次男として生まれ、佐野家に養子となった。修学の過程などは不明であるが、数冊の翻訳書を手掛けており、英語に堪能であったようである。一八八五年頃には大阪で僧徒英学校という学校を開いていたようである。また大内青巒や南條文雄らと交わり、出版事業を通じて護法活動に従事していた。佐野は一九一七（大正六）年二月に没し、その直後に遺族が新聞に出した死亡広告には、親戚総代の筆頭に藤枝正観（実兄）の名前が記されている。正観は長源寺住職を継職し、佐野の活動を支援したようであり、オルコットの招聘義捐金の寄付名簿にも名を連ねている。

佐野正道は、一八八四年七月に「僧侶宜シク人心ノ向フトコロヲ詳ニセヨ」という論説を『令知会雑誌』に寄せ

ている。そこでは、競争によって文明は進歩するというギゾーの主張を紹介した上で、次のように指摘している。

今ヤ基督教アリ進化説アリ而テ諸君ノ智力仏ノ威神力ニ及ハサル遠シ是レ実ニ人心ノ向フトコロヲ詳ニシ鞠躬黽勉同心戮力以テ他教他説ニ競争スルニ非スンハ奚ソ十全ノ勝ヲ得テ我カ説留此経ノ金言ヲシテ宇内ニ欽仰セシムルコトヲ得ンヤ我等方ニ粉骨摧身勉テ蘊奥ヲ発揚シ真理ヲ琢磨シ必勝ノ効ヲ奏スヘキノミ(38)

この当時、仏教教団側は教導職が廃止されたことで名目上の特権を失い、直接にキリスト教と対峙せざるを得ない状況に追い込まれていた。キリスト教に対する脅威が高まりつつあるなかで、佐野は同年一二月に南條に『仏教十二宗綱要』の英訳を依頼し、一八八六年四月頃には本格的な英訳作業に着手したようであり、当時発行の『令知会雑誌』には次のように記されている。

会員佐野正道氏は兼てより仏書英訳の急務なるを感じ居られしが愈今回該事業に取掛らる、由にて第一着に八宗綱要次に七十五法次に観心覚夢鈔等の順にて出版の計画及び資本の準備は粗出来したりと又翻訳の手順は最初漢文の八宗綱要に真宗日蓮宗等を加へ之を時文に訳し討論会議し後之を英訳し其上に精密の校閲を経たる後出版の見込なり会議者校閲者は凡て現今有名の学師及ひ西洋人にて帰仏の学士達に依頼せらる、ことなりに一大美挙と云ふへし編者の如きは指を屈して其成功の日を待つ所なり(39)

この記事から、佐野正道も令知会会員であったことが判明し、その活動には、令知会を通じて本願寺派・大谷派

の関係者の協力があったことがうかがえる。また佐野は南條文雄や令知会会員を通じて神智学協会に対して英語により日本仏教各宗の教義を得ていたことであろう。『仏教十二宗綱要』の英訳を急いだのも、神智学協会に対して英語により日本仏教各宗の教義を説明する必要性を痛感したためと考えられる。佐野は同年一二月に『仏教十二宗綱要』の英語版・日本語訳版を刊行したが、翌年七月に平井金三とオルコット招聘事業に着手している。佐野にとって、『仏教十二宗綱要』英語版刊行はオルコット来日前になすべき事業であったのかもしれない。

その後、佐野は京都に朝陽館を設立し、一八八九年一〇月に同館から創刊された『欧米之仏教』の編集に従事した。同誌第一編巻頭の「欧米之仏教発行ノ趣意」では、「抑モ仏教ノ欧米ニ伝播シ近世ニ至リ著シキ進歩ヲナセシ所以ハ全ク神智学会ノ設立アリシニ依ルモノナリ今ヤ神智学会ハ五洲都府勝邑ニハ殆ド此会ノ設立サラザルナク」と神智学会の隆盛にふれ、「欧米宗教改革ノ時機已ニ熟セリ」と記している。さらに神智学への「小乗教ヲ信ズルモノニシテ未ダ我邦大乗ノ真味ヲ知ラザル者ナリ」との批判に対しては、「小乗決シテ空理ニ非ルナリ」といい、「南方仏教徒ハ宛然世尊ノ遺誡ヲ遵奉シ戒律ヲ守リ威儀ヲ正フシ実ニ仏弟子ニ恥ヂザルナリ」と反論している。

その上で、雑誌刊行の意図を次のように結んでいる。

宜シク先ツ欧米仏教及ビ南方仏教徒ノ説ヲ討究シ又タ広ク日本現時ノ仏教ヲ欧米及ビ南方ニ知ラシメ以テ彼此仏教徒ノ連合ヲ謀リ円滑ニ宣教ノ方法ヲ議シ軋轢ヲ未萌ニ防ガザル可ラズ果シテ然ルトキハ独リ将来仏教ノ旺盛ヲ期スノミナラズ我邦西洋心酔者ノ迷夢ヲ攪破シ以テ国家ノ元気ヲ奮起スルニ足ラン(40)

佐野は神智学協会との双方向での交流を期して『仏教十二宗綱要』の英訳も手掛けたのであろう。その一方で佐

第Ⅰ部　解説論文編　20

野は、大谷派の改革運動にも関わったが、一八九一年一一月の『明教新誌』に、次のような記事を見出す。

○大谷派本願寺改革党の運動　同党の巨魁龍華空音宗制寺に依り奪班に処せられ入海雑誌の発行人平野恵粋氏は停班三年の処分を受け佐野正道氏は依願脱班となりしよりさしもに劇しかりし同党の気焔も全く消滅せしが如く（以下略）

大谷派改革党への宗務当局の処分に対し、自ら堂班を返上したようであり、以後、佐野は大谷派との関係を断ったようである。前述一九一七年の佐野の死亡告知によれば、友人総代として、藤沢幾之輔（衆議院議員・宮城県郡部選出）、櫻内幸雄（株式会社日本電気製鉄所社長、石巻電灯株式会社取締役など）、小林久治（明治電気株式会社・石巻電灯株式会社取締役など）の三名の名前が挙がっている。佐野の自宅は東京にあったが、石巻で死亡しており、晩年は石巻で電気事業に関わっていたと推察される。

六、ツループ訳『英訳真宗教旨』刊行の事情

『真宗教旨』を英訳したのは、英国領事ゼームス・ツループ（James Troup）であるが、その刊行に至った経緯は必ずしも詳らかではない。『真宗教旨』は、小栗栖香頂が中国布教実施のために漢文で著したもので、一八七六（明治九）年に真宗東本願寺教育課より刊行された。『英訳真宗教旨』の序文によれば、ツループが小栗栖の『真宗教旨』を読んだのは、一八八五年八月のことであり、その直後から英訳にとりかかったようである。同年一二月発

行の『令知会雑誌』には、次のような記事がある。

大坂及ひ神戸英国領事ゼームスツループ氏は嘗て大谷派本願寺に於て刊行せし真宗教旨を英文に翻訳し近々出版する都合にて同書中仏教の成語（隠顕頓斬等）にして解釈し難き箇所を南條文雄師に質疑致し越されたり編者曰仏教の大意を簡単に述へたる英文の書籍を出版することは目下の急務なりと余輩は常に論したることなりか之も亦先鞭を外人に著られたり（45）

ツループは南條に英訳の指導を仰いだようであり、『英訳真宗教旨』の表紙には校閲者として南條とともに赤松連城の名前も挙がっている。さらに翌八六年四月発行の『令知会雑誌』には、次のように記されている。

在神戸港英国領事ヂェームス、ツループ氏は大谷派の準一等学師小栗栖香頂師の編集にして同派本山教育課に於て刊行せし真宗教旨を鈔訳して昨年十月二十一日築地居留地三十三番地館で開きたる亜細亜学会に於て朗読せられたる講案に脚註を加え十七頁の小冊子として頃日南條師の許へ一本を寄せられたり（46）

この頃までには、すでに草稿本の小冊子の印刷が終了し、各方面に配布されていたようであり、同年四月発行の『奇日新報』にも次の記事を見出す。

〇大坂通信　四月五日在神戸英領事ゼームス、ツループ氏よりオン、ゼ、テネッツ、オフ、ゼ、シンシユ、オ

アー「ツルーセクト」オフ、ブヂスツ即ち予て同君が小栗栖香頂師編次の真宗教旨の英訳一冊を郵贈せられた り十七ページの小冊子にして印刷鮮明なり該書は訳文の間往々諸書より引用栖香頂師のツループ氏の脚注あり外人の初めて読むものには大に便利なるべし

しかし、公刊は二年近く遅れた一八八八年五月のことであった。公刊が遅れたのは一八八六年一〇月に起こったノルマントン号事件の影響もあったのかもしれない。この事件では、横浜港から神戸港に航行中のイギリス貨物船ノルマントン号が、和歌山県潮岬沖で暴風雨によって難破、座礁沈没した。その際、英国人ら外国人乗組員二六名が全員救命ボートで脱出したのに対して、日本人乗客二五名が船中に取り残され全員が溺死した。翌月、領事裁判権にもとづき海難審判を行なったのが、英国領事のツループであり、ツループは、日本人は英語が理解できず救助できなかったという船長の陳述を認めて、船長以下船員全員に無罪判決を下した。この事件に対する国民の反発は強く、ツループの英訳書の公刊も見送られたのかもしれない。

ツループはオルコットとも親交があったようである。一八八三年一月水谷に宛てたオルコットの書簡の末尾には、「末毫ナカラツループ君御帰着ノ上ニ候得者宜御伝声奉願候」と記されている。また、一八八七年九月の『奇日新報』は、オルコットの日本招請に「大谷派の渥美契縁氏又神戸の英領事ゼームス、ツループ氏等も大に賛成尽力さる、由」と報じているが、ツループ自身は神智学協会に直接的に関与していなかったようである。一方、一八八七年四月発行の『令知会雑誌』は、ツループのことを次のように記し、真宗信徒を自称した最初の西欧人としている。

神戸駐剳の英国領事ゼームス、ツループ氏が真宗教旨を訳述せられしことは嘗て報道したりしが這回再訂の書

を会員水谷涼然氏の許へ寄贈せられたるを見るに一頁ごとに皆仏教真宗信徒ゼームス、ツループと認め置かれたり欧人にして真宗信徒の称を用ゐるしは是を以て嚆矢とすべし(50)

ツループと本願寺派の関係は深く、一八八七年八月に『反省会雑誌』の創刊号に、ツループは禁酒・節酒を勧める文(松山松太郎訳)を寄稿しており、同誌には松山宛のツループの書簡、『英文真宗教旨』の一部も掲載されている(51)。こうして翌八八年五月に『英文真宗教旨』が公刊され、同年九月ツループは『縮刷蔵経』を贈られた謝礼のため本願寺派本山を訪問している(52)。本願寺派がツループに『縮刷蔵経』を贈ったのは、『英文真宗教旨』の翻訳事業への褒賞の意味があり、その出版に本願寺派側からの支援もあったと考えられる。

おわりに

オルコットらの神智学協会の活躍は、キリスト教への脅威が高まりつつあるなかで、一面において日本仏教界に大きな期待をもって迎えられた。しかし、その立場は、日本仏教が「小乗仏教」と蔑称してきた南方仏教に依拠し、神智学協会の提唱するアジア仏教勢力の結集に消極的な側(本願寺派)だけでなく、その提唱に賛意を表する側(大谷派)も、英語により日本仏教・真宗教義を説明する必要に迫られたのである。

こうして本願寺派と大谷派の協力のもとに編纂された仏教英書は、従来の教義解説書や談義本などとは異なり、外国語による新たな説明原理と内容を必要とした。『英文真宗大意略説』は、一八九三年のシカゴ万国宗教会議の

しかし、キリスト教への脅威が減退し、神智学協会も衰微に向かうと、その存在は忘れられていった。近代以降に大きな社会変動に対応した仏教教化・真宗教化の再構築には、いまだ大きな課題を残している。これを考える上でも、仏教英書の先駆的試みをいま一度検証してみる必要があるのかもしれない。

註

（1）海外宣教会については、中西直樹・吉永進一著『仏教国際ネットワークの源流――海外宣教会（1888年～1893年）の光と影――』（三人社、二〇一五年）を参照。また、同会の英文機関誌『THE BIJOU OF ASIA』第三巻（亜細亜之宝珠）は、中西直樹・吉永進一監修『海外仏教事情・THE BIJOU OF ASIA』第三巻（三人社、二〇一五年）に収録されている。

（2）管見の限りでは、英国人ロゼルスの英訳抄訳『発句経（ダンマハダ）』に英語と日本語訳を併記して出版した加藤正廓（本願寺派）『法の道芝』（島地黙雷・赤松連城同閲、一八八二年三月）が、英語表記された仏教書として日本最初のものと考えられる。

（3）「英文仏教書」（『教学論集』五八編、一八八八年一〇月五日）。

（4）「寄南條文雄書第七」（一八八一年一〇月一〇日）・「寄南條文雄書第八」（同月一九日）・「寄南條文雄書第九」（同月二七日）（『教学論集』二七～二九集、一八八六年三～五月。後、南條文雄編纂『笠原遺文集』〈博文堂、一八九九年七月〉収録）。

（5）「仏教ノ西漸」西京　榕陰道人（一八八四年八月一三・一五日付『奇日新報』）。ちなみに、榕陰道人とは赤松連城の号である。

（6）「寄水谷君書簡」（『教学論集』三二編、一八八六年七月五日）。

（7）「写真に関するヲルコット氏書束の抄訳」（『法之雨』九編、一八八八年九月一五日）。

（8）「海外仏教徒通信」（一八八八年二月二八日付『明教新誌』）。英国領事ゼームス、ツループ著『TRUE SECT OF BUDDHISTS（英文真宗教旨 和文付）』（一八八八年五月）にも「広告」として掲載。

（9）「デイヴィット氏の手簡」（一八八八年七月一六日付『明教新誌』）、「オルコット氏を招聘せんとす」（一八八七年八月二四日付『明教新誌』）。

（10）オルコット編『仏教金規則』（佐野正道訳、平井金三校、東洋堂出版、一八八八年）掲載広告。

（11）一八八九年一月二七・二九日付『奇日新報』掲載広告。

（12）吉永進一「仏教ネットワークの時代――明治20年代の伝道と交流――」（水谷大菩薩伝）（水谷仁海著『仏教要論』付録、新書社、一八八八年所収）。また水谷仁海の経歴に関しては、前掲『仏教国際ネットワークの源流』を参照。

（13）「外人の真宗信徒」（『令知会雑誌』三七号、一八八七年四月）。

（14）水谷了然編『帝王護法録』（無外書房、一八九六年）。

（15）『法之雨』九編、一八九八年九月一五日）。

（16）例えば、菅龍貫編纂『現行類纂両本願寺末派寺院明細録大全』（共益義会、一八九二年）によれば、順照寺の住職は「水谷了阿」となっており、記録所編纂『本派本願寺寺院名簿』（一九〇八年）に同寺の住職は「水谷了明」と記されている。

（17）「義援金募集広告」（一八八八年一月二・一四日付『明教新誌』）。

（18）大谷派の中国・朝鮮布教に関しては、中西直樹著『植民地朝鮮と日本仏教』（三人社、二〇一三年）、中西直樹著『植民地台湾と日本仏教』（三人社、二〇一六年）を参照されたい。

（19）「米国通信将に開けんとす」（『令知会雑誌』四〇号、一八八七年八月）。関係記事・書簡は、「米国神智学協会」（一八八七年八月一九日付『奇日新報』）、「反省会雑誌」初号（一八八七年八月）などに掲載。

（20）一八八七年七月九日付『奇日新報』掲載の「普通校と神智学会との往復」に「普通教校にては米国の神智学会社及び印度の神智学会社と通信するの道を開き以て東西仏教の気脈を通ぜんことを計画し」とあることから、欧米通

第Ⅰ部 解説論文編 26

信会もスリランカとの交流も視野に入れていたのかもしれない。しかし、松山松太郎のジヤツジ宛書簡に「合衆国民ノ如キ白人種ノ間ニ仏教ノ弘布スルハ小生等ノ甚夕希望スル処ニ御座候」と記されているように、欧米との交流により大きな関心が寄せられていたことは間違いないであろう（一八八七年七月一二日付『奇日新報』、『反省会雑誌』初号、一八八七年八月）。

(21) 前掲『植民地朝鮮と日本仏教』及び『植民地台湾と日本仏教』を参照されたい。

(22) 『反省会雑誌』三号（一八八八年二月一〇日）。

(23) 「雄ルコット氏仏教問答ノ駁論」（『反省会雑誌』二〇号、一八八九年七月一〇日）。この批評が対象としている『仏教問答』は、水谷了然が翻刻出版人となり一八八六年四月に仏典協会本局より刊行されたものとは別に、東京国文社より刊行されたものである。東京国文社刊行のものは未見であるが、引用箇所をみる限り、仏典協会本局刊行のものと大差はない。

(24) 註(19)参照。

(25) 註(5)参照。

(26) フェノロサの遺したメモから、一八八四年八月三日から七日の間に、フェノロサらは本願寺を訪問し、赤松連城と会い、その後も交流したと視察される（村形明子著「フェノロサの京都社寺什宝調査メモ──ハーヴァード大学ホートン・ライブラリー蔵遺稿（Ⅲ）──」《英文学評論》四三集、一九八〇年五月）。赤松とフェノロサとは、その後も親交を深め、仏教教義についても討論している（一八八四年十二月八日付『明教新誌』）。

(27) 註(5)参照。

(28) 本願寺派側の資料としては、『明如上人日記抄』前編・奥日次抄、六二二頁（本願寺室内部、一九二七年）、『明如上人伝』略年表一〇頁（明如上人伝記編纂所、一九二七年）、上原芳太郎著『明如上人略年表』三五頁（真宗本願寺派護持財団、一九三五年）などに記述がある。またリードと川村純義の動向は、当時の『朝日新聞』『読売新聞』などに記事が散見する。

(29) 『興隆雑誌』三号（一九七九年五月）、『教学論集』一編（一八八三年一〇月）。内容は福嶋寛隆ほか編『赤松連城資料』上巻・下巻（本願寺出版部、一九八二・一九八四年）にも収録されている。

(30) 『教学論集』二六編掲載広告(一八八六年二月五日)、「英文真宗大意の評」(一八八六年四月一日付『奇日新報』)。刊行後に本書は各方面に頒布され、海外へは南條文雄によりインド・アイルランド・イギリスロンドン等へ郵送された(「英文真宗大意」〈一八八六年二月一五日付『奇日新報』〉)。
(31) 米国人エッチ、エス、ヲルコット著『仏教問答』(京都中学校今立吐酔訳、仏書出版会、一九八六年)。
(32) 前掲『赤松連城資料』下巻所収「年譜」。
(33) 南條文雄訳『A SHORT HISTORY OF THE TWELVE JAPANESE BUDDHIST SECTS(仏教十二宗綱要)』(仏教書英訳出版舎、一八八六年)。
(34) 南條文雄著『南條文雄自叙伝』五一頁(沈石山房、一九二四年)には、一八八四年「十二月、佐野正道氏大阪より来り、十二宗綱要の英訳を余に嘱せられき」と記されている。
(35) 『僧侶英学校』(一八八五年四月九日付『奇日新報』)、「大坂通信」(一八八五年五月三日付『奇日新報』)。
(36) 一九一七年二月九日付『東京朝日新聞』朝刊。
(37) 註(17)。
(38) 『仏書英訳』(『令知会雑誌』二五号、一八八六年四月)。
(39) 『僧侶宜シク人心ノ向フトコロヲ詳ニセヨ』佐野正道(『令知会雑誌』四号、一八八四年七月)。
(40) 『欧米之仏教発行ノ趣意』(『欧米之仏教』一編、一八八九年一〇月)。『欧米之仏教』は、六編までの刊行を確認できる。また三編(一八九〇年三月)の巻頭には、発行元の朝陽館の館則が掲出されており、「一本館ノ主意ハ万国仏教徒連合ノ方法ヲ講シ汎ク仏教ノ光輝ヲ五洲ニ輝カスニ在リ」と記している。
(41) 現時点で『欧米之仏教』は、一編(一八八九年一〇月)、二編(一八九〇年三月)、五編(一八九一年七月)、六編(一八九一年八月)の存在しか確認できていない。一・二編の掲載は神智学協会関係を中心とする欧米人の論説の翻訳が中心であるのに対し、五・六編では、大谷派改革派の得明会の関係記事が誌面のかなりの比重を占めるようになった。
(42) 一八九一年一一月二日付『明教新誌』。

(43) 註(36)及び『人事興信録』(一九一八年九月刊行)を参照。
(44) 『東本願寺上海開教六十年史』五頁(東本願寺上海別院、一九三七年。中西直樹ほか編『仏教植民地布教史資料集成〈満州・諸地域編〉第一・二巻〈三人社、二〇一六年〉収録)。
(45) 「仏書英訳」《令知会雑誌》二一号、一八八五年一二月。
(46) 「英人真宗教旨を鈔訳す」《令知会雑誌》二五号、一八八六年四月。
(47) 「大坂通信」(一八八六年四月二五日付『奇日新報』)。
(48) 註(5)参照。
(49) 「京都通信」(一八八七年九月三日付『奇日新報』)。
(50) 註(13)参照。
(51) 『反省会雑誌』初号(一八八七年八月)。
(52) 『明如上人略年表』五一頁(沈石山房、一九二四年)。本願寺派は、一八八六年にもツループに「七祖聖教」一部を贈与している(『大阪通信』〈一八八六年三月一七日付『奇日新報』〉)。
(53) 『海外仏教事情』三九号(一八九三年一〇月)。
(54) 廣田一乗編『明治二十六年夏期講習会 仏教講話集』(仏教学会、一八九三年)。

【付記】本論執筆にあたり、佐野正道の出身寺院である長源寺(大阪市西成区)の住職藤枝正樹師より佐野と長源寺との関係について貴重な情報をご教示いただいた。記してお礼を申し上げる。

〔関係略年表〕

一八七九年（明治一二年）
二月二七日、英国議員リード、海軍卿川村純義の案内で本願寺を訪問。赤松連城、リードの求めに応じて『英文真宗大意』を執筆。
五月、『興隆雑誌』の付録として『英文真宗大意』が刊行。

一八八二年（明治一五年）
三月、加藤正廓（本願寺派）、笠原研寿（大谷派）、イギリス留学の帰路、セイロンに立寄り、現地の神智学協会支部を訪問（帰国後、一八八三年七月六日に笠原死去）。
一一月一日、水谷、オルコット宛に書簡を発送。

一八八三年（明治一六年）
一月一四日、オルコット、水谷宛に返信を発送し、『A BUDDHIST CATECHISM』を同封。
三月一三日、赤松連城、熊本県下へ出張のため山口県下筑後へ出張（三一日福岡県下筑後へ出張）。
三月中下旬、赤松連城、水谷了然（涼然）と熊本で会い、オルコットの書簡と『A BUDDHIST CATECHISM』を見せられる。
一〇月二七日、神智学会社書記ダモダル・ケー・マーバランカ、水谷宛に書簡を発送。

一八八四年（明治一七年）
七月一五日、横浜刊行の『ジャパン・メール』新聞。ロンドン発行の『ポールメールガゼト』新聞掲載の「セヲソフィストノ高僧」を抄出。
八月上旬、フェノロサ、京都を訪れ赤松連城と会談、ビゲローも同席。シネット著『イソテリク、ブヂスム（秘密仏教）』、『ジャパン・メール』新聞のオルコットの記事等が話題となる。
八月一三-一五日、赤松連城、『仏教ノ奇日新報』に『仏教ノ西漸』を発表。
一二月、佐野正道、東京の南條文雄を訪ね『十二宗綱要』の英訳を依頼。

一八八五年（明治一八年）
四月一八日、普通教校開校式。
八月頃、英国領事ジェームス・ツループ、小栗栖香頂編『真宗教旨』（漢文）を読み英訳に着手。南條らの指導を得て一〇月英訳完了し、亜細亜学会で朗読発表。

一八八六年（明治一九年）
二月、赤松連城、普通教校に反省会が創立。
四月六日、英国領事ジェームス・ツループ著『A BRIEF ACCOUNT OF SHINSHIU（英文真宗大意略説）』刊行（発兌：無外書房）。
四月、HENRY S. OLCOTT 著『A BUDDHIST CATECHISM』刊行（翻刻出版人：水谷了然、発兌所：仏典協会本局）。
四月、米国人エッチ、エス、ヲルコット著『仏教問答』刊行（京都中学校今立吐酔訳、発兌：仏書出版会）。
四月、英国領事ツループ、『英文真宗教旨』小冊子を南條文雄らに送付。
四月頃、佐野正道、『十二宗綱要』英訳事業に本格的着手。
五月一三日、『英文真宗大意』が普通教校の課業となる。

一八八七年（明治二〇年）	六月、赤松連城、普通教校の法話で『英文真宗大意』を講ずる。 七月、『教学論集』、水谷宛の神智学会社書記ダモダル・ケー・マーバランカ書簡（一八八三年一〇月二七日発送）を掲載。 一〇月二四日、ノルマントン号事件起こる。一一月一日神戸の英国領事ツループ、海難審判で外国人乗組員全員の無罪判決を下す。 一二月、南條文雄訳『A SHORT HISTORY OF THE TWELVE JAPANESE BUDDHIST SECTS』（仏教十二宗綱要）』刊行（発兌元：仏教書英訳出版舎）。 一二月、小栗栖香頂編纂『仏教十二宗綱要』刊行（発兌元：仏教書英訳出版舎）。
一八八八年（明治二一年）	三月七日、松山松太郎、ニューヨークの神智学会社社長ジャッジに書簡を送付。以後文通がはじまり、普通教校に欧米通信会が組織。 四月一九日、平井金三、オルコットに書簡を送付。 四月頃、英国領事ツループ、『英文真宗教旨』の小冊子再訂版を作成し、令知会会員水谷涼然に贈る。 五月三〇日、神智学協会書記エッチ・ドン・ダビット（ダルマパーラ）、平井金三へ返書を送る。 七月六日、オルコット、水谷涼然に書簡発送（印度霊智協会東洋図書館での集会の記念写真を同封）。 七月七日、オルコット、平井金三に書簡発送（八月、平井金三・佐野正道、「米人ヘンリー、エスオルコット氏招聘義捐金募集広告を発表」し、オルコット招聘に着手。 八月、『反省会雑誌』創刊。ツループ、禁酒の必要性を求める文（松山松太郎訳）を寄稿。ツループ訳『英文真宗教旨』も抄録。 一〇月七日、オルコット、平井金三らによる神智学協会京都支部の設置を承認。 一二月一四日、神智学協会書記エッチ・ドン・ダビット、水谷涼然宛に書簡を発送。オルコット著『仏教問答』の訳述出版と協会への賛助を求める。
一八八九年（明治二二年）	二月、『反省会雑誌』、オルコット招聘よりも欧米布教が重要との論説を掲載。 二月、オルコット編『仏教金規則』刊行（佐野正道訳、平井金三校）。 五月、"TRUE SECT" OF BUDDHISTS（英文真宗教旨 和文付）』刊行（英国領事ゼームス、ツループ訳 南條文雄・赤松連城同校）。 八月頃、普通教校に欧米通信会が海外仏教宣教会に改組（会長、赤松連城）。 九月、英国総領事ツループ、『縮刷蔵経』を贈られた謝礼のため本願寺を訪問。 一二月、海外宣教会の和文機関誌『海外仏教事情』が創刊。 一月一四日、『明教新誌』に「オルコット招聘の義援金募集広告」掲載、寄付者名簿等を記載。 一月一八日、オルコット、印度コロンボを出港。来日。二月九日神戸着。 七月、海外宣教会の英文機関誌『THE BIJOU OF ASIA（亜細亜之宝珠）』創刊。 七月、『反省会雑誌』に「ジャパン・メール」新聞掲載の「雄ルコット氏仏教問答ノ駁論」を日本語訳転載。

復刻資料の解説

那須英勝

文献解題（1）

『A BUDDHIST CATECHISM』BY HENRY S. OLCOTT（英文）　和文タイトル：仏教問答

翻刻出版人：水谷了然　発兌所：仏典協会本局　一八八六年四月出版

本書は、水谷了然（涼然）が一八八三（明治一六）年一月にオルコットから送られた書籍が底本となっていると考えられる。中西論文でも述べられたように、本書の日本語訳は英文と同月に刊行されており、国立国会図書館のデジタルコレクションで全文を閲覧することができる。その奥付には次のような内容が記されている。

『仏教問答』　訳述者：今立吐酔　出版人：阿部準輔　発兌：仏書出版会　一八八六年四月出版

オルコットの『仏教問答』は、改訂されて数種が刊行されたようである。『奇日新報』は、一八八八年末調査の神智学会の統計を翻訳・掲載している。その内容から神智学会の概要を知ることができる。以下にその全文を掲出

しょう。

「神智学会の統計年表」(一八八九年六月九・一一日付『奇日新報』)

本年一月発行神智学会の報告書に依り確然たる諸々の新統計を号を追ふて掲ぐること、為せり

◎万国学会の総数　一百七十三箇（昨年十二月三十一日調）

明治二十一年中増加せし会数を掲ぐれば

亜細亜　三箇　欧羅巴　四箇　北米合衆国　十三箇　新西蘭　一箇

更に新旧学会の総数を地理上に分配せば

錫蘭島　十箇　マドラス州　四十六箇　バンガル州　二十六箇　ボンベイ州　七箇

中央印度　四箇　但本部ハマドラス港に在りて此統計に入れず　其他印度　二十三箇

緬甸国　三箇　英国　四箇　スコットランド　二箇　愛蘭土　一箇　仏国　二箇

米国　二十五箇　希臘　一箇　和蘭陀　一箇　魯西亜　一箇　西印度　二箇

亜米利加　一箇　豪州　二箇　日本　未定一箇

計一百七十三箇

更に明治八年紐育府に神智学会の起りたるを始めとし学会進歩の度を示せば

明治九年　一　明治十年　二　明治十一年　二　明治十二年　四

明治十三年　十一　明治十四年　二十七　明治十五年　五十一

明治十六年　九十三　明治十七年　百〇四　明治十八年　百二十一

明治十九年　百三十六　明治廿年　百五十八　明治廿一年　百七十九

内六個は合併に付取消

◎昨明治廿一年中出版書数　三十九種（但龍動出版会社其他各区支部の刊本は此外と知るべし）

○仏教問答　昨年中出版せしもの六種

魯西亜語　瑞典語　加那利語　賓豆語　ベンカル語　英語（龍動版）

右にウルヅー語　日本語　パリ語　仏語　独語　支那語　緬甸語

其他印度地方の語を合せて都合十有九種の訳本あるなり

○機関新聞　昨年中発行せし者三種（但し本部より直接管理するもの、み他の支部の分は之を除く）

ゼ、フツデイスト新聞　ゼ、ヘスチア新誌　イニシエーション新誌

右に印度セオソフヒスト（神智学雑誌）仏国ロトス（蓮華雑誌）米国パツス新誌　英国リユーシフハー雑誌

及印度サラサビサンデレサ新聞　ヘラデユーワナ新聞　独逸国スフヒンクス新誌等を合せて凡て十種となるなり（外略す）

この記事によれば、一八八八年中だけでも六種の『仏教問答』が刊行されており、一九種の言語に翻訳されている。また、『奇日新報』は、三年前にロンドンのツルブナー商会より販売された『仏教問答』が四三版も重版され、発行部数が三〇万部に及んでいることを考慮すると、全発行部数は五〇万部を下らないと推計している。日本語訳も、原成美訳（一八八九年七月刊）、大久保一枝訳（法藏館西村七兵衛、一八九〇年十一月刊、書名『通俗仏教問答』）など数種が確認できる。

35　復刻資料の解説（那須）

なお、一八八六年三月一五日付『奇日新報』によれば、数校の仏教関係教育機関が本書を英語教育のテキストとして使用する予定であったようだが、実際に使用した事例は確認できなかった。また本書発行元の仏典協会本局の住所は「東京府芝公園第八号浄運院内」、和訳版発行元の仏書出版会の住所は「東京本郷区湯島天神町一丁目四十五番地」と記されている。『仏教問答』以外に、両出版所から刊行された書籍は確認できていないが、仏書出版会は京都に支会仮事務所を置いていたようであり、その住所は「三条通柳馬場東」となっている。いずれも短期間で閉鎖になったようである。

文献解題（2）

『A SHORT HISTORY OF THE TWELVE JAPANESE BUDDHIST SECTS』南條文雄著訳（英文）

和文タイトル：仏教十二宗綱要　発兌元：仏書英訳出版舎　一八八六年一二月出版

原著編集：小栗栖香頂

本書の日本語版も同時刊行されており、国立国会図書館のデジタルコレクションでも全文を閲覧することができる。その奥付には次のような内容が記されている。

『仏教十二宗綱要』編集人：小栗栖香頂　出版人：佐野正道　発兌：仏教書英訳出版舎　一八八六年一一月出版

本書が出版に至る状況については、イントロダクションの前に付された、南條文雄の英文の「序文」(Preface)

に比較的詳しく説明されている。

まず南條は本書の英語版の編纂を引き受けたものの、翻訳すべき原稿が全て揃わない状況で作業を始めることになり、さらに原稿そのものも担当者によって執筆のスタイルが統一されておらず、しかもそれらを・他の仕事をこなしながら短期間で英訳しなければならなかったという困難な状況があったことを正直に伝えている。また、実際に提出された原稿は、必ずしも英訳することを前提に書かれていなかったようで、それを英語にする際に、あまりにも複雑な記述が用いられているものについてはその部分を抄訳し、場合によっては一部を省略しなければならなかったことも記している。

なお、本書のイントロダクションから以下の部分の和文原稿の著者は、英文本文には記されていないが、南條の「序文」によると、イントロダクション、五章（三論宗）、六章（華厳宗）、八章（真言宗）の原稿は真宗の小栗栖香頂が執筆し、一章（倶舎宗）も真宗の江村秀山が、二章（成実宗）、三章（律宗）は真言宗の上田照遍、四章（法相宗）は同じく真言宗の高志大了、七章（天台宗）は天台宗の上郊教観がそれぞれ執筆したとある。九章以下のいわゆる「八宗」以外についての原稿は、福田行誠（九章：浄土宗）、辻顕高（一〇章：禅宗）、赤松連城（一一章：真宗）、小林是純（一二章：日蓮宗）と、各宗の学匠による執筆であることを伝えている。

また、これは本書の日本語版と比較していただければわかることであるが、一章（倶舎宗）の原稿は、真言宗の佐伯旭雅に、五章（三論宗）は真言宗の上野相憲、六章（華厳宗）は時宗の卍山（かずやま）実弁にそれぞれ執筆が依頼されていたようであるが、原稿が届くのが英語版の出版に間に合わず、止むを得ず別の執筆者のものを使用したことも記されている。なおこのうち、卍山以外の原稿は、日本語版の出版には間に合ったようで、それぞれの著者名で出版されている。

サンスクリット語の文献学者である南條は、本書の原稿の翻訳にあたり、漢語で記述された仏教思想の独特な表現を英語にするのにかなりの苦労をしたようであり、「序文」末尾に、本書の英訳については、W・S・ビゲロー（William Sturgis Bigelow）とB・H・チェンバレン（Basil Hall Chamberlain）の助力を得たことを記していることも興味深い。

本書発行元の仏教書英訳出版舎が他に刊行した書籍を確認できないが、一八八七（明治二〇）年二月には京都にも支局を設置したようである。同年二月二七日付『奇日新報』には「支局設立広告」が掲載されており、その趣旨を「今回南條文雄氏著訳英文日本仏教十二宗綱要出版致候処各宗諸大学林ノ教科ニ編入被成下候ニ付関西売捌上ノ便宜ヲ謀リ西京ニ支局設立致候」と記しており、仏教系諸学校のテキストとして販売するため京都に支局を置いたようである。仏教書英訳出版舎の所在地を「西京上京木屋町二条下ル七番」としている。一八八七年一二月二六日付『明教新誌』には、「都合有之当分の間本所亀沢町一丁目四十九番地渡部謙三方に於て御取引仕候」との広告を載せている。さらに一八八九年一〇月発行の『欧米之仏教』一編掲載の広告によれば、『仏教十二宗綱要』の和文・英文版、『仏教問答』の和訳・英文版などの販売が「都屋書店」の取扱いとなっており、その住所は「京都市下京油小路北小路下ル」と記されている。しかし、都屋書店のことは、『京都書肆変遷史』（京都府書店商業組合、一九九四年）にも記述はなく、単なる取次店として短期間しか存在しなかったようである。

ところで、『仏教十二宗綱要』は普通教校で成績優秀者への記念品としても活用されたようである。一八八七年六月五日付『奇日新報』掲載の「普通教校申報」には、「学力優等にして第三等賞（和文十二宗綱要の一部）を与ふる者四名（松谷慈乗、小林洵、平山寿海、西原百寿）なり」とあり、小林洵（後の高楠順次郎）も成績優秀者として本

文献解題（3）

『"TRUE SECT" OF BUDDHISTS（英文真宗教旨　和文付）』（英文・和文）

英国領事ゼームス、ツループ君著　南條文雄・赤松連城同校

発行者：船井政太郎　一八八八年五月出版

　本書は、その表紙に記されているように、中国布教推進のために小栗栖香頂によって漢文で執筆された『真宗教旨』を英国領事として神戸に赴任していたゼームス・ツループ（James Troup, 1840-1925）が、英文で紹介するために、一八八五（明治一八）年秋に東京で開催された日本アジア協会（The Asiatic Society of Japan）の総会（General Meeting）で発表した報告論文に、漢文で出版された『真宗教旨』の和文（抄出訳）を付して、書籍として出版されたものである。本書の和訳タイトルは『英文真宗教旨』とあり、また内容の大部分が漢文原文の翻訳ではあるが、正確には漢文『真宗教旨』抄出訳というべき性格のものである。

　本書の原漢文である『真宗教旨』の著者、小栗栖香頂は大分県妙正寺の出身で、一八七三年に「支那国布教掛」に任じられて中国布教に着手し、一八七六年には上海別院を創立した。『真宗教旨』は、一時帰国していた際に執筆されたもので、『東本願寺上海開教六十年史』（五頁）は、この間の事情を次のように記している。

　書を授与されている。また本書は、本願寺派の藤島了穏によってフランス語にも翻訳されている（「仏文十二宗綱要」〈一八八九年一月二日付『奇日新報』〉）。

日本仏教徒として、支那開教に先鞭をつけた東本願寺の小栗栖香頂師は、明治六年六月長崎を出帆して、初めて支那に渡航し、上海を経て北京に入り、龍泉寺清慈庵に於て本然法師等について北京音を習ひ、仏教の現状を観察しつつ「北京記事」を著して之を俗語に訳し、また雍和宮に洞濶爾胡図克図と交つて喇嘛教の意を以て上京就任した。かくて師は十一月「真言宗大意」を完成し、翌九年五月「喇嘛教沿革」十四巻及び漢文の「真宗教旨」一冊を編述し、支那開教の準備に資したのである（以下略）。

漢文版は、国立国会図書館のデジタルコレクションで全文を閲覧することができる。その表紙・奥付には次のような内容が記されている。

『真宗教旨』　真宗東派本願寺教育課蔵版　編集者：小栗栖香頂　校閲兼出版人：石川舜台　一八七六年十二月出版

本書英文の初出であるゼームス・ツループの報告論文は、一八八五年一〇月二一日に東京築地の日本アジア協会の図書室で開催された総会で "Tenet of the Shinshu, or 'True Sect' of Buddhists" として発表された報告論文であり、一八八六年に、同協会の年次報告書である *Transactions of Asisatic Society of Japan*, vol. XLV（１〜１７頁）に "On the Tenet of the Shinshu, or 'True Sect' of Buddhists" として出版されたのが初出である。

第Ⅰ部　解説論文編　40

先にも述べた通り、このツループの報告論文は、もともと漢文の『真宗教旨』に基づいて書かれたものであるので、ツループは本書に付した英文注36（二二頁）において、『真宗教旨』が中国での布教のために著されたものであることに読者の注意を促しているが、本書に付された和文にもその末尾に、

本書は元来支那布教の為めに著述せしものなれば他邦人に在ては或は適合せざるの条項あるを免れず故今爰に原文中より抜粹抄出して其の要領を記しぬ読者幸に其意を了せよ（和文一三～一四頁）。

と記されているように、この和文テキストは、漢文で書かれた原著とは異なる部分もあり、またその部分については原著と英文の記述との間に、内容の合致しないところがあることにも注意されたい。また原著の漢文が東本願寺の中国布教のために書かれたこともあってか、原文の第二章には東本願寺の厳如・現如法主についての記述があり、ツループの日本アジア協会における報告論文にも記されているが、本書では、この部分は英文、和文ともに削除されている。

最後に、本書には、『真宗教旨』の本文の訳だけでは理解しにくい真宗教義に関する用語や概念については、ツループによる、かなり詳しい注が追加されている。この注記については、英文注2（五頁）の末尾に「関連事項についての日本の専門家」から得た情報に基づいて記述したという断り書きが付されており、原文の読解に際してのツループの丁寧な作業の姿勢が現れているとともに、当時、英語圏ではほとんど知られていなかった真宗の教義についてどのような説明が必要であったかが、この注記を通して知られることも大変興味深いことである。

【付記】執筆にあたり、中西直樹先生には各文献に関する書誌情報やその他の資料などのご提供を受けましたことを拝謝申し上げます。

赤松連城著「A BRIEF ACCOUNT OF "SHINSHIU"」について

嵩　満也

一、「A BRIEF ACCOUNT OF "SHINSHIU"」執筆の動機

この「A BRIEF ACCOUNT OF "SHINSHIU"」という英文は、一八七九(明治一二)年五月八日に発行された『興隆雑誌』第三号の付録として印刷されたもので、英語で真宗教義の大意を概説した最初の事例であると考えられる。著者は、明治期に、西本願寺の教団の近代化や宗門の教育改革を推進した赤松連城である。また本書は、真宗英書伝道の嚆矢であるだけでなく、日本人によって著された最初の英文で書かれた仏教書であると考えられる。

同文執筆の直接の動機は、一八七九年二月に海軍卿川村純義の案内で本願寺を訪問した英国議員リードが、応対をした赤松に対して、真宗の大意と歴史について略説することを求めたことによる。そのことは、『興隆雑誌』第一号に、「明治十二年三月二十七日、英国議員リード氏我本山ニ来リシ時、本宗ノ大意及本刹ノ歴史ヲ聞カンコトヲ請フ。因テ英文ヲ以テ記シテ之ヲ贈ル」(『赤松連城資料』上巻、本願寺出版部、五二八頁)と記されていることから知ることが出来る。リードは、当時、英国造船局の専務であり、軍備増強をすすめていた明治政府にとり重要な

人物であった。①そのリードが本願寺を訪れた際に、英語で真宗教義の大意を紹介するよう求めたことから、急遽、短期間のうちに英語で同文を執筆して贈ったようである。また、『興隆雑誌』第三号の末尾に「右英国議員リード氏ニ贈ル所ノ原文ハ付録ニ在リ」とあることから、どうも赤松は、先に英語の文章を書き、その後自分でそれを日本語に訳したようである。

このように赤松が、先に英語で文章を書くことができるほど高い語学力を有していたのは、西本願寺の命により、一八七二（明治五）年からおよそ二年間、イギリス留学を経験していたからである。留学中の赤松の英語の上達ぶりについては、たとえば同じく西本願寺より海外教状視察団の一員として、同時期に欧州へ派遣された島地黙雷が、久しぶりにロンドンで再会した赤松について、「赤松ノ進歩驚愕セリ、通弁モ能ク出来、書物モ余程能ク読ム、頓テ大翻訳家トナルベシ」（『赤松連城資料』下巻「年譜」、本願寺出版部、六〇九頁）と手紙の中で書いていることから窺い知ることができる。また、明治初期に日本を訪れていたようである。三〇歳を超える年齢であったにもかかわらず、赤松は短期間に相当の英語力を身につけていたようである。また、明治初期に日本を訪れ Unbeaten Tracks in Japan（高梨健吉訳［一九七三］『イザベラバードの日本紀行』平凡社）という紀行記を書いた、イギリス人女性イザベラ・バートも、リードが本願寺を訪問する一年前の一八七八（明治一一）年に本願寺で赤松に会っているが、「赤松氏はとても紳士的で礼儀正しく、英語を非常にうまく話し、表現力豊かで、私には驚くほど率直に話してくれているように思えました」と、その英語力を高く賞賛している。

一八七四（明治七）年に日本へ帰国した赤松は、島地らとともに本願寺の教団運営において中心となって活躍した。とりわけ、イギリスの教育制度を学んでいた赤松は、宗門の教育改革を主導し、龍谷大学の前身である大教校校長、普通教校校長、仏教大学綜理を務め、後には学階の最高位である勧学にも任命されている。また、宗務政治

でも教団の近代化を推進し、内事局長や執行長など教団内の要職を歴任した。

二、「A BRIEF ACCOUNT OF "SHINSHIU"」への反響

最初に述べたように、「A BRIEF ACCOUNT OF "SHINSHIU"」は、『興隆雑誌』三号の付録として刊行されたが、同号には「真宗大意略説（訳文）」というタイトルで赤松による日本語訳も掲載されたことが分かっている。しかし、この最初の日本語訳は、現時点まで筆者は資料として目にすることができていない。ただ赤松の「真宗大意略説（訳文）」は、その後何度かにわたり活字化され、出版されている。

まず、一八八三年に刊行された『教学論集』一編には、日本語の「真宗大意略説（訳文）」だけが同じタイトルで収録されている。また、一八八六年には『A BRIEF ACCOUNT OF "SHINSHIU"（英文真宗大意略説）』というタイトルで、東京の無外書房から、英語と日本語の二つの文章を収録した単行本として出版されている。『教学論集』第二六編に掲載された広告文から、出版にあたり南條文雄が赤松の英文を校閲していることが知られるが、同書についても残念ながら未見である。また、一八八六年に刊行された『真宗大意』という本には、日本語の文章だけが収録されている。ただ『真宗大意』では、本文のタイトルは「譯文真宗大意略説」と若干『興隆雑誌』とは異なっている。

『興隆雑誌』第三号の付録として刊行された「A BRIEF ACCOUNT OF "SHINSHIU"」の英文には、何カ所か意味が取りにくいところや誤植が見られるものの、全体として赤松が伝えようとしていた内容は十分に伝わったと考えられる。そのことは、同文に対する国内外の反応からも知ることが出来る。

45　赤松連城著「A BRIEF ACCOUNT OF "SHINSHIU"」について（嵩）

たとえば、出版からわずか七カ月後の一八七九年一二月に、アメリカのキリスト教宣教会の雑誌である The Missionary Herald の Volume LXXV, Number 12 には、赤松の「A BRIEF ACCOUNT OF "SHINSHIU"」が、日本の仏教界において近代化がすすめられていることを示す一つの事例として紹介されている。どのような経緯で赤松の「A BRIEF ACCOUNT OF "SHINSHIU"」を入手したのかは不明であるが、記事では同文に見られる誤植やいくつかの文法的な誤りを訂正されたかたちで転載されている。記事では、真宗という仏教の宗派は、古くからある信条（蓮如の『領解文』を指すと考えられる）に新しい解釈を加え、キリスト教から幾らかの思想を付け足し、キリスト教宣教に対抗するための変革に努めているという紹介がおこなわれている。

また一方では、一八八六（明治一九）年に無外書房から出版された『A BRIEF ACCOUNT OF "SHINSHIU"（英文真宗大意略説）』が、刊行後各方面に頒布され、海外へは南條文雄によりインド・アイルランド・イギリスロンドン等へ郵送されたという記事が、一八八六年二月一五日付『奇日新報』に掲載されているが、真宗の側でも積極的に海外に向けて発信している。さらに、東京で刊行されていた英字独立新聞『The Tokyo Independent』では、一八八六年二月一三日号の記事が同書を取り上げて、赤松が祈禱などを行なわないと書いていることに対して、好意的な論評をしている。

さらに、一八八六年五月には、同書は赤松が校長を務めていた普通教校の英語の講義テキストとして用いられていることが記録に残っている。宗門内でも、大いに活用されたようである。ただ残念ながら、現時点では、そのテキストの原稿は確認できていない。また、一八九三年のシカゴ万国博覧会にあわせて開催されたシカゴ万国宗教会議の時には、日本仏教の代表者たちが持参し、参加者に配布した、英語で日本仏教について紹介する本の中の一冊として選ばれている。

このように、赤松が書いた「A BRIEF ACCOUNT OF "SHINSHIU"」は、初めての真宗教義の英書伝道の試みであったが、さまざまなかたちで海外に紹介され、反響を呼んだだけでなく、その後国際的に活躍することになる若い真宗学徒に大きな刺激を与えたと考えられる。

既に述べたように、赤松は「A BRIEF ACCOUNT OF "SHINSHIU"」の刊行と同時に、「真宗大意略説（訳文）」という、その日本語訳も書いている。両者の構成はほとんど同じであるが、内容を細かく見ていくと英文の方がかなり簡略な内容になっている。また、「他力」、「浄土」、「大願」、「摂受」といった、真宗教義の核心をなす概念については、「the power of others」と直訳的に訳している場合もあれば、「help through another」と説明的に訳している場合もある。また、英語圏の読者を意識してのことかもしれないが、一般にキリスト教で用いられる「mercy」や「paradise」といった用語を訳語として使っている。これらの点からは、赤松が前例のない真宗教義の英語翻訳作業の中で、特に翻訳語の選択に苦心していたことが見えてくる。

では、実際に赤松が書いた「A BRIEF ACCOUNT OF "SHINSHIU"」は、どのような内容を持っているのか。既に紹介したように、同文については、赤松自身が自分で「真宗大意略説（訳文）」という日本語訳を作成している。しかしながら、英文で書かれた内容は、赤松自身が「真宗大意略説（訳文）」の内容に比べると、説明が簡略なものとなっている。訳文とは謳っているが、慣れた日本語では、やはり日本人の読者を意識してか、直訳ではなく英語表現では十分伝えきれていないところまで言及したのであろう。また、いくつかの箇所で、日本語に訳す場合には、日本語としては十分伝えきれていないところまで言及したのであろう。たぶん赤松は、英語による説明順序を意識して原文を書いたものの、日本語に訳す場合には、日本語としてわかりやすい説明順序に変えたものと考えられる。いずれにしても、訳文と言いながらも、英語原文と日本語訳の間にはそのようなちがいが見られる。そこで参考までに、「A BRIEF ACCOUNT OF "SHINSHIU"」英語原文

47　赤松連城著「A BRIEF ACCOUNT OF "SHINSHIU"」について（嵩）

の意味を尊重しつつ、筆者が直訳的に日本語に訳したものを次に示しておきたい。

三、筆者による「A BRIEF ACCOUNT OF "SHINSHIU"」の日本語訳

「真宗大意略説」

赤松連城

この世界のすべての物事、抽象的なものも具体的なものも (abstract and concrete)、ある原因とさまざまな状況 (circumstances) により生まれそして滅する。現在の私たちの境遇は、前世の存在から現在に至るまでの間に自らが行ったことにその原因がある。

私たちの行為に、善悪あるいは優劣において程度のちがいがあるのと同じように、それらの行為によりさまざまな苦楽の程度をもった異なった果を生むことになる。私たち人間と生きとし生けるものは、休止することのない存在を持っており、ある存在の形態において死すと、また別の存在に再生する。従って、人がもしそのような悲惨な転生の境遇から免れようと願うならば、その因となっている貪欲や瞋恚といった煩悩を断じなければならない。仏教の根本の目的は、煩悩の滅尽 (extinction of passion) により、私たちにそのような惨めな境遇から救済 (salvation) を可能にしようとするところにある。この教義 (doctrine) が救済の因となる。救済はこの教義の果である。

この救済のことを、私たちは涅槃 (Nirvāna) と呼ぶ。涅槃とは永遠の幸福を意味し、仏の境涯のことである。しかし、すべての煩悩を断じることはとても難しいことである。しかし、仏教はこの目的に到達する多くの道を説こうとする。

インドの聖者である龍樹は、仏教にはこの世の道と同じように、行き易い道と行くことが難しい道があると説かれた。ある道は山道のように険しく、またある道は海を船で行くように楽しいものもあると説いている。これらの道は、二つに分けて整理することが出来る。一つは「自力（the power of others）」すなわち「他者の助力（help through another）」による道である。もう一つは「自力（help through self）」道であり、私たちの宗派は真宗と呼ばれるが、この言葉の意味は「真実の教え（Ture doctrine）」ということである。真宗は親鸞聖人により開かれた教義で、「他者の助力」の教義を説く。

さて、「他者の助力」とは何か。それは阿弥陀仏（Amita Buddha）の大いなる力である。阿弥陀とは「量ることの出来ない（無量）」という意味であり、私たちは、阿弥陀仏の光明と寿命は共に完全なものであり、また他の諸仏たちは阿弥陀仏の助力により本質を得たのであると信じている。それ故に、阿弥陀仏は諸仏の主であると呼ばれる。

阿弥陀仏は常にすべての生きとし生けるものに対して、量ることの出来ないほどの慈悲（mercy）をはたらかせ、諸功徳を成就し、浄土（Paradise [Nirvāṇa]）に往生（reborn）するために、阿弥陀仏に帰依するあらゆる人々に力を貸し、その影響力を及ぼそうと願っているのである。

私たちの宗派では、他の諸仏に対して心を向けることはない。ただ阿弥陀仏の大いなる願いを信じるだけである。阿弥陀仏の救済の願い（saving desire）を信じた時から、私たちは自ら助けるいかなる力も必要ではない、ただ阿弥陀仏の慈悲を心に入れて、来世の生では浄土に転入することを願うだけである。阿弥陀仏の慈悲を心に留めるために、阿弥陀仏の名前を称える（invoke）だけである。

私たちの宗派では、救済にあずかることおいて、僧侶と在家信者との間で区別をしない。その職業と仕事にお

て違いがあるだけである。そのことから、他の仏教の宗派では禁止されている僧侶の結婚も肉や魚を食べることも許されている。

さらに、私たちの宗派では、他のいかなる仏や、阿弥陀仏に対しても、祈禱、すなわち現世における幸福の祈願は禁止されている。なぜならば、現世での出来事は、他者の力によって変えることが出来ないからである。その上で、宗派の信徒に対しては、道徳的な義務を守り、互いに睦み合い、秩序と政府の法律を守ることを教えている。私たちの宗派には、教えを説く多くの書物がある。ただここでは、第八代目の宗主である蓮如上人が書いた次の信条（creed）だけを翻訳しておくことにする（以下蓮如の領解文〔creed〕の日本語については省略する）。

四、「A BRIEF ACCOUNT OF "SHINSHIU"」の構成と内容

「A BRIEF ACCOUNT OF "SHINSHIU"」において赤松は、まず仏教の根本教説である縁起の理法について明らかにすることから説明を始めている。すなわち、最初の三つの段落では、縁起の思想、善因善果・悪因楽果、解脱と涅槃という仏教の根本的な教説を取り上げている。次に赤松は、仏教には自力の道と他力の道の二つの仏道があることを明らかにした上で、親鸞が説いた真宗の教えは他力の道を説く教えであることを説いている。そして、阿弥陀仏がどのような存在であり、自分たちがどのようにして苦の世界から救われ、仏の涅槃の世界である浄土に往生することができるのかという、真宗教義の根本原理について説明している。そして、真宗信仰の特色として、阿弥陀仏一仏への帰依、他力の救いをただ信じ人間の側の自力のはたらくことがないこと、また他の宗派と異なり、僧侶が結婚し、肉や魚を食べることを認めてい

このように、赤松の「A BRIEF ACCOUNT OF "SHINSHIU"」は短い文章ではあるが、簡明直截に真宗の教えの特色がまとめられているばかりでなく、最初期の英語伝道の書物として、注目される資料である。

なぜなら、翻訳とは単なる言葉の置き換えではなく、原文が伝えようとする意味を他の言語の文法的な構文だけでなく、文化的・社会的な背景も含めた脈絡の中で表現しようとする作業である。従って、翻訳文とその原文との間には、一定の解釈の余地が生まれる。「A BRIEF ACCOUNT OF "SHINSHIU"」と「真宗大意略説（訳文）」の場合には、その両方を作成した人物が同じであるという点で、非常に稀なケースである。したがって、両者を比較することで、母語である日本語で書かれた内容と意図が、英語としてどのように表現され、両者の間にどのような対応関係と意味のズレが生じているかを考える格好の材料ともなる。ただここでの目的は、そのような翻訳そのものをめぐる議論を紹介することにはないので、そのことを指摘するだけに留めておきたい。いずれにしても、真宗教義の英語伝道の最初の試みとして「A BRIEF ACCOUNT OF "SHINSHIU"」は、非常に注目されるべき一文であることは確かである。

最後に、参考までに、一八九四（明治二七）年に出版された『真宗大意　全』に収められた、「譯文真宗大意略説」の原文を掲載しておく。

＊＊＊＊＊

ること、さらに救いにおいて僧侶と信徒の間にちがいはないことや、信徒に対しては、道徳的な義務を守り、互いに睦み合い、秩序と政府の法律を守ることなどが簡潔に語られている。そして最後に、真宗の代表的な聖教として蓮如の「領解文」をあげて、その英訳文を最後に付している。

[譯文眞宗大意略說]

佛教ニハ凡事及物、皆因及緣ノ結合ニ由テ生ジ、且滅スト教ユ、故ニ我等ガ現在ノ境界ハ、其原因等カ過去世ヨリ、今マテ作セシ所ニ存セリ、而シテ我等ガ今日ノ所作ハ、我等ガ未來世ノ境界ノ因ト爲ル。

我等ガ所作或ハ善或ハ惡、其優劣ニ等級アルガ如ク、種々ノ等級アル、種々ノ苦樂ノ果ヲ生ズ、凡人及其他ノ衆生、無窮ノ果報ヲ受ケ、一趣ニ死シ他趣ニ生ズ、故ニ人輪廻ノ苦境ヲ免レント欲スレバ、必ズ其原因ヲ斷ズベシ、其原因トハ煩惱ナリ、即チ貪欲瞋恚等是ナリ。

佛教ノ本旨ハ、煩惱ヲ斷尽スル法ニ由テ、苦界ヲ出離スルヲ得ントスルニ在リ、此法卽チ出離解脫ノ因ニシテ、解脫ハ卽チ此法ノ果ナリ、此ノ解脫ヲ涅槃ト稱ス、常樂ノ謂ニシテ、卽チ佛ノ境界ナリ。

然ルニ一切ノ煩惱ヲ斷尽スルコト、甚ダ難トス、然レドモ佛教ハ、此目的ヲ達スル種々ノ法門ヲ設ケリ、印度ノ聖者那伽閼刺樹那（此ニ譯シテ龍樹ト云フ）曰ク佛法ニ無量ノ門アリ、世間ノ道ニ難アリ易アリ、陸道ノ歩行ハ卽チ苦ク、水道ノ乘船ハ則チ樂シキガ如シト、此ノ如キノ法門、二途ニ分ツコトヲ得ベシ、一ハ曰ク自力、曰ク自ラ攝クルナリ、一ニハ曰ク他力、曰ク他ニ攝ケラル、ナリ。

我宗ハ眞宗ト稱ス、眞實ノ教法ト云フ意ナリ、見眞大師之ヲ開創セリ、卽チ他力ノ法門ヲ教ユ、今何ヲカ稱シテ、他力トスルヤトイフニ、是卽チ阿彌陀佛ノ大ナル力ナリ、阿彌陀トハ量ナキヲ云フ、我等此佛ノ壽命及光明、共ニ無量ナリト信ズ、又彼智慧及慈悲共ニ圓滿セリ、故ニ阿彌陀佛ハ諸佛中ノ王ト稱ス、阿彌陀佛常ニ一切衆生ニ於テ、無量ノ慈悲ヲ垂レ、彼佛ヲ信ズルモノヲシテ、功德成就セシメ、樂邦卽涅槃界ニ往生セシメントイヘル、大願ヲ示シ玉ヘリ。

我宗ハ自餘ノ諸佛ヲ念ゼズ、唯阿彌陀ノ大願ヲ信ジ、此苦界ヲ離レ、順次ノ生ニ於テ、彼樂邦ニ入ランコトヲ期

ス、彼佛ノ攝受衆生ノ本願ヲ信ゼシヨニ、自力自攝ヲ要スルコトナク、唯彼大悲ヲ心ニ念ジ、彼佛ヲ憶想スルガ爲メニ、彼佛ノ名号ヲ稱スベキノミ、此ノ如キノ所作ヲ名ケテ、攝受ノ恩ヲ報謝スト云リ。我宗ニハ出離ノ法ニ關シテ、僧ト俗トノ差別ナシ、唯其職業ニ於テ區分アルノミ、故ニ僧ト云ヘドモ佛教中、他ノ宗派ニ於テ禁ゼシ所ノ肉食及妻帶ヲ遮セズ。又復我宗ニハ現在ノ幸福ノ爲メニ、他佛ハ元ヨリ、阿彌陀佛ニ向ツテモ、祈願スルコトヲ禁ズ、是今生ノ報ハ他ノカニ由テ、轉ズベカラザレバナリ、而シテ宗徒ニ教フルニ當行ノ義務ヲ盡クシ、人々相愛シ、政府ノ命令法律ヲ守ルベキヲ以テス。

本宗ヲ教ユル所ノ大旨ヲ記シタル種々ノ書アリ、然レドモ余ハ唯ダ次下ニ、領解文ノ譯文ヲ示ス、此文ハ開祖ヨリ第八世ノ宗主蓮如上人述シ玉ヘル所ノモノナリ。

【付記】本文を執筆するにあたり、アメリカ・カリフォルニア州在住のワンドラ睦美氏より、赤松連城の「A BRIEF ACCOUNT OF "SHINSHIU"」が転載された、アメリカのキリスト教宣教会の雑誌 *The Missionary Herald* の情報及び原文資料の提供を受けた。記して感謝の意を表したい。

註
(1) 明治政府は手厚くもてなしていたようで、リードの大阪での動向について一八七九年二月一九日付の『朝日新聞』では、その訪問先や浄瑠璃を観劇したことなどが詳細に紹介されている。
(2) 掲載された原稿には、編集の手が入っており、意味が取りにくい部分やスペルミスは改められている。
(3) 一八八六年四月一日付の『奇日新聞』五五三号。

興隆雜誌

第三號

明治十二年五月八日發兌

○興產ノ急務第壹回
○眞宗大意略說

明治十二年(即西暦一千八百七十九年)三月
日本京都本願寺ニ於テ　　赤松連城
○右英國議員リード氏ニ贈ル所ノ原文ハ附錄ニ在リ

明治十二年五月八日刊行　毎週發兌

本局
京都府下下京區花屋町新町西
東松屋町八百九番地

編輯　赤松連城
印刷　野村淳達

興隆社

雜誌定價每號一册金貳錢
二十部前金　三十二錢

for happiness in the present life, to any of the Buddhas, even to Amita Buddha, because the events of the present life cannot be altered by the power of others; and teaches the followers of the sect to do their moral duty; loving each other, keeping order and the laws of the Government.

We have many writings stating the principles inculcated by our sect, but I give only the translation of the following creed which was written by Rennyo Shonin who was the chief priest of the 8th generation from the founder.

Creed.

Rejecting all religions austerities and other action, giving up all idea of self power, rely upon Amita Buddha with the whole heart, for we our salvation in the future life, which is the most important thing: believing that at the moment of putting our faith in Amita Buddha, our salvation is settled. From that moment, invocation of his name is observed to express gratitude and thankfulness for Buddhas mercy: Moreover, being thankful for the reception of this doctrine from the founder and succeeding chief priests whose teachings were so benevolent, and as welcome as light in a dark night: we must also keep the laws which are fixed for our duty during our whole life.

classed in two divisions, one being called //self power// or help through self, and the other called //the power of others// or help through another.

Our sect, called //Shinshiu,// literally, meaning: //True doctrine,//which was founded by Shinran Shonin, teaches the doctrine of //help from another.//

Now what is the //power of another?// It is the great power of Amita Buddha. Amita means //boundless,// and we believe that the life and light of Buddha are both perfect, also that other Buddhas obtained their state of Buddhaship, by the help of Amita Buddha. Therefore Amita Buddha is called the chief of the Buddhas.

Amita Buddha always exercises his boundless mercy upon all creatures and shows a great desire to help and influence all people who rely on him to complete all merits and be reborn into Paradise (Nirvâna).

Our sect pays no attention to the other Buddhas and putting faith only in the great desire of Amita Buddha, expect to escape from the miserable world and to enter into Paradise in the next life. From the time of putting faith in the saving desire of Buddha we do not need any power of self help, but need only keep his mercy in heart and invoke his name in order to remember him. These doings we call: //thanksgiving forsalvation.//

In our sect we make no difference between priest and layman, as concerns their way of obtaining salvation, the only difference being in their profession or business; and consequently the priest is allowed to marry and to eat flesh and fish which is prohibited to the members of other Buddhist sects.

Again, our sect forbids all prayers or supplications

A Brief account of "Shinshiu."

Buddhism teaches that all things, both abstract and concrete, are produced and destroyed by certain causes and combination of circumstances: and that the state of our present life has its cause in what we have done in our previons existence up to the present; and our present actions will become the causes of our state of existence in the future life.

As our doings are good or bad aud of different degrees of excellence or evil, so these produce different effects having many degrees of suffering or happiness, all men and other sentient beings have an interminable existence, dying in one form and being reborn in another; so that if men wish to escape from a miserable state of transmigration, they must cut off the causes, which are the passions, such for example as covetousness, anger, &c.

The principal object of Buddhism is to enable men to obtain salvation from misery according to the doctrine of "extinction of passion." This doctrine is the cause of salvation, and salvation is the effect of this doctrine.

This salvation we call Nirvâna which means eternal happiness and is the state of Buddha.

It is however very difficult to cut off all the passions, but Buddhism professes to teach many ways of obtaining this object.

Nâgârdjuna, the Indian saint, said that in Buddhism there are many ways, easy and difficult as in worldly ways, some painful like a mountainous journey, others pleasant like sailing on the sea. These ways may be

眞宗大意略說

興隆雜誌附錄

A BRIEF ACCOUNT OF "SHINSHIU"

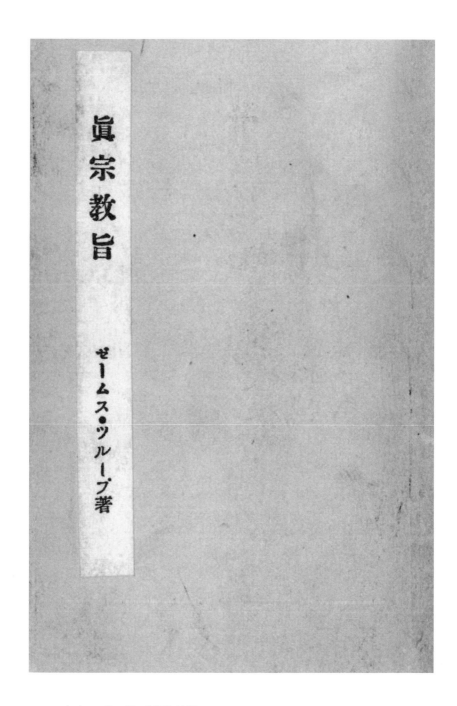

眞宗教旨

ゼームス・ツループ著

眞宗敎旨

第一章　七祖

第一祖龍樹菩薩
其易行品ヲ作ルヲ祖トシテ其華嚴中論ヲ講布スルヲ祖トセス

第二祖天親菩薩
其淨土論ヲ作ルヲ祖トシテ其俱舍唯識ヲ講布スルヲ祖トセス

第三祖曇鸞大師
其往生論註ヲ作ルヲ祖トシテ其四論ヲ講布スルヲ祖トセス

第四祖道綽禪師
其安樂集ヲ作ルヲ祖トシテ其涅槃經ヲ講布スルヲ祖トセス

第五祖善導大師
其一向ニ專ラ彌陀ノ佛名ヲ稱スルヲ祖トシテ其持戒禪定ヲ祖トセ

第六祖源信和尚其念佛ヲ先トスルチ祖トシテ其天台部ヲ講布スルチ祖トセス
第七祖源空大師其念佛チ本トスルチ祖トシテ其圓頓戒チ祖トセス
盖七祖ノ意素ト念佛ニ在リ而テ傍ラ餘事ニ及フモノハ時ニ聖道自力ノ機アルニ係ル空海氏ノ所謂賢者ノ説默時ヲ待チ人ヲ待ツモノ是ナリ

第二章 傳燈

日本ニ十四宗アリ曰ク俱舍宗曰ク成實宗曰ク律宗曰ク法相宗曰ク三論宗曰ク華嚴宗曰ク天台宗曰ク眞言宗曰ク禪宗曰ク大念佛宗曰ク淨土宗曰ク時宗曰ク日蓮宗

本宗ハ淨土眞宗ト名ヲ念佛成佛是眞宗ノ語ニ據リ親鸞聖人ヲ以テ始祖トス聖人ハ大織冠鎌足公ノ裔而テ藤原有範公ノ男ナリ夫人ハ玉日氏攝政關白兼實公ノ女ナリ初メ源空大師淨土宗ヲ倡フ海内風靡門人三百餘聖人實ニ其上足タリ關白大師ニ歸シ大檀越トナル一日ヨク大師持戒ニシテ念佛ス弟子畎肉畜妻ニシテ念佛ス孰ヲ勝劣アルコト無キヤト大師曰ク同一念佛何ノ差カ之レ有ラン曰ク弟子女アリ一上足チ屈シテ婿ト爲シ以テ天下後世ノ疑ヲ斷タン大師聖人ヲ以テ之レニ應ス聖人辭スレ可カス

第三章

判教

聖道淨土ノ二門ヲ以テ一代教ヲ判ス大小半滿權實顯密ヲ聖道門トス是ニレ此土入聖ノ教ニ係ル大無量壽經觀無量壽經阿彌陀經ヲ淨土宗トス是ニレ往生淨土ノ教ニ係ル

三

又聖道門中堅出堅超アリ法相三論ヲ堅出トシ華厳天台密禅ヲ堅超トス浄土門中横出横超アリ諸行往生ヲ以テ横出トシ是レ自力ニ係ル念仏往生ヲ以テ横超トス是レ他力ニ係ル

第四章 三時

法ニ三時アリ仏滅後五百年間ヲ正法トシ教行証アリ五百年後一千年間ヲ像法トシ教行アリテ証ナシ一千五百年後一万年間ヲ末法トシ教アツテ行証ナシ方今仏滅後二千八百二十余年人劣リ才闇ク聖道ヲ践テ大果ニ登ルコト能ハズ是レ聖道門ノ振ハサルノ所以ナリ行スヘカラサルノ法ヲ以テ行スル能ハズ是レ能ハサルノ人ニ強ユルコレ難ヲ推テ水ニ入ラシムルカ如シ理アランヤ但弥陀仏ノ本願ハ三時ニ亘テ五乗ヲ該ス故ニ行ヘカラサルノ時ナク行スル能ハサルノ人ナシ経ニ曰ク○特リ○此○経○ヲ○留○ム○コ○ト○止○住○百○歳○ト末法万年ノ後尚ホ住スルコト百歳況

ヤ萬年間オヤ教ハ時ト契ヒ行ハ機ト符ス故ニ淨土門ノ眞證今ヲ以テ盛ナリトス末法ニ入テ尚ホ聖道ヲ戀ユ夏ニ當テ裘ヲ着ケ冬ニ當テ葛ヲ着クカ如シ豈ニ理アランヤ

第五章　四法

大無量壽經ヲ眞實教トス彌陀ノ名號ヲ眞實行トシ第十七願ニ出ッ三心ヲ眞實信トシ第十八願ニ出ッ必至滅度ヲ眞實證トシ第十一願ニ出ッ大導師アリ敎ユルニ名號ヲ以テシ衆生之ヲ聞信スレハ往生ヲ得ル是ヲ四法トス

第六章　三願

四十八願ノ中ニ於テ第十八願ヲ以テ眞實トシ其所被ノ機ヲ正定聚トシ眞實報土ニ生ス十九二十ヲ方便トシ十九ノ機ハ諸行ヲ回向シテ化

土ニ至ルカ故ニ邪定聚トシ二十ノ機或ハ第十八願ニ進入シ或ハ第十九ニ退堕スルカユヘニ不定聚トナス
十八願ヲ開說シテ大經トシ第十九願ヲ開說シテ觀經トシ第二十願ヲ開說シテ小經トナス大經ハ機教俱ニ頓ナリ觀經ハ機教俱ニ漸ナリ
經教ハ頓ニ機ハ漸ナリ
諸行ヲ捨テ一念佛ヲ取ル是ヲ十九ノ二十ニ入ルトナシ自力念佛ヲ捨テ他力信心ヲ取ル是ヲ二十ノ十八ニ入ルトナス

第七章　隱顯

大經ハ眞實教ニ係リ隱顯ノ義ナシ觀經ハ方便ノ教ニ係ルカ故ニ隱顯アリ定散ヲ顯說トシ弘願ヲ隱彰トス觀經ノ觀ハ顯ヲ以テ之ヲ見ル日想水想ノ觀ト爲ス隱ヲ以テ之ヲ取ル觀佛本願ノ觀ト爲ス一文兩義是ヲ隱顯トナス小經モ亦隱顯アリ一箇名號ヲ佛邊ニ約スルヲ眞實トシ衆

生ニ約スルヲ方便トナス、若シ但其隱ヲ取ルトキハ則チ三經一ニ歸ス
是レ千古ノ未タ道ヒ及ハサル所而テ祖師ノ首唱スル所ナリ

第八章 本願名號

我等凡夫安樂國ニ往生セント欲スレハ須ラク他力信心ヲ發スヘシ他力
信心ヲ發サント欲スレハ須ラク本願ノ名號ヲ聞クヘシ本願ノ名號ヲ聞
カント欲セハ須ラク善知識ニ見ユヘシ既ニ善知識ニ見エ本願ノ名號ヲ
聞キ歸命ノ心ヲ發スル是チ他力信心トナス方今末法ニ係リ聖道修シ難
シ飲酒噉肉何ソ克ク持戒セン愛妻愛子何ソ克ク割愛セン既ニ富メハ
益ス貪ホル豈ニ肯テ布施セン東セサレハ則チ西ス豈ニ禪觀ニ暇アラ
ン漁色弋利何ソ精進スルチ得ン妬賢罵善何ソ忍辱スルヲ得ン素ト般
若ナク眞如ヲ認メ難シ故ニ一時勇進奮テ六度ヲ作ス亦其久キニ勝ヘ
ス、旣ニ才力ノ六度ヲ修スルナキトハ則チ其レ解脫ヲ得サルヤ必セリ

善導曰ク自身ハ現ニ是レ罪惡生死ノ凡夫曠劫ヨリ以來常ニ沒シ常ニ
流轉シ出離ノ緣アルコトナシト○
彌陀佛久遠劫前大悲心ヲ發シ五劫ニ思惟セサルヘケンヤ然ルニ阿
就スル日ク十方衆生至心信樂シテ我國ニ生ント欲スレハ乃至十念セン
若シ生セスハ正覺ヲ取ラスト十方衆生ノ語ハ在家出家ヲ問ハス破戒
無戒ヲ問ハス有妻無妻ヲ問ハス有子無子ヲ問ハス吃酒吃肉ヲ問ハス
農ト商ト其人ヲ攝取シ命終ノ時ニ臨テ極樂ニ往生シ大涅槃ヲ證スヘシ
ヲ放チ其人ヲ攝取シ命終ノ時ニ臨テ極樂ニ往生シ大涅槃ヲ證スヘシ
無涯ノ大悲ニ非スヤ其恩ヲ報セント欲セハ須ク佛名ヲ稱スヘシ

第九章　他力信心

單ニ佛名ヲ稱スト雖モ然レモ眞實報土ニ往生スヘカラス必ス信心ヲ
發スニ由ルニ而テ後始テ往生ヲ得ル信心ヲ發スト雖モ然レモ自力ノ信

ハ以テ眞實報土ニ往生スヘカラス必ス他力ノ信ヲ發スニ由テ而テ後ニ始テ往生ヲ得ルナリ

信心ハ他力ニ從テ發ルカユヘニ他力信心ト名ク佛力ヲ他力ト爲ス明
信佛智ヲ信心ト爲ス佛智ヲ明信スルノ心ハ佛力ヨリ生ス我ヨリ發ス
ニ非ス

我心ヨリ之ヲ發スヲ自力信心ト名ク是レ心堅牢ナラサレハ條々變移
スルコト水ニ畫クカ如シ然レモ他力ノ信ハ堅牢ニシテ退カサルコト

猶ホ金剛ノ如シ

信心ト釋尊ハ之ヲ信心ト謂フ天親之ヲ一心ト云佛ハ此心ヲ回
一ナルカ故ニハ彌陀本願ノ中ニ成ス曰ク至心、信樂、欲生我國、ト此ノ三ハ体
シテ諸ノ衆生ニ施ス是ヲ他力信心ト爲ス

信心ハ彌陀ノ名號ノ中ヨリ成ス善導ノ曰ク南無ト云フハ卽チコレ歸
命ナリト祖師云ク歸命ハ本願招喚ノ勅命ナリト歸命ノ心我ヨリ生

スルニアラス佛勅ヨリ生ス故ニ他力信心ト名クルナリ
因願ニハ三心ト云ヒ果號ニハ歸命ト云因願ニ若シ生セス
ハ正覺ヲ取ラスト云果號ニ阿彌陁ト云祖師ハ攝取シテ捨テス故ニ阿彌陁ト名ク
ト云因願果號其撰一ナリ
信心ト其體一ナルコトヲ知ルヘシ
心歡喜ト第十七ノ名號ノ衆生ノ心中ニ入ルヲ是ヲ信心ト云名號ト
名號ハ第十七願ニ成ル信心ハ第十八願ニ成ル經曰ク其名號ヲ聞テ信
凡ソ心ハ濁水ノ如ク佛心ハ淨摩尼珠ノ如シ摩尼珠ノ濁水ニ入ルトキ
ハ水變シテ清トナル佛心ノ凡心ニ入ルトキハ心變シテ信トナル
第十七ノ名號ノ所信ノ行トシ第十八ノ三信ヲ能信ノ心トス十七ノ名
號衆生ノ心中ニ入レハ三信トナル十八ノ三信其聲ニ發スルモノハ十
念トナラサルヲ得ス是ヲ信行體一トナス
心ニ在ルモノヲ信トナシ聲ニ發スルヲ行ト爲ス既ニ此信アルトキハ

此行ナキ能ハサルコト火ノ必ス煙アルカ如シ

自力ノ信ハ心ニ安ンスルコト能ハス曰ク果タ往生ヲ得ルヤ否或ハ往生ヲ得サルヤ否故ニコノ信、實ニ疑ト名ク龍樹曰ク疑ヘハ則チ花開ケス。

他力ノ信ハ心ニ安ンス曰ク彼願力ニ乘シテ定テ往生ヲ得毫モ狐疑ノ心ナシ自力ノ徒ハ念佛ヲ回向シテ往生ノ業ト爲ス他力ノ徒ハ念佛ヲ以テ報恩ノ事ト爲ス

自力ノ徒ハ雜行雜修ヲ修ス他力ノ徒ハ之ヲ修セス

自力ノ徒ハ兼テ餘佛ヲ信ス他力ノ徒ハ唯一佛ヲ信スルコト忠臣ノ二主ニ事ヘサルカ如シ

自力ノ信ニ九品アリ所生ノ土モ亦九品アリ經ニ胎生ト云ヒ他力ノ信ハ一相ニシテ別ナク所生ノ土モ亦タ一無量光明土ナリ經ニ化生ト云

第十章

俗諦

眞俗ノ名重々ノ義アリ本宗ハ假ニ安心門ヲ以テ眞諦トナシ倫常門ヲ以テ俗諦トナス

本宗既ニ蓄妻ヲ開許スルトキハ五倫ナキ能ハス既ニ五倫アルトキハ其道ヲ履サル丶ヲ得ス是ヲ俗諦トナス

經ニ十方衆生ト云フトキハ其在家出家ヲ問ハサルナリ故ニ人民噉肉蓄妻ニシテ往生スコレ聖道ト殊カニ別ナリ

凡夫ノ罪大ナリト雖モ諸レノ願力ニ較フルトキハ管ニ滄海ノ一粟ノミナラス噉肉蓄妻ヲ問ハサル所以ンナリ

石ノ性重シ諸レヲ水中ニ投スレハ必ス沈ム諸レヲ大船ニ載スルトキハ必ス浮フ凡夫ノ罪重シ諸レヲ三界ニ投スレハ必ス沈ム諸レヲ願船ニ載スルトキハ必ス輕シ

衆生ノ善ヲ有漏トナシ彌陀ノ報土ヲ無漏トナス有漏ノ善ハ以テ無漏

ノ土ニ往生スヘカラス

本宗ハ戒律ヲ立テストモ然レトモ必ス倫常ヲ以テ自ラ處スヘシ

倫常ノ源大經ニ出ツ曰ク臣ハ其君ヲ欺キ子ハ其父ヲ欺キ兄弟夫婦中

外知識更ニ相ヒ欺誑スト是レ釋尊ノ敗倫斁行ヲ訶禁スル者ナリ

念佛ノ地ニ於テハ必ス佛陀アッテ之ヲ護ル經ニ云ク天下和順シ日月

清明ナリ風雨時ヲ以テシ災厲起ラス國豐カニ民安シ兵戈用ナクト豈

ニ報國ノ冥策ニアラスヤ

念佛ノ人ハ君ニ報スルコト大ナリ曰ク我ヲ養フニ太平ヲ以テシ我ヲ

飽シツ念佛ヲ以テス生ノ死ト主恩ナラサルハナシ

本宗最モ不孝ヲ惡ムト經ニ曰ク父母教誨スレハ瞋目怒鷹スト又曰ク

子ナキニ如カスト蓮師曰ク不孝ヲ萬惡ノ首トス

○

本書ハ元來支那布敎ノ爲メニ著述セシモノナレハ他邦人ニ在テハ

三十

書名	編著者	価格
近代西本願寺を支えた在家信者　評伝　松田甚左衛門	中西直樹著	一、九〇〇円
日本近代の仏教女子教育	中西直樹著	二、六〇〇円
薗田宗恵　米国開教日誌	薗田香勲編	一、六〇〇円
近代仏教スタディーズ　仏教からみたもうひとつの近代	大谷栄一・吉永進一・近藤俊太郎編	二、三〇〇円
アジアの開教と教育	小島勝・木場明志編	六、六九九円
ブッダの変貌　交錯する近代仏教	末木文美士・林淳・吉永進一・大谷栄一編	八、〇〇〇円
新装版　講座　近代仏教　上・下	法藏館編集部編	一六、〇〇〇円

法藏館　　価格税別

龍谷大学アジア仏教文化研究叢書Ⅲ
仏教英書伝道のあけぼの

二〇一八年一月三一日　初版第一刷発行

編著者　那須英勝
　　　　嵩　満也
　　　　中西直樹

発行者　西村明高

発行所　株式会社 法藏館
　　　　京都市下京区正面通烏丸東入
　　　　郵便番号　六〇〇-八一五三
　　　　電話　〇七五-三四三-〇〇三〇（編集）
　　　　　　　〇七五-三四三-五六五六（営業）

装幀者　大杉泰正（アイアールデザインスタジオ）
印刷・製本　中村印刷株式会社

©N.Nakanishi, E.Nasu, M.Dake 2018
Printed in Japan
ISBN978-4-8318-5553-4 C3021
乱丁・落丁の場合はお取り替え致します。

編著者紹介

中西直樹（なかにし　なおき）

一九六一年生まれ

龍谷大学文学部歴史学科（仏教史学専攻）教授

主要編著

『仏教海外開教史の研究』（不二出版、二〇一二年）

『植民地朝鮮と日本仏教』（三人社、二〇一三年）

『仏教国際ネットワークの源流――海外宣教会（1888年～1893年）の光と影』（共著、三人社、二〇一五年）

『植民地台湾と日本仏教』（三人社、二〇一六年）

那須英勝（なす　えいしょう）

一九六一年生まれ

龍谷大学文学部真宗学科教授

主要編著

Engaged Pure Land Buddhism: Challenges Facing Jōdo Shinshū in the Contemporary World (共著、Wisdom-Ocean Press、一九九八年)

『犀の角：世界に拓く真宗伝道』（共著、永田文昌堂、二〇〇五年）

Memory and Imagination: Essays and Explorations in Buddhist Thought and Culture (共著、永田文昌堂、二〇一〇年)

嵩　満也（だけ　みつや）

一九五八年生まれ

龍谷大学国際学部国際文化学科教授

龍谷大学現代南アジア研究センター長

主要編著

『親鸞読み解き事典』（共著、柏書房、二〇〇六年）

"Shinran's Understanding of Amida Buddha: an example of the embodiment of hope in Buddhism, Ed.by Elizabeth Harris *Hope: A Form of Delusion?* (EOS Publication、二〇一三年)

「仏教は共生を語るのか？――「きょうせい」と「ともいき」の相克をめぐって」、権五定・斎藤文彦編『多文化共生を問い直す――グローバル化時代の可能性と限界』（日本経済評論社、二〇一四年）

In Search of Well-being――Genealogies of Religion and Politics in India (龍谷大学現代インド研究センター［現、南アジア研究センター］、二〇一四年)

をさらに推進し、日本仏教を世界的視野から通時的共時的にとらえるとともに、日本仏教が直面する諸課題を多文化共生の文脈で学際的に追究し、今後の日本仏教の持つ意義を展望するものです。このような研究のあり方を有機的に進めるため、本研究プロジェクトでは通時的研究グループ（ユニットA「日本仏教の形成と展開」、ユニットB「近代日本仏教と国際社会」）と共時的研究グループ（ユニットA「現代日本仏教の社会性・公益性」、ユニットB「多文化共生社会における日本仏教の課題と展望」）の二つに分け、基礎研究等に基づく書籍の刊行や講演会等による研究成果の公開などの諸事業を推進していくことになりました。

このたび刊行される『仏教英書伝道のあけぼの』は、右のような研究プロジェクトの共同研究の成果の一つであります。今後とも、世界仏教文化研究センターの傘下にあるアジア仏教文化研究センターが、日本仏教をテーマとして国内外に発信する諸成果に、ご期待いただければ幸いです。

平成三〇年一月一〇日

「龍谷大学アジア仏教文化研究叢書」刊行について

アジア仏教文化研究センター
センター長　楠　淳證

龍谷大学は、寛永一六年（一六三九）に西本願寺の阿弥陀堂北側に創設された「学寮」を淵源とする大学です。その後、明治維新を迎えると学制の改革が行われ、学寮も大教校と名を変え、さらに真宗学庠、大学林、仏教専門学校、仏教大学と名称を変更し、大正一一年（一九二二）に今の「龍谷大学」となりました。

その間、三百七十有余年もの長きにわたって仏教の研鑽が進められ、龍谷大学は高い評価を得てまいりました。そして平成二七年四月、本学の有する最新の研究成果を国内外に発信するとともに仏教研究の国際交流の拠点となるべき新たな機関として、本学に「世界仏教文化研究センター」が設立されました。アジア仏教文化研究センターは、そのような意図のもと設立された世界仏教文化研究センターの傘下にある研究機関です。

世界仏教文化研究センターが設立されるにあたって、その傘下にあるアジア仏教文化研究センターは、文科省の推進する「私立大学戦略的研究基盤形成支援事業」に、「日本仏教の通時的・共時的研究――多文化共生社会における課題と展望――」と題する研究プロジェクト（平成二七年度～平成三一年度）を申請し、採択されました。

本研究プロジェクトは、龍谷大学が三百七十有余年にわたって研鑽し続けてきた日本仏教の成果を踏まえ、これ

第Ⅱ部
復刻資料編

（資料の復刻にあたって）
一、原本を適宜、縮小・拡大して収録しました。
一、原本の状態により判読困難な箇所があります。
一、資料の中に、人権の視点からみて不適切な語句・表現、明らかに学問上の誤りがある場合でも、歴史的資料の復刻という性質上、そのまま収録しました。

A BUDDHIST CATECHISM
BY
HENRY S. OLCOTT

NAMO TASSA BHAGAVATO ARAHATO SAMMA SAMBUDDHASSA.

A BUDDHIST CATECHISM,

According to the Canon of the Southern Church,

BY

HENRY S. OLCOTT,

PRESIDENT OF THE THEOSOPHICAL SOCIETY, ETC.

Approved, and recommended for use in Buddhist schools, by H. SUMANGALA, High Priest of the Sripada (Adam's Peak) and Galle, and Principal of the Widyodaya Parivena (Buddhist College).

FOURTEENTH THOUSAND.

COLOMBO, CEYLON,
THE ILANGAKOON CATECHISM FUND.
LONDON,
TRÜBNER AND CO., LUDGATE HILL.

1882.

[*All Rights Reserved.*]

Printed by Kokubunsha, Tokio.

東京國文社印刷

PREFACE.

It is a very well known fact that Catechisms are much used not only by the missionaries of Christianity everywhere, but also by the teachers of common education throughout all the Christendom. Nothing is more easy to impress the minds of the young or uneducated than a work like a Catechism. I remember I was once staying in a Christian family in London, where there were three children, seven, five and three years old; and the eldest girl just learning the Catechism in the school, could answer any question out of it, and in turn teach it to her little sisters. Witnessing this, I often reflected that I had never seen any child in my own community, who was able to answer even so simple a question as to 'Was Buddha a God?' I therefore wanted such a book as the present very much. When my ever lamented fellow-worker, Kenjiu Kasawara, visited Ceylon on his way home, he was given there with a copy of the present Catechism and several publications of the Theosophical Society. As he says in one of his letters to me, he saw the venerable Sumangala, and was present at a

meeting of the Ceylon Branch of the Society, but did not meet Colonel Olcott. This same thing is mentioned by Col. Olcott in his letter to R. Midzutani Esq., under the date of the 14th January, 1883, i. e. the 15th year of the Meiji period. On the 16th July of that year, Kasawara died from consumption in Tokio. So he did not see Mr. Midzutani, who was then in a different part of Japan. In the following year, I came home from England by America, and at once saw my learned friend, Mr. R. Akamatsu, who then spoke to me about this book, and even told me that he had it almost translated into Japanese. Meanwhile, examining Kasawara's books, I found the very copy which he had brought with him from Ceylon, and wished very much to make it known in this country.

Now the time comes when this Buddhist Catechism in English is republished here by Mr. Midzutani. A Japanese translation has already been done by T. Imadate Esq., Principally the Kioto Academy, and published by the Society of Publication of the Buddhist Books in Tokio. As to the nature and object of the work, the author explains himself so minutely in his two prefaces, that I need say nothing. I sincerely hope that our Buddhist brethren will earnestly read this Catechism, and become more or less able to understand one hundred and sixty-eight questions and answers, which this book contains. They are also to know that an American officer has become a true

Buddhist, and is trying to do for Buddhism what Paul did for Christianity more than eighteen centuries ago.

BUNYIU NANJIO.

Tokio, 13th March, 19th year of the Meiji period.

CERTIFICATE.

WIDYODAYA COLLEGE,
Colombo, 7th July, 1881.

I hereby certify that I have carefully examined the Sinhalese version of the Catechism prepared by Col. H. S. OLCOTT, and that the same is in agreement with the Canon of the Southern Buddhist Church. I recommend the work to teachers in Buddhist schools, and to all others who may wish to impart information to beginners about the essential features of our religion.

H. SUMANGALA,
High Priest of the Sripada & Galle, and Principal of Widyodaya Parivena.

NOTICE.—*This Catechism is published, in the English and Sinhalese languages, at the expense of* MRS. FREDRIKA CECILIA DIAS ILANGAKOON, F.T.S., *of Matara Ceylon; who makes the offering as a contribution to the cause of religion and a tribute of affection to the Theosophical Society.*

PREFACE TO THE THIRTEENTH THOUSAND.

The demand for a succinct exposition of the beliefs of Sinhalese Buddhists has been proved by the large sales of this little work, and the general favour with which it has been received by the non-Buddhistic, as well as the Buddhistic public. It is within bounds to say that it has already found its way into ten thousand Sinhalese households, and that many thousands of Buddhist children are now for the first time deriving from it that elementary knowledge of their religion which until now they could get neither from parents nor school teachers. The translation of the Catechism into the German, Siamese, Japanese and Tamil languages, is additional evidence of its circulation. It was announced and has, by the learned High Priest Sumangala Thero, been endorsed as a presentation of orthodox Southern Buddhism; *as such only should it be regarded*, and not as the creed of any particular Buddhistic *sect*, or individual Buddhist. The author, confining himself strictly to his subject, did not make the comparison he easily might between the ideas respectively held by the Northern and Southern

Buddhists; those of Tibet, on the one hand, and those of Ceylon, on the other:—countries which are the acknowledged foci of the purest doctrine prevalent in their respective geographical divisions. He is even less disposed to do so now, since there is reason to expect that the Tibetan philosophy will shortly be made public, for the first time, by Tibetan proficients most amply qualified to speak. Orientalists will then have the means of comparing, and possibly of understanding more clearly than hitherto, the texts that have so long puzzled them. The first steps are also taken—in part through the obliging help of British officials—to bring the Buddhistic scholars of Ceylon into closer communion with their co-religionists of Japan and Burma than heretofore; a relationship which cannot fail to do good. Letters received from several non-Buddhistic countries since the first appearance of the Catechism, show that various agencies—among them, conspicuously, the wide circulation of Mr. Edwin Arnold's beautiful poem. "The Light of Asia"—have created a sentiment in favour of Buddhistic philosophy, which constantly gains strength. It seems to commend itself especially to Freethinkers of every shade of opinion. Three French gentlemen of high position who recently visited Ceylon, and made public prefession of Buddhism by taking the " Three Refuges" at Colombo and Galle temples, told the High Priest that the whole school of French Positivists were practically Buddhists, and would not hesitate to follow

the above example set by themselves. And it is reported to the author by a Sinhalese gentleman of high birth that the eminent Professor Ernst Hæckel, in a conversation which occurred during his recent visit to the Island, told him that, so far as explained to him, the Buddhistic theory of the eternity of matter and force and other particulars were identical with the latest deductions of Science. This good opinion of Buddhism must increase in strength among scientific men as its corruptions are dissected away, and the veritable teaching of Lord Buddha is discovered. In common with Esoteric Hindu philosophy, and other esoteric cults derived from the pre-Aryan and Irano-Aryan parent source, Esoteric Buddhism, wherever found rests upon the assumption of a true Individualism, unerringly developing effects from causes under the Universal Reign of Law; and all utterly scout the theory of miracle. How identical this is with the position of modern Science need not be discussed since we have, amid the testimony of a cloud of witnesses, that of the lamented Professor J. W. Draper that " the spirit that imparted life to this movement [that of Science], that has animated these discoveries and inventions, is Individualism." (*Conflict, p. 324.*)

The author, in fulfilment of the promise given in the first edition, has embodied in the present text such changes as have, by impartial critics, been shown to be advantageous or have suggested themselves to his own

mind. Additional questions have been also introduced to define points not previously covered. Among these subjects, are the Five and Ten Precepts; the relationship between the *personalities* evolved, in successive births, along any given line of individual life, or *vital undulation* —if a new phrase be permitted; the better definition of Bodhisatship; the cause of lapse of memory between successive births; the nature of *Tanha*; the anti-Buddhistic character of certain superstitious rites; the innate distinction between Buddhism and religions, properly so called; Arahatship; etc. He will thankfully receive, at all times, recommendations for further improvements.

A few explanatory notes have also been added in an Appendix, to which the reader is referred.

H. S. O.

Galle, Ceylon.
August 2, 1882.

PREFACE.

Being intended for the use of beginners, this little work aims only to present the main facts in the life of Gautama Buddha and the essential features of his Doctrine. Strange to say, it is unique of its kind in Ceylon, notwithstanding that the Missionaries have scattered their Christian catechisms broadcast in the Island, and for many years have been taunting the Sinhalese with the puerility and absurdity of their religion. To whatever cause it may be due this apathy is something to be deplored by every Buddhist or admirer of the Buddhist philosophy. The present Catechism is largely a compilation from the works of T. W. Rhys Davids, Esq., Bishop Bigandet, Sir Coomara Swamy, R. C. Childers, Esq., and the Revs. Samuel Beal and R. Spence Hardy; in a few cases, their exact language has been used. But having been assisted by the Venerable High Priest H. Sumangala, Principal, and the Priest H. Devamitta, of Widyodaya College, the author's treatment of some of the subjects will be found to differ from that of those authors in some respects. Truth to say, a very incomplete popular notion of what orthodox Buddhism is seems to prevail in Western countries. The folk-lore and fairy stories

upon which some of our principal Orientalists, cited above, have mainly based their commentaries, are no more orthodox Buddhism than the wild monkish tales of the middle ages are orthodox Christianity. Only *the authenticated utterances of Sakya Muni himself* are admitted as orthodox. Deeper analysis will unquestionably prove to Western scholars that the Kapilawastu Sage taught, six centuries before the Christian Era, not only a peerless code of morals, but also a philosophy so broad and comprehensive as to have anticipated the inductions of modern research and speculation. The signs abound that of all the world's great creeds that one is destined to be the much talked-of Religion of the Future which shall be found in least antagonism with nature and with law. Who dare predict that Buddhism will not be the one chosen?

Though the author gratefully acknowledges his obligations to Messrs. E. F. Perera, Proctor, and W. D'Abrew, for their services as interpreters between the reverend priests and himself, yet he claims the indulgence of all who have tried to do such work as this through intermediaries, for the many imperfections that will doubtless be found in the following pages. His ignorance of Pali and Sinhalese has prevented his doing full justice to the subject, but he hopes to avail in future editions, of the criticisms the present one may call forth.

A BUDDHIST CATECHISM.

1. Q. *Of what religion* are you?*
A. The Buddhist.
2. Q. *What is a Buddhist?*
A. One who professes to be a follower of our Lord Buddha and accepts his doctrine.
3. Q. *Was Buddha a God?*
A. No.
4. Q. *Was he a man?*
A. In form a man; but internally, not like other men. That is to say, in moral and mental qualities he excelled all other men of his own or subsequent times.
5. Q. *Was Buddha his name?*
A. No. It is the name of a condition or state of mind.
6. Q. *Its meaning?*
A. Enlightened; or, he who has the perfect wisdom.
7. Q. *What was Buddha's real name then?*

---

* The asterisks refer to Notes in the Appendix.

Siddartha was his royal name, and Gautama, or Gotama, his family name. He was Prince of Kapilavastu.

8. Q. *Who were his father and mother?*
A. King Suddhodana and Qneen Maya.
9. Q. *What people did this King reign over?*
A. The Sakyas; an Aryan tribe.
10. Q. *Where was Kapilavastu?*
A. In India, 100 miles north-east of the city of Benares, and about 40 miles from the Himalaya mountains.
11. Q. *On what river?*
A. The Rohini; now called the Kohana.
12. Q. *When was Prince Siddartha born?*
A. 623 years before the Christian era.
13. Q. *Did the Prince have luxuries and splendors like other Princes?*
A. He did; his father, the King, built him three magnificent palaces, for the three Indian seasons, of nine, five and three stories respectively, and handsomely decorated. Around each palace were gardens of the most beautiful and fragrant flowers; with fountains spouting water, the trees full of singing birds, and peacocks strutting over the ground.

14. Q. *Was he living alone?*

A. No, in his sixteenth year he was married to the Princess Yasodhara, daughter of the King Suprabuddha. Many beautiful maidens, skilled in dancing and music, were also in continual attendance to amuse him.

15. Q. *How, amid all this luxury, could a Prince become all-wise?*

A. He had such a natural wisdom that when he was but a child he seemed to understand all arts and sciences almost without study. He had the best teachers, but they could teach him nothing that he did not seem to immediately comprehend.

16. Q. *Did he become Buddha in his splendid palaces?*

A. No: he left all, and went alone into the jungle.

17. Q. *Why did he do this?*

A. To discover the cause of our sufferings and the way to escape from them.

18. Q. *It was not selfishness that made him do this?*

A. No; it was boundless love for all beings that made him sacrifice himself for their good.

19. *Q. What did he sacrifice?*

A. His beautiful palaces, his riches, his luxuries, his pleasures, his soft beds, his fine dresses, his rich food, his kingdom; he even left his beloved wife and his only son.

20. *Q. What was this son's name?*

A. The Prince Rahula.

21. *Q. Did any other man ever sacrifice so much for our sake?*

A. Not one: this is why Buddhists so love him, and why good Buddhists try to be like him.

22. *Q. How old was he when he went to the jungle?*

A. He was in his 29th year.

23. *Q. What finally determined him to leave all that men usually love so much, and go to the jungle.*

A. A deva* appeared to him when driving out in his chariot, under four impressive forms on four different occasions.

24. *Q. What were these different forms?*

A. Those of a very old man broken down by age, of a sick man, of a decaying corpse, and of a dignified hermit.

25. Q. *Did he alone see these visions?*

A. No, his attendant Channa also saw them.

26. *Why should these sights, so familiar to everybody, have caused him to go to the jungle?*

A. We often see such sights: he had not, and they made a deep impression on his mind.

27. Q. *Why had he not also seen them?*

A. The Astrologers had foretold at his birth that he would one day resign his kingdom and become a Buddha. The King, his father, not wishing to lose his son, had carefully prevented his seeing any sights that might suggest to him human misery and death. No one was allowed to even speak of such things to the Prince. He was almost like a prisoner in his lovely palaces and flower-gardens. They were surrounded with high walls, and inside everything was made as beautiful as possible, so that he might not want to go and see the sorrow and distress that are in the world.

28. Q. *Was he so kind-hearted that his father feared he might really want to sacrifice himself for the world's sake?*

A. Yes, he seems have felt for all beings so strong a pity and love as that.

29. Q. *And how did he expect to learn the cause of sorrow in the jungle?*

A. By removing far away from all that could prevent his deeply thinking of the causes of sorrow and the nature of man.

30. Q. *How did he escape from the palace?*

A. One night when all were asleep, he arose, took a last look at his sleeping wife and infant son; called Channa, mounted his favorite white horse Kantaka, and rode to the palace gates. The devas had thrown a deep sleep upon his father's guards who watched the gate, so they heard not the noise of his horse's hoofs.

31. Q. *But the gate was locked, was it not?*

A. Yes; but the devas caused it to open without the slightest noise, and he rode away into the darkness.

32. Q. *Whither did he go?*

A. To the river Anoma, a long way from Kapilavastu.

33. Q. *What did he then do?*

A He sprang from his horse, cut off his beautiful hair with his sword, and giving his ornaments and horse to Channa, ordered him to take them back to his father, the King.

34. *Q. What then?*

A. He went afoot towards Râjagriha the capital city of Mâgadha.

35. *Q. Why there?*

A. In the jungle of Uruwela were hermits—very wise men, whose pupil he afterwards became, in the hope of finding the knowledge of which he was in search.

36. *Q. Of what religion were they?*

A. The Hindu religion: they were Brahmans.

37. *Q. What did they teach?*

A. That by severe penances and torture of the body a man may acquire perfect wisdom.

38. *Q. Did the Prince find this to be so?*

A. No, he learned their systems and practised all their penances, but he could not thus discover the reason for human sorrow.

39. *Q. What did he then do?*

A. He went away into the forest near a place called Buddha Gaya, and spent several years in deep meditation and fasting.

40. *Q. Was he alone?*

A. No, five companions attended him.

41. *Q. What were their names?*

A. Kondanya, Bhaddaji, Wappa, Mahanama, and Assaji.

42. Q. *What plan of discipline did he adopt to open his mind to know the whole truth?*

A. He sat and meditated, shutting out from his sight and hearing all that was likely to interrupt his inward reflections.

43. Q. *Did he fast?*

A. Yes; through the whole period. He took less and less food and water, until it is said, he ate scarcely more than one grain of rice or sesamum seed a day.

44. Q. *Did this give him the wisdom he longed for?*

A. No: he grew thinner and thinner in body and fainter in strength, until, one day, as he was slowly walking here and there and meditating, his vital force suddenly left him and he fell to the ground, unconscious.

45. Q. *What did his companions think of that?*

A. They fancied he was dead; but after a time he revived.

46. Q. *What then?*

A. The thought came to him that knowledge could never be reached by mere fasting

or bodily suffering, it must be gained by the opening of the mind. He had just barely escaped death from self-starvation but had not obtained the Perfect Wisdom. So he decided to eat, that he might live at least long enough to become wise. He therefore received some food of a nobleman's daughter who saw him lying at the foot of a nuga tree. After that his strength returned to him; he arose, took his alms-bowl, bathed in the river Niranjara, ate the food, and went into the jungle.

47. *Q. What did he there?*

A. Having formed his determination after these reflections, he went at evening to the Bodhi, or Asvattha, tree.

48. *Q. What did he do there?*

A. He determined not to leave the spot until hs attained the Buddhaship.

49. *Q. At which side of the tree did he seat himself.*

A. The side facing the East.*

50. *Q. What did he obtain that night?*

A. The knowledge of his previous births, of the causes of rebirth, and of the way to extinguish desires. Just before the break of the

next day his mind was entirely opened, like the full-blown lotus flower; the light of supreme knowledge, or the Four Truths, poured in upon him; he had become Buddha—the Enlightened, the All-knowing.

51. Q. *Had he at last discovered the cause of human misery?*

A. At last he had. As the light of the morning sun chases away the darkness of night, and reveals to sight the trees, fields, rocks, seas, rivers, animals, men and all things, so the full light of knowledge rose in his mind, and he saw at one glance the causes of human suffering and the way to escape from them.

52. Q. *Had he great struggles before gaining this perfect wisdom?*

A. Yes, mighty and terrible struggles. He had to conquer in his body all those natural defects and human appetites and desires that prevent our seeing the truth. He had to overcome all the bad influences of the sinful world around him. Like a soldier fighting desperately in battle against many enemies, he struggled: like a hero who conquers, he gained his object, and the secret of human misery was discovered.

53. *Q. Can you tell me in one word what is that secrect?*

A. Ignorance.

54. *Q. Can you tell me the remedy?*

A. To dispel Ignorance and become wise.

55. *Q. Why does Ignorance cause suffering?*

A. Because it makes us prize what is not worth prizing, grieve for that we should not grieve for, consider real what is not real but only illusionary, and pass our lives in the pursuit of worthless objects, neglecting what is in reality most valuable.

56. *Q. And what is that which is most valuable?*

A. To know the whole secret of man's existence and destiny; so that we may estimate at no more than their actual value this life and its relations; so that we may live in a way to ensure the greatest happiness and the least suffering for our fellow-men and ourselves.

57. *Q. What is the light that can dispel this ignorance of ours and remove all sorrows?*

A. The knowledge of the "Four Noble Truths," as Buddha called them.

58. *Q. Name these Four Noble Truths.*

A. 1. The miseries of existence; 2. The

cause productive of misery, which is the desire, ever renewed, of satisfying one's self without being able ever to secure that end; 3. The destruction of that desire, or the estranging of one's self from it; 4. The means of obtaining this destruction of desire.

59. Q. *Tell me some things that cause sorrow?*

A. Birth; growth, decay, illness, death; separation from objects we love, hating what cannot be avoided, craving for what cannot be obtained.

60. Q. *These are individual peculiarities?*

A. Yes: and they differ with each individual; but all men have them in degree, and suffer from them.

61. Q. *How can we escape the sufferings which result from unsatisfied desires, and ignorant cravings?*

A. By complete conquest over, and destruction of this eager thirst for life and its pleasures, which cause sorrow.

62. Q. *How may we gain such a conquest?*

A. By following in the Noble Eightfold Path which Buddha discovered and pointed out.

63. Q. *What do you mean by that word: what*

is this *Noble Eightfold path?*

A. The eight parts of this path are called *angas;* they are: 1. Right Belief; 2. Right Thought; 3. Right Speech; 4, Right Doctrine; 5. Right Means of Livelihood; 6. Right Endeavour; 7. Right Memory; 8. Right Meditation. The man who keeps these *angas* in mind and follows them will be free from sorrow and may reach salvation.

64. Q. *Salvation from what?*

A. Salvation from the miseries of existence and of rebirths, all of which are due to ignorance and impure lusts and cravings.

65. Q. *And when this salvation is attained, what do we reach?*

A. Nirvana.

66. Q. *What is Nirvana?*

A. A condition of total cessation of changes, of perfect rest; of the absence of desire, and illusion, and sorrow; of the total obliteration of every thing that goes to make up the physical man. Before reaching Nirvana man is constantly being reborn: when he reaches Nirvana he is reborn no more.

67. Q. *What causes us to be reborn?*

A. The unsatisfied desire for things that belong to the state of personal existence in the material world. This unquenched thirst for physical existence is a force, and has a creative power in itself so strong that it draws the being back into mundane life.

68. Q. *Are our rebirths in any way affected by the nature of our unsatisfied desires?*

A. Yes: and by our individual merits or demerits.

69. Q. *Does our merit or our demerit control the state, condition, or form in which we shall be reborn?*

A. It does. The broad rule is that if we have an excess of merit, we will be well and happily born the next time; if an excess of demerit, our next birth will be wretched and full of suffering.

70. Q. *Is this Buddhistical doctrine supported or denied by the teachings of modern science?*

A. It is in reconciliation with science, Since it is the doctrine of cause and effect. Science teaches that man is the result of a law of development, from an imperfect and lower, to a higher and perfect condition.

71. *Q. What is this doctrine of Science called?*
A. Evolution.

72. *Q. Can you show any further endorsement of Buddhism by science?*

A. Buddha's doctrine teaches that there were many progenitors of the human race; also that there is a principle of differentiation among men; certain individuals have a greater capacity for the rapid attainment of Wisdom, and arrival at Nirvana, than others. Of Bódhisats there are three kinds—

73. *Q. Stop: what is a Bódhisat?*

A. A being who has outstripped other men in moral development, and who in some future birth is sure to appear upon earth as a Buddha. He will so appear, because his pity for human ignorance is so deep, and his benevolent desire to teach mankind the cause of sorrow and the means of escape, is so strong, that he voluntarily reincarnates himself in many births; until, at last, he has become pure enough to attain the Buddahood. Having reached that state, and preached the Law, he only then consents to pass out of the circle of birth into the perfect release of Paranirvana.

74. *Q. Proceed. How are these three kinds of Bódhisats called?*

A. Panyâdika, or Udghatitagnya—" he who attains quickly;" Saddhadhika, or Vipachitagnya—" he who attains less quickly;" and Wiriadhika, or Gneyya—" he who attains least quickly."

75. *Q. Well, proceed?*

A. Just so modern science teaches that, out of the millions of beings that appear upon earth, some reach perfection most quickly, some less quickly, and others least quickly. Buddhists say that the nature of the rebirth is controlled by the Karma—the preponderance of merit or demerit—of the previous existence. The men of science say the new form is partly the result of the influences (Environment) that surrounded the previous generation. There is thus an agreement between Buddhism and science as to the root-idea.

76. *Q. And then, do not both Buddhism and science teach that all beings are alike subject to universal law?*

A. Both do so teach.

77. *Q. Then may all men become Buddhas?*

A. It is not in the nature of every man to become a Buddha; for a Buddha is developed only at long intervals of time, and, seemingly when the state of humanity absolutely requires such a teacher to show it the forgotten Path to Nirvána. But every being may equally reach Nirvána, by conquering Ignorance and gaining Wisdom.

78. Q. *Does Buddhim teach that man is reborn only upon our earth?*

A. No: we are taught that the inhabited worlds are numberless; the world upon which a person is to have his next birth, as well as the nature of the rebirth itself, being decided by the preponderence of the individual's merit or demerit. In other words, it will be controlled by his attractions, as science would describe it.

79. Q. *Are there worlds more perfect and developed, and others less so, than our Earth?*

A. Buddhism teaches this, and also that the inhabitants of each world correspond in development with itself.

80. Q. *Has not the Buddha summed up his whole religion in one* SUTTA, *or verse?*

A. Yes.

18 BUDDHIST CATECHISM.

81. *Q. Repeat it?*

   Sabbapápassa akaranam
   Kusalassa upasampadá
   Sa chitta pariyo dapanam—
   Etam Buddhánu sásanam.*

   "To cease from all sin,
   To get virtue,
   To cleanse one's own heart,—
   This is the religion of the Buddhas."

82. *Q. Do these precepts shew that Buddhism is an active, or a passive religion?*

A. To 'cease from sin,' may be called a passive, but to 'get virtue,' and to 'cleanse one's own heart', are altogether *active* qualities. Buddha taught that we should not merely *not* be evil, but that we should be *positively* good.

83. *Q. Who or what are the "Three Guides"* that a Buddhist is supposed to follow?*

A. They are disclosed in the formula called the *Tisarana:*—"I follow Buddha as my Guide: I follow the Law as my Guide: I follow the Order as my Guide."

84. *Q. What does he mean when repeating this formula?*

A. He means that he regards the Lord Buddha as his all-wise Teacher and Exemplar; the Law or Doctrine, as containing the essential and immutable principles of Justice and Truth and the path that leads to *summum bonum;* and the Order as the teachers and expounders of that excellent Law revealed by Buddha.

85. Q. *But are not many of the members of this "Order" men intellectually and morally inferior to ourselves?*

A. Yes: but we are taught by Buddha that only those who diligently attend to the Precepts, discipline their minds, and strive to attain or have attained one of the eight stages of holiness and perfection, constitute his "Order." It is expressly stated that the Order referred to in the "*Tisarana*" refers to the "*Attha Ariya Puggala*"—ascetics who have attained one of the eight stages of perfection.

86. Q. *What are the five observances or Precepts called the Panca Sîla § imposed on the Buddhist laity in general?*

A. They are included in the following formula which Buddhists repeat publicly at the Vihâras (temples):—

(1.) I observe the precept to refrain from destroying the life of beings.
(2.) I observe the precept to refrain from stealing.
(3.) I observe the precept to abstain from unlawful sexual intercourse.
(4.) I observe the precept to refrain from falsehood.
(5.) I observe the precept to abstain from using intoxicating liquors, and drugs that tend to procrastination.

87. Q. *What benefits does a Buddhist derive by the observance of these Precepts?*

A. He is said to acquire more or less merit according to the manner and time of observing the precepts, and the number observed, That is, if he observes only one precept, violating the other four, he acquires the merit of the observance of that precept only; and the longer he keeps that precept the greater will be the merit. He who keeps all the precepts inviolate will cause himself to have a higher and happier existence hereafter.

88. Q. *Are there any other observance which*

---

§ Pronounced Pancha Seela.

it is considered meritorious for the laity to voluntarily undertake to keep?

A. Yes: the *Atthanga Síla*, or the Eight-fold Precept, which embraces the five above enumerated with three additional; viz:—

    (6.) I observe the precept to abstain from eating at unseasonable times.*

    (7.) I observe the precept to abstain from dancing, singing and unbecoming shows.

    (8.) I observe the precept to abstain from using garlands, scents, perfumes, cosmetics, ointments and ornament.

    To the above are added two other to form the *Dasa Síla* or the Tenfold Obligation of a Priest, viz:—

    (9.) I observe the precept to abstain from using high and broad beds.

    (10.) I observe the precept to abstain from receiving gold or silver.

    The *Dasa Síla* is binding on *all* Priests and *Samaneras*, or novitiates, but optional with lay devotees.

89. Q. *Are there separate Rules and Precepts for the guidance and discipline of the Order?*

22 BUDDHIST CATECHISM.

A. Yes: they are many, but all come under the following four heads :—

(1.) Principal Disciplinary Rules (*Pátimokkha samvara síla.*)
(2.) Observances for the repression of the senses (*Indriya samvara síla*).
(3.) Regulations for justly procuring and using food, diet, robes, &c., (*Paccayasannissitasíla*).
(4.) Directions for leading an unblemished life (*Ajivapárisuddhasíla*).

90. Q. *Enumerate some crimes and offences that priests are particularly prohibited from committing?*

A. The priests ought to abstain from :—
Destroying the life of beings,
Stealing,
Sexual intercourse,
Falsehood,
The use of intoxicating liquors, and eating at unseasonable times,
Dancing, singing, and unbecoming shows,
Using garlands, scents, perfumes, &c.
Using high and broad beds,

Receiving presents of gold, silver, raw grain and meat, women and maidens, slaves, cattle, elephants, &c.

Defaming,

Using harsh and reproachful language,

Idle talk,

Reading and hearing fabulous stories and tales,

Carrying messages to and from laymen,

Buying and selling,

Cheating, bribing, deception and fraud,

Imprisoning, plundering, and threatening others; and

From the practice of certain specified arts and sciences, &c., &c.

91. *Q. What are the duties of priests to the laity?*

A. Generally, to set them an example of the highest morality; to teach and instruct them; to preach and expound the Law; to recite the *Paritta,* (comforting texts) to the sick, and publicly in times of public calamity, when requested to do so; and to exhort the people to virtuous actions.

92. Q. *How would a Buddhist describe true merit?*

A. There is no great merit in any outward act; salvation depends upon the inward motive that provokes the deed.

93. Q. *Give an example?*

A. A rich man may expend lakhs of rupees, in building Dàgobas or Vihàras, in erecting statues of Buddha, in festivals and processions, in feeding priests, in giving alms to the poor, or in digging tanks or constructing rest-houses by the roadside for travellers, and yet have comparatively little merit, if all this is done for the mere sake of display and to make himself praised by men, or for any other selfish motives. But he who, whether rich or poor, does the least of these things with kind motive, or from a warm love for his fellow-men, gains great merit. A good deed done with a bad motive benefits others, but not him who does it. And one who approves of a good deed when done by another, shares in the merit; if his sympathy is *real, not pretended.*

94. Q. *In what books is written all the most excellent wisdom of Buddha's teachings?*

A. In the three collections of books called *Tripitikas*.

95. Q. *What are the names of the three Pitakas, or groups of books?*

A. The *Vinaya Pitaka*, the *Sutta Pitaka* and the *Abidhamma Pitaka*.

96. Q. *What do they respectively contain?*

A. The first contains rules of discipline, for the government of the priests; the second contains instructive discourses for the laity; the third explains the metaphysics of Buddhism.

97. Q. *Do Buddhists believe these books to be inspired, in the sense that Christians belive their Bible to be?*

A. No: but they revere them as containing all the parts of that Most Excellent Law, by the knowing of which man may save himself.

98. Q. *Do Buddhists consider Buddha as one who by his own virtue can save us from the consequences of our individual sins?*

A. Not at all. No man can be saved by another; he must save himself.

99. Q. *What, then, was Buddha to us and all other beings?*

A. An all-seeing, all-wise counsellor; one who discovered the safe path and pointed it out; one who showed the cause of, and the only cure for human suffering. In pointing to the road, in showing us how to escape dangers, he became our Guide. And as one leading a blind man across a narrow bridge, over a swift and deep stream saves his life, so in showing us, who were blind from ignorance, the way to salvation, Buddha may well be called our 'Saviour.'

100. Q. *If you were to try to represent the whole spirit of Buddha's Doctrine by one word, which word would you chose?*

A. JUSTICE.

101. Q. *Why?*

A. Because it teaches that every man gets under the operations of universal law, exactly that reward or punishment which he has deserved; no more, and no less. No good deed or bad deed, however, trifling, and however secretly committed, escapes the evenly-balanced scales of Karma.

102. Q. *Were all these points of Doctrine that you have explained meditated upon by Buddha near the Bó-tree?*

A. Yes, these and many more that may be read in the Buddhist Scriptures. The entire system of Buddhism came to his mind during the Great Meditation.

103. Q. *How long did Buddha remain near the Bó-tree?*

A. Forty-nine days.

104. Q. *What did he then do?*

A. He went to the tree called Ajapála, where he decided after meditation to teach his law to all without distinction of sex, caste or race.

105. Q. *To whom did he first preach the Doctrine?*

A. To the five companions, or disciples, who had abandoned him when he broke his severe fast.

106. Q. *Where did he find them?*

A. At Isipatana, near Benares.

107. Q. *Did they readily listen to him?*

A. They meant not to do so. However, so great was the beauty of his appearance and the

power of his influence, all five were forced to pay the closest attention to his preaching.

108. *Q. What is this discourse of Buddha's called?*

A. The Dhammacakka-ppavattana Sutta,—the Sutra of the Definition of the Rule of Doctrine.*

109. *Q. What effect had the discourse upon the five companions?*

A. The aged Kondanya was first to enter the path leading to arahatship; afterwards the other four.

110. *Q. Who were the next converts?*

A. A young, rich layman, named Yasa, and his father. By the end of five months the disciples numbered sixty persons.

111. *Q. What did Buddha at that time do?*

A. Called together his disciples, and sent them in various and opposite directions to preach. He himself went to a town called Senani which was near Uruwela.

112. *Q. Are there many Buddhists at present in all the world?*

---

* The High Priest Sumangala gave me the translation of the title, but see *Appendix*.

A. There are more Buddhists than any other class of religionists.

113. *Q. How many people are there supposed to be living on the earth?*

A. About 1,300 millions.

114. *Q. Of these how many are Buddhists?*

A. About 500 millions; not quite half.

115. *Q. You say that after Buddha had been preaching five months, his followers numbered only sixty in all?*

A. He had that many disciples only.

116. *Q. After becoming Buddha how long did he teach his Doctrine on earth?*

A. Forty-five years. During this time he made a vast number of converts among all classes; among rajahs and coolies, the rich and the poor, the mighty and the humble. And among his followers were also some of the most learned men of his day.

117. *Q. What became of his former wife and his son Rahula?*

A. First Rahula, and, later, Yasódhara gave up the world and became followers of his Doctrine.

118. *Q. What of his father, the King?*

A. He accepted the true Doctrine also.

119. Q. *Throughout his career was it Buddha's habit to travel about the conntry?*

A. During the eight dry months of the year he went from city to city, and from province to province, teaching and preaching to the people. During the four rainy months he would remain in one place, giving especial instruction to his declared followers.

120. Q. *Do Buddhist priests still imitate this custom?*

A. Yes, many do.

121. Q. *Of Buddha's own disciples, who were his favourites?*

A. Sàriputra and Moggallána.

122. Q. *How do Buddhist priests differ from the priests of other religions?*

A. In other religions the priests claim to be intercessors between men and God, to help to obtain pardon of sins; the Buddhist priests do not acknowledge or expect anything from a Divine Power, but they ought to govern their lives according to the Doctrine of Buddha and teach the true path to others. A personal god Buddhists regard as only a gigantic shadow

thrown upon the void of space by the imagination ef ignorant men.

123. Q. *Do they accept the theory of everything having been formed out of nothing by a Creator?*

A. Buddha taught that two things are eternal, viz, 'Akása' aud 'Nirvána:' everything has come out of Akása in obedience to a law of motion inherent in it, and, after a certain existence, passes away. No thing ever come out of nothing. We do not believe in miracles; hence we deny creation, and cannot conceive of a Creator.

124. Q. *Did Buddha hold to idol worship?*

A. He did not, he opposed it.

125. Q. *But do not Buddhists offer flowers and make reverence before the statue of Buddha, his relics, and the monuments enshrining them?*

A. Yes, but not with the sentiment of the idolator.

126. Q. *What is the difference?*

A. Our Pagan brother not only takes his images as visible representations of his unseen God or gods; but the refined idolator in worshipping considers that the idol contains in its substance a portion of the all-pervading divinity.

The Buddhist reverences Buddha's statue and the other things you have mentioned only as mementos of the greatest, wisest, most benevolent, and compassionate man who ever lived. All races and peoples preserve, treasure up, and value the relics and mementos of men and women who have been considered in any way great. Buddha, to us, seems more to be revered and beloved by every human being who knows sorrow, than any one else in the history of the world.

127. *Q. Are charms, incantations, the observance of lucky hours, and devil-dancing a part of Buddhism?*

A. They are positively repugnant to its fundamental principles. They are the surviving relics of fetishism and pantheistic and other foreign religions. In the *Brahmajala Sutta* Buddha has categorically described these and other superstitions as pagan, mean and spurious.

128. *Q. What striking contrasts are there between Buddhism and what may be properly called " religions" ?*

A. Among others, these: It teaches the highest goodness without a God: a continued

existence without what goes by the name of 'soul'; a happiness without an objective Heaven; a method of salvation without a Vicarious Saviour; a redemption by oneself as the Redeemer, and without rites, prayers, penances, priests or intercessory saints; and a *summum bonum* attainable in this life and in this world.

129. Q. *Does popular Buddhism contain nothing but what is true, and in accord with science?*

A. Like every other religion that has existed many centuries, it doubtless contains untruth mingled with truth; even gold is found mixed with dross. The poetical imagination, zeal, or lingering superstitions of Buddhist devotees, have no doubt, in various ages, caused the noble principles of Buddha's moral doctrines to be coupled more or less with what might be removed to advantage.

130. Q. *Is Buddhism opposed to education, and to the study of science?*

A. Quite the contrary: in the *Singálowáda Sutta*, a discourse preached by Buddha in the bambu grove near Rajagriha, he specified as one of the duties of a teacher that he should give

his pupils "instruction in science and lore."

131. *Q. Are there any dogmas in Buddhism which we are required to accept on faith?*

A. No: we are earnestly enjoined to accept nothing whatever on faith; whether it be written in books, handed down from our ancestors, or taught by the sages. Our Lord Buddha has said that we must not believe in a thing said merely because it is said; nor in traditions because they have been handed down from antiquity; nor rumours, as such; nor writings by sages, because sages wrote them; nor fancies that we may suspect to have been inspired in us by a deva [that is, in presumed spiritual inspiration]; nor from inferences drawn from some haphazard assumption we may have made; nor because of what seems an analogical necessity; nor on the mere authority of our teachers or masters. But we are to believe when the writing, doctrine, or saying is corroborated by our own reason and consciousness. "For this," says he in concluding, " I taught you not to believe merely because you have heard, but when you believed of your own consciousness, then to act accordingly and

abundantly." (See the *Kálámá Sutta of the Anguttara Nikaya*.)

132. Q. *Does Buddhism countenance hypocrisy?*

A. The *Dhamma-pada* says: Like a beautiful flower full of colour without scent, the fine words of him who does not act accordingly are fruitless."

133. Q. *Does Buddhism teach us to return evil for evil?*

A. In the *Dhamma-pada* Buddha said: "a man who foolishly does me wrong, I will return to him the protection of my ungrudging love: the more evil comes from him, the more good shall go from me." This is the path followed by the Arahats.* To return evil for evil is positively forbidden in Buddhism.

134. Q. *Is Buddhism a chart of science, or a code of morals?*

A. It is chiefly a pure moral philosophy. It assumes the universal operation of the law of motion and change, by which all things, the worlds and all forms, animate, and inanimate, upon them are governed. It is unprofitable to waste time in speculating as to the origin of things. In the *Málunka Sutta* we read that

when Málunka asked Buddha to explain the origin of things he made him no reply; as he considered that the iniquiry tended to no profit. Buddhism take things as they are, and shows how the existing evil and misery may be overcome.

135. *Q. Does Buddhism teach the immortality of the soul?*

A. "Soul," it considers a word used by the ignorant to express a false idea. If every thing is subject to change, then man is included, and every material part of him must change. That which is subject to change is not permanent: so there can be no immortal survival of a changeful thing.

136. *Q. If the idea of a human "soul" is to be rejected, what is that in man which gives him the impression of having a permanent individuality?*

A. *Tanha*, or the unsatisfied desire for existence. The being having done that for which he must be rewarded or punished in future, and having Tanha, will have a rebirth through the influence of Karma.

137. *Q. What is it that is born?*

A. A new aggregation of Skandhas, or

personality * caused by the last yearnings of the dying person.

138. Q. *How many Skandhas are there?*
 A. Five.

139. Q. *Name the five Skandhas?*

 A. Rúpa, Vêdanâ, Sanná, Samkhárá, and Vinnána.

140. Q. *Briefly explain what they are?*

 A. Rúpa, material qualities; Vêdanâ sensation; Sanná, abstract ideas; Samkhárá, tendencies of mind; Vinnána, mental powers. Of these we are formed; by them we are conscious of existence; and through them communicate with the world about us.

141. Q. *To what cause must we attribute the differences in the conbination of the Five Skandhas which make every individual differ from every other individual?*

 A. To the *Karma* of the individual in the next proceeding birth.

142. Q. *What is the force or energy that is at work, under the guidance of Karma, to produce the new being?*

 A. *Tanha*—the "WILL TO LIVE."*

143. Q. *Upon what is the doctrine of rebirths founded?*

A. Upon the perception that perfect justice, equilibrium, and adjustment are inherent in the universal law of nature. Buddhists do not believe one life long enough for the reward or punishment of a man's deeds. The great circle of re-births will be more or less quickly run through according to the preponderating purity or impurity of the several lives of the individual.

144. Q. *Is this new aggregation of Skandhas, this new personality, the same being as that in the previous birth, whose Tanha has brought it into existence?*

A. In one sense it is a new being, in another it is not. During this life, the Skandhas are constantly changing; and while the man A.B. of forty is identical, as regards personality, with the youth A.B. of eighteen, yet, by the continual waste and reparation of his body, and change of mind and character, he is a different being. Nevertheless, the man in his old age justly reaps the reward or suffering consequent upon his thoughts and actions at every previous stage of his life. So the new being of a re-birth,

being the same individulity as before with but a changed form, or new aggregation of Skandhas, justly reaps the consequences of his actions and thoughts in the previous existence.

145. Q. *But the aged man remembers the incidents of his youth, despite his being physically and mentally changed. Why, then, is not the recollection of past lives brought over by us from our last birth into the present birth?*

A. Because memory is included within the Skandhas; and the Skandhas having changed with the new existence, a new memory, the record of that particular existence, develops. Yet the record or reflection of all the past lives must survive; for, when Prince Siddhárta became Buddha, the full sequence of his previous births was seen by him. If their several incidents had left no trace behind, he could not have done this, as there would have been nothing for him to see. And any one who attains to the state of *Jhana* can thus retrospectively trace the line of his lives.

146. Q. *What is the ultimate point towards which tend all these series of changes in form?*

A. NIRVANA.

40 BUDDHIST CATECHISM.

147. Q. *Does Buddhism admit that man has in his nature any latent powers for the production of Phenomena, commonly called ' miracles.' ?*

A. Yes; but they are natural, not supernatural. They may be developed by a certain system which is laid down in our sacred books.

148. Q. *What is this branch of science called?*

A. The Pali name is Iddhividhanâna.

149. Q. *How many kinds are there?*

A. Two: "Laukika" (*i.e.*, one in which the phenomena-working power is obtained by resort to drugs, the recitation of *mantras* (charms), or other extraneous aids), and "Lokôttara" (that in which the power in question is acquired by interior self-development).

150. Q. *What class of men enjoy these powers?*

A. They gradually develop in one who pursues a certain course of ascetic practice called *Dhyana*.

151. Q. *Can this Iddhi power be lost?*

A. The Laukika can be lost, but the Lokothra never, when once acquired.

152. Q. *Had Buddha this last-named Iddhi?*

A. Yes, in perfection.

153. Q. *What did Buddha's wisdom embrace?*

A. He knew the nature of the KNOWABLE and the "UNKNOWABLE," the Possible and the Impossible, the cause of Merit and Demerit; he could read the thoughts of all beings; he knew the laws of nature, the illusions of the senses and the means to suppress desires; he could distinguish the births and rebirths of individuals; and other things.

154. Q. *You spoke of a 'deva' having appeared to the Prince Siddartha under a variety of forms; what do Buddhists believe respecting races of invisible beings having relations with mankind?*

A. They believe that there are such being; which inhabit worlds, or spheres, of their own. It is Buddhist doctrine that by interior self-development and conquest over his baser nature, the Arahat becomes superior to the best of the devas, and may subject and control the lower orders.

155. Q. *How many kinds of devas are there?*

A. Three: "Kâmâwachera" (those which are still under the dominion of the passions): "Rûpâwachera,' (a higher class, but which still retain an individual form); "Arûpawachera,"

(the highest in degree of purification, and which are devoid of material forms.)

156. *Q. Should we fear any of them?*

A. He who is pure in heart and of a courageous mind need fear nothing: no bad deva can injure him. But some have power to torment the impure, as well as those who invite their approach.

157. *Q. Give me the particulars about the death of the body of Buddha, and his departure to Nirvána?*

A. Having accomplished his self-appointed task, perfected his Doctrine, and pointed out the path to Nirvàna to thousands of people, he was ready to depart. The 45th season after his attaining Buddhahood, at the full-moon day of May, he came at evening to Kusi-nagara, a place about 120 miles from Benares, and his end approaching, he caused his couch to be spread between two Sâl trees, the head towards the North. He preached in the first part of the night to the Malliya princes; in the second part of the night he converted a great Brahmin pandit, Subhadra; after that he discoursed to the assembled priests

about his Doctrine; at daybreak he passed into the interior condition of "Samadhi."

158. *Q. What were Buddha's last words, and to whom addressed?*

A. To his disciples: he said "Mendicants! I now impress it upon you, the parts and powers of man must be dissolved; WORK OUT YOUR SALVATION with diligence." After this he spake no more.

159. *Q. Give the important dates connected with his life?*

A. He was born under the constellation Wissa on a Friday in May, in the year 2478 of the Kaliyuga; went into the jungle in the year 2506; became a Buddha in the year 2513, on a Wednesday, at early dawn; and in the year 2558, at the full moon of May, on a Tuesday, he expired at the age of eighty years.

160. *Q. Did he write in books his Doctrine?*

A. No; it was not the Indian custom. During the forty-five years of his teaching he developed his Doctrine in all the minute details. He recited te his disciples, who committed it to memory, word by word. But as there was no prohibition against writing it, it appears from

44   BUDDHIST CATECHISM.

the *Dhatu Wibhanga Sutta* that King Bimbisàra caused the chief points to be inscribed on golden leaves. In the season of *was* following his death a council, consisting of 500 Arahats under the presidency of Mahá Kásyapa, one of Buddha's greatest disciples, was held to settle the rules and doctrines of the Order.

161. Q. *Where did this Council meet?*

A. At the Sattapanni cave near Rájagriha. The whole council chanted together the words of the Teacher.

162. Q. *When were other Councils held?*

A. A second, at Vaisàli, in the Wâlukarama temple, a century after, under the presidency of Yasat Thera; a third, at Patna, in the 226th year of the Buddhist Era, in the Asokarama temple, under the presidency of Moggaliputtatissa and the patronage of the great King Asoka.

163. Q. *Who was King Asoka?*

A. King of Magadha, and the most powerful monarch of his time in Asia. He was converted to Buddhism in the 10th year of his reign and most devoted to its spread throughout

the world. He was a good King and his name is honoured and beloved wherever there are Buddhists.

164. Q. *What did he for Buddhism?*

A. Built dagobas and monasteries, established gardens and hospitals, not only for men but also for animals, and enjoined all his subjects to observe the moral precepts of Buddha. He also sent missionaries after the Council of Patna to carry the religion to many different countries, and ambassadors to four Greek Kings to inform them about Buddha's Doctrine. To keep the religion pure he established in his own country the office of Minister of Justice and Religion. The King also appointed officials to promote the education of women in the principles of Buddha.

165. Q. *What tangible proof is there of all this?*

A. Within the last fifty years there have been discovered in various parts of India and Afghanistan, the edicts of King Asoka engraven on rocks and stone pillars. They have been translated into English and published at the Government Press in India.

166. Q. *In what light do these edicts make Buddhism appear?*

A. As a religion of noble tolerance, of universal brotherhood, of righteousness and justice. They have done much to win for it the respect in which it is now held in Europe and America by all the great pandits.

167. Q. *How does a recent English writer express himself about these edicts, in a work published by a Christian Educational Society?* (*Buddhism,* by T. W. Rhys.-Davids, Esq.)

A. He says: "the edicts are full of a lofty righteousness......Obedience to parents; kindness to children and friends; mercy towards the brute creation; indulgence to inferiors; reverence towards Brahmins and members of the Order; suppression of anger, passion, cruelty or extravagance; generosity, and tolerance, and charity—such are the lessons which 'the kindly King, the delight of the gods,' inculcates on all his subject."

168. Q. *When was Buddhism introduced into Ceylon?*

A. In the reign of King Devanam Piya Tissa, it was brought to Ceylon by Mahinda,

king Asoka's own son, who had become a priest. The King of Ceylon received him and the six priests accompanying him with great favour; became a convert to Buddhism, and built the Thúpàràma Dágoba, at Anurádhapura. The sister of Mahinda—Sanghamitta—who had also entered the Order, came to Ceylon, some time after, with a party of Buddhist nuns, and instructed many Sinhalese ladies in religion. Sanghamitta brought over with her a branch of the Bó-tree at Buddha-Gaya, under which the Teacher had gained the Buddhahood. This was planted at Anurádhapura and is still living. It is acknowledged to be the oldest historical tree in the world.

APPENDIX.

Q. 1. The word " religion " is most inappropriate to apply to Buddhism; which is not a religion, but a moral philosophy, as I have shown in Q. 121. But by common usage it has been applied to all groups of people who profess a special moral doctrine, and is so employed by statisticians. The Sinhalese Buddhists have never yet had any conception of what Europeans imply in the etymological construction of the Latin root of this term. In their creed there is no such thing as a " binding," in the Christian sense;—a submission to or merging of self in a divine being. *Agama* is their vernacular word to express their relation to Buddhism and Buddha. It is pure Sanskrit, and means Approach, or Coming; and as '*Buddha*' is Enlightenment, the compound word by which they indicate Buddhism—*Buddhagama*—would be properly rendered as an Approach or Coming to Enlightenment or possibly as a following of the Doctrine of Sakya Muni. The Missionaries, finding *agama* ready to their hand, adopted it as the equivalent for 'religion'; and 'Christianity' is written by them *Christianiagama*, whereas it should be *Christianibandhana*, for *bandhana* is the etymological equivalent for 'religion.'

50   APPENDIX.

With this explanation, I continue to employ under protest the familiar word when speaking of Buddhistic philosophy, for the convenience of the ordinary reader.

* Q. 23. See definition of " Deva " above.

* B. 49. No reason is given in the canonical books for the choice of this side of the tree, though an explanation is to be found in the popular legends upon which the books of Bishop Bigandet and other European commentators are based. Translated into the simpler garb of scientific language it might be thus rendered: There are always certain influences coming upon us from the different quarters of the sky. Sometimes the influence from one quarter will be best, sometimes that from another quarter. This time the influence from the East was best, as he sat at the Western side so as to face the East.

* Q. 81. This celebrated verse has a meaning that should not be overlooked by the student of Buddhistic philosophy. The first line embodies the whole spirit of the *Vinaya*, the second line that of the *Sutta*, the third that of the *Abbidhamma*; thus in three lines, collectively comprising only eight Pali words, are condensed the entire essence of the Buddhist scriptures. According to Mr. Rhys Davids there are about 1,752,800 words in the whole text of the three Pitakas.

* Q. 83. *Saranam*. Wijesinha Mudaliyar writes me:—
" This word has been hitherto very inappropriately and erroneously rendered " *Refuge* " by European Pali

scholars, and thoughtlessly so accepted by native Pali scholars. Neither Pali etymology nor Buddhistic philosophy justifies the translation. "*Refuge*," in the sense of "*a fleeing back*" or "*a place of shelter*," is quite foreign to true Buddhism, which insists on every man working out his own emancipation. The root *Sri* in Sanskrit (*Sara* in Pâli.) means to move, to go; so that Saranam would denote a moving, or he or that which goes before or with another—a Guide or Helper. I construe the passage thus: *Gacchami* I go, *Buddham* to Buddha-*Saranam* as my Guide. The translation of the *Tisarana* as the "Three Refuges, has given rise to much misapprehension, and has been made by Anti-Buddhists a fertile pretext for taunting Buddhists with the absurdity of taking refuge in non-entities and believing in unrealities. The term Refuge is more applicable to Nirvâna of which *Saranam* is a synonym." The High Priest also calls my attention to the fact that the Pali root *Sara* has also the secondary meaning of killing him or that which destroys. *Buddham Saranam gacchami* might thus be rendered "I go to Buddha, the Law, and the Order, as the destroyers of my fears;—the first by his preaching, the second by its axiomatic truth, the third by their virtuous example and precepts."

* Q. 88. An "unseasonable time" is after the sun has passed the meridian. Buddha was wise enough to know that his 'mendicants' could think deeper and be

52 APPENDIX.

healthier by resting the digestive organs half of each day.

* Q. 108. Since the appearance of the first edition I have received from one of the ablest English-Pali, scholars of Ceylon, L. Corneille Wijesinhe, Esq: Mudaliyar of Matale, what seems a better rendering of *Dhammacakka ppavattana* than the one previously given. He makes it " The establishment of the Reign of Law. " Mr. Rhys-Davids' prefers " The Foundation of the Kingdom of Righteousness." Mr. Wijesinha writes me " you may use ' Kingdom of Righteousness,' too, but it savours more of dogmatic theology than of philosophic ethics, *Dhammackka ppvattana suttam* is " The discourse entitled ' The Establishment of the Reign of Law'."

P. S. Having shown this to the High Priest, I am happy to be able to say that he assents to Mr. Wijesinha's rendering.

* Q. 133. A Buddhist ascetic who by a prescribed course of practice, has attained to a superior state of moral and intellectual development. Arahats may be divided into the two general groups of the *Samathayanika, and Sukkha Vipassaka*. The former have destroyed their passions and developed to the fullest their intellectual capacity, or mystical insight; the latter have equally conquered passion, but not acquired the superior mental powers. The Arahat of the former class, when fully developed, is no longer a prey to the

APPENDIX.   53

delusions of the seasons, nor the slave of passion or moral frailty. *He penetrates to the root of whatsoever subject his mind is applied to* without following the slow *processes of reasoning.* His self-conquest is complete; and in place of the emotion and desire which vex and enthral the ordinary man, he is lifted up into a condition which is best expressed in the term ' Nirvamic.' There is in Ceylon a popular misconception that the attainment of Arahatship is now impossible; *that the Buddha had himself prophesied that the power would die out in one millenium after his death.* This rumour, and the similar one that is everywhere heard in India, viz., that this being the dark cycle of the " Kali Yug," the practice of Yoga Vidya, or sublime spiritual science is impossible—I ascribe to the ingenuity of those who should be as pure and *psychically* (to use a non-Buddhistic but very convenient term) wise as were their predecessors, but are not, and seek an excuse. The Buddha taught quite the contrary idea. In the *Digha Nikaya* he said : " Hear, Subhadra—The world will never be without Rahats if the ascetics (Bhikku) in my congregations *well and truly keep my precepts.*"

Imecha Sabadda Bhikku Samma Viharaiyum asanyo loke Arahantehi.

* Q. 137. Upon reflection, I have substituted " personality " for " individuality " as written in the first edition. The successive appearances upon one or many earths, or " descents into generation," of the

APPENDIX.

tanhaically—coherent parts (Skandhas) of a certain being, are a succession of personalities. In each birth the *personality* differs from that of the previous or next succeeding birth. Karma, the *deus ex machina*, masks (or, shall we say, reflects?) itself now in the personality of a sage, again as an artisan, and so on throughout the string of births. But though personalities ever shift, the one line of life along which they are strung like beads, runs unbroken; it is ever *that particular line*, never any other. It is therefore individual, an individual vital undulation, which began in Nirvana, or the subjective side of nature, as the light or heat undulation through æther began at its dynamic source; is careering through the objective side of Nature, under the impulse of Karma and the creative direction of Tanha; and tends, through many cyclic changes, back to Nirvana. Mr. Rhys-Davids calls that which passes from personality to personality along the individual chain, "character" or "doing." Since "character" is not a mere metaphysical abstraction, but the sum of one's mental qualities and moral propensities, would it not help to dispel what Mr. Rhys-Davids calls " the desperate expedient of a mystery" [*Buddhism*, p. 101] if we regarded the life-undulation as individuality, and each of its series of natal manifestations as a separate personality? The perfected individual, Buddhistically speaking, is a Buddha, I should say; for a Buddha

APPENDIX. 55

is but the rare flower of humanity, without the least supernatural admixture. And, as countless generations ("four asankheyyas and a hundred thousand cycles." Fausböll and Rhys-Davids' *Buddhist Birth Stories*, p. 13) are required to develop a man into a Buddha, and *the iron will to become one runs throughout all the successive births*, what shall we call that which thus wills and perseveres? *Character?* Or individuality: an individuality but partly manifested in any *one* birth, but built up of fragments from all the births?

The denial of "Soul" by Buddha (see Sanyutto Nikàya the Sutta Pitaka) points to the prevalent delusive belief in an independent, transmissible personality; an entity that could move from birth to birth unchanged, or go to a place or state where, as such perfect entity, it could eternally enjoy or suffer. And what he shows is, that the "I am I" consciousness is, as regards permanency logically impossible, since its elementary constituents constantly change, and the "I" of one birth differs from the "I" of every other birth. But everything that I have found in Buddhism accords with the theory of a gradual evolution of the perfected man —viz. a Buddha—through numberless natal experiences. And in the consciousness of that person who, at the end of a given chain of beings attains Buddhahood, or who succeeds in attaining the fourth stage of Dhyana, or mystic self-developement, in any one of his births

anterior to the final one, the scenes of all these serial births are perceptible. In the Jatakatthavannanà—so well translated by Mr. Rhys Davids—an expression continually recurs which, I think, rather supports such an idea, viz: "Then the Blessed One *made manifest an occurence hidden by change of birth.*" Or "that which had been hidden by, &c." Early Buddhism then, clearly held to a permanency of records in the Akasa, and the potential capacity of man to read the same, when he has evoluted to the stage of true individual ENLIGHTENMENT.

*Q. 142. The student may profitably consult Schopenhauer in this connection. Arthur Schopenhauer, a modern German philosopher of the most eminent ability, taught that " the Principle, or Radical, of Nature, and of all her objects, the human body included, is intrinsically what we ourselves are the most conscious of in our own body, viz., Will. Intellect is a secondary capacity of the primary will, a function of the brain, in which this will reflects itself, as nature and object and body as in a mirror * * * Intellet is secondary * * but may lead, in saints, to a complete renunciation of "will," as far as it urges life and is then extinguished in Nirvana." (L. A. Sanders, in the *Theosophist*, for May, 1882, p. 213.)

明治十九年四月一日御屆
同年四月十二日出版

翻刻出版人 京都府平民 水谷了然

發兌所 東京府芝公園地第八號淨運院內 佛典協會本局
　　　　東京府下京橋區松屋町貳丁目六番地寄留

賣捌所 全三十間堀町壹丁目貳番地 明教社

全南鍋町壹丁目六番地 鴻盟社

大坂府備後町四丁目

博聞分社

西京府下花屋町

永田調兵衛

全 日本橋區通三丁目

丸善書肆

東京府銀坐四丁目

博聞社

ERRATA.

In the Page 4, line 3, of second preface " Fiveand" is " Five and "

„ „ 9, section 43, " hs " is " he "

„ „ 17, „ 78, "Buddhim" is "Buddhism"

„ „ 37, „ 141, must be reduce the period under " every "

„ „ 39, „ 144, " individulity " is " individuality "

„ „ 43, „ 160, " te " is " to "

„ „ 50, line 5, " B. 49." is " Q. 49."

A SHORT HISTORY
OF THE
TWELVE JAPANESE BUDDHIST SECTS

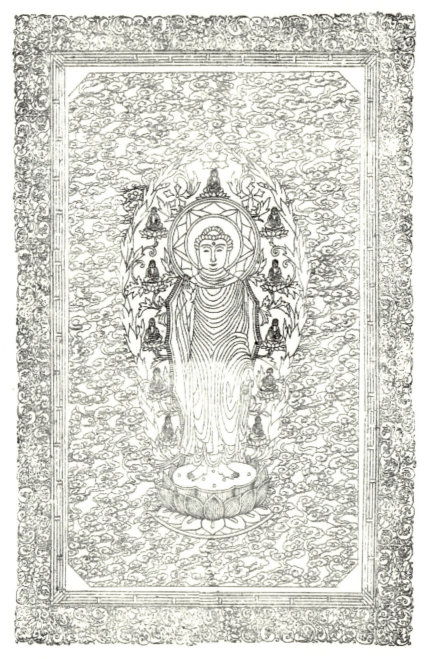

A SHORT HISTORY

OF THE

TWELVE JAPANESE BUDDHIST SECTS.

TRANSLATED FROM THE ORIGINAL JAPANESE

BY

BUNYIU NANJIO, M. A. OXON;

MEMBER OF THE ROYAL ASIATIC SOCIETY, LONDON;
LECTURER ON THE SANSKRIT LANGUAGE
IN THE IMPERIAL UNIVERSITY, TŌKYŌ.

TOKYO:
BUKKYŌ-SHO-EI-YAKU-SHUPPAN-SHA.
MEIJI 19TH YEAR.

CONTENTS.

	page
Preface...	V
Introduction	VIII
Chapter I, the Ku-sha-shū	1
Chapter II, the Jō-jitsu-shū	13
Chapter III, the Ris-shū	20
Chapter IV, the Hossō-shū	32
Chapter V, the San-ron-shū	44
Chapter VI, the Ke-gon-shū	57
Chapter VII, the Ten-dai-shū	68
Chapter VIII, the Shin-gon-shū	78
Chapter IX, the Jō-do-shū	104
Chapter X, the Zen-shū	114
Chapter XI, the Shin-shū	122
Chapter XII, the Nichi-ren-shū	132
Sanskrit-Chinese Index	149

PREFACE.

The aim of the following work is defined by its title; it is a short history, not of Buddhism in general, but of the twelve Japanese Buddhist sects. It is a translation of a Japanese Ms., which consists of an introduction and twelve chapters written separately by nine living Japanese priests within the last seven months. When I was requested by Mr. S. Sano to undertake this work in May last, the Ms. was not yet complete. As my translation was going on, the writers, gradually sent me their respective Ms. from various parts of the country, saying that they wrote in a great hurry. Their style of composition is not always the same, and this has given me a special difficulty to render their words exactly into the English language, with which I am not at all very well acquainted. Moreover the subject itself is of course a very hard one though I have already spent many years in studying it. Whenever the original text is too complicated, I have been obliged to make it short, or to leave certain portions untranslated.

The following are the names of the writers of the text, and some other matters : —

The introduction and the fifth, sixth and eighth chapters on the sects of San-ron, Ke-gon and Shin-gon were written by my friend the Rev. Kō-chō

VI PREFACE.

Ogurusu of the Shin-shū. The first chapter on the Ku-sha-shū was written by the Rev. Shū-zan Emura of the Shin-shū. Another and longer text on the same sect was written by the Rev. Kyoku-ga Saiki of the Shin-gon-shū, but it was too late to be used for this translation. The second and third chapters on the sects of Jō-jitsu and Ritsu are the productions of the Rev. Shō-hen Ueda of the Shin-gon-shū. The writer of the fourth chapter on the Hossō-shū is the Rev. Dai-ryō Takashi of the Shin-gon-shū, and that of the seventh chapter of the Ten-dai-shū is the Rev. Kyō-kwan Uemura of that sect. Another text on the San-ron-shū was written by the Rev. Sō-ken Ueno of the Shin-gon-shū; and that on the Ke-gon-shū, by the Rev. Jitsu-ben Kazuyama of the Ji-shū. But these were also too late to be used for this work. The Revs. Gyō-kai Fukuda, Ken-kō Tsuji, Ren-jō Akamatsu and Ze-jun Kobayashi have each written a chapter on their own sect. Their subjects are the Jō-do-shū (the 9th chapter), the Zen-shū (10th), the Shin-shū (11th) and the Nichi-ren-shū (12th) respectively.

The text is full of proper names and technical terms, which I have mostly restored to their Sanskrit forms, adding the Japanese sound of the Chinese translation or transliteration, and also giving an English translation.

For the orthography of the Sanskrit names and

PREFACE. VII

terms, Professor Max Müller's missionary alphabet has been adopted, as it avoids the use of diacritical marks. It has this peculiarity that italic *k* and *g* are emplyed to represent ch and j as usually pronounced in English. This is because these palatal sounds are derived from gutturals.

For the orthography of the Japanese sound of the Chinese and Japanese names and terms, the alphabet of the Rō-ma-ji-kwai or 'Roman Letter Society' has been adopted.

I greatly regret that the scale of the present work has hindered me from giving in detail the authorities for every statement. In the original text, the authorities are not given, and I have also had no time to look through even the principal books of the tweleve sects, during the progress of this work, as my time has been much occupied by professional duties. Nevertheless I have done my best, though the work be very imperfect indeed.

I have now only most sincerely to thank Dr. W. S. Bigelow for his kindness in correcting some parts of this translation, and Professor Chamberlain for similar assistance with regard to certain others.

Bunyiu Nanjio.

Asakusa, Tōkyō, Japan:
6th December, 19th year of Meiji (1886).

VIII

INTRODUCTION.

Those whose minds are confused are called the ignorant. Those whose minds are enlightened are called Buddhas.

Among the confused, there are insects whether flying quickly or moving slowly, such as wasps and caterpillars. There are animals of the scaly tribes, and those covered with shells or crusts. There are animal tribes which are either hairy or naked. Some are one-horned, and others two-horned. Some are two-footed, and others many-footed. Some have wings with which they fly, and others have talons with which they seize their prey. There are large animals called whales; the ferocious are tigers and wolves; the poisonous are vipers and waterbugs; and the cunning are foxes and badgers. There are horned owls which eat their mothers. There are some animals called owl-cats which eat their fathers. Thus there are several different kinds of animals, of which the weaker are always injured by the stronger. Such is the state of the beings who have entered into the nature of animals (Tiryag-yoni-gata, or Chiku-shō-dō, or Tō-shō-shu).

There are Pretas (Ga-ki) or 'departed spirits,' whose bellies are as large as a hill, while their mouths are as small as the eye of a needle; so that

INTRODUCTION. IX

they can neither eat nor drink. There are Pretas, for whom water is always changed into fire, as soon as they desire to drink; so that they can never satisfy their thirst. There are Pretas, who eat nothing but excrements and matter. There are Pretas, whose bodies are pierced by their own hairs, the points of which are as sharp as swords. Again there are Pretas, who eat their own children. Such is the state of the Pretas. This state is not seen by human eyes; but among mankind there is often seen something like the above.

The eight hot hells are the states of blazing fire, and the eight cold hells are those of freezing water. The former eight are called Sam*g*îva (Tō-kwatsu), Kâlasûtra (Koku-jō), Sa*m*ghâta (Shu-gō), Raurava (Kyō-kwan), Mahâ-raurava (Dai-kyō-kwan), Tapana (Shō-netsu), Pratâpana (Dai-shō-netsu), and Avî*k*i (Mu-ken). The latter eight are called Arbuda (A-bu-da), Nirarbuda (Ni-ra-bu-da), A*tat*a (A-se-ta), Apapa (Ko-ko-ba), Hâhâdhara (Ko-ko-ba), Utpala (U-ha-ra), Padma (Ha-do-ma), and Mahâ-padma (Ma-ka-ha-do-ma). No words can sufficiently express the several kinds of sufferings in these hells. Such are the states of the beings in these hells (Nârakas). Both the blazing fire and freezing water are not made by any other being, but by their own thought alone.

Not only the beings who have entered into the

nature of the above three states of the lower animals, departed spirits, and those in the various hells, are confused or perplexed; but also the Devas or heavenly beings, Nâgas or serpents, and the other eight classes of beings (Ten-ryū-hachi-bu) are the same. They are called Mahoragas ('great serpents'), Kinnaras (lit. 'what sort of men?'), Garu*d*as, Râhu ('the seizer'), Asuras, Gandharvas, Râkshasas, Yakshas, Nâgas ('serpents'), Vi*s*vakarma*n* ('all-doer'), Sûrya ('the sun'), Soma ('the moon'), Marî*k*i, Mahe*s*vara, *S*akra Devânâm Indra ('the king of gods named *S*akra'), Mahâbrahman, beings of the four Dhyâna-go*k*aras (Shizen-ten), and the four Arûpas (Shi-mu-shiki). Though their pains and pleasures are somewhat different from each other, being themselves either holy or ignorant; yet they all belong to the three worlds of desire, form, and formlessness, and are not free from confusion.

Among the beings of the three worlds, men are more thoughtful than all others. Thinking is their mental faculty. Being thoughtful, they are confused. Being thoughtful, they are enlightened, Being thoughtful, they become rich and noble. Being thoughtful, they become poor and mean. Being thoughtful, they keep peace. Being thoughtful, they begin to fight. Being thoughtful, they plan to strengthen themselves. Being thoughtful, they fear to be weakened by others. Thus, whether their thinking be skilful or not, some people are flourishing, while others

INTRODUCTION. XI

are put to shame.

There are wise princes and clever ministers. There are rebellions ministers and villainous sons. Some people are appointed to high office, given large salaries and intrusted with the power of government. Some people are always picking up things which are rejected or useless. Some dwell in splendid houses and halls, and eat excellent food at every meal. Some live in the dilapidated houses, wear torn clothes, and suffer hunger. Some are in fear of assasins; and others in dread of epidemic disease. Some are in dread of inundation and conflagration; and others are afraid of theives and robbers. Some are drowned in the water, and others are hanged by the neck. There are people either deaf, dumb, or blind. Thus greatly do they differ in happiness and unhappiness; some being joyful, and others sorrowful. This difference depends only on the goodness and badness of their thinking; and they are the effects of the causes of the former existence.

In short, all those who are only careful for the present life and can not see into the future, are called the confused, whether they be wise or ignorant, rich or poor. It is quite impossible for human power to cause every man in the world to become rich and noble, wise and healthy, and long-lived. No religion except the doctrine of Buddha can place all beings in the true state of permanence, joy, self and **purity**

XII INTRODUCTION.

(Jō-raku-ga-jō, i. e. the four virtues of Nirvâna). This Buddhism does out of compassion, being itself independent of all the troubles of the three worlds.

Buddha Sâkyamuni appeared in the world to perform the most important thing, namely, to cause beings to become enlightened. There are many different accounts given of his life. We shall give here an outline of one of these accounts.

LIFE OF BUDDHA.

Buddha was born in the kingdom of Kapila-vastu (Ka-bi-ra-e) in Central India, on the eighth day of the fourth month of the twenty fourth year of the reign of the king Shō of the Shū (Chow) dynasty in China, 1027 B. C. At the moment of his birth, he said: 'I alone, of all beings in heaven above and under the heavens, am worthy of honour.' His father was the Mahâ-râga or 'great king' Suddhodana (Jō-bon Dai-ō), and his mother was the Devî or 'queen' Mâyâ (Maya Bu-nin).

At the age of seven he was thoroughly acquainted with astronomy, geography, arithmetic and military science. At ten he surpassed other princes in shooting through seven iron targets. At fifteen he was formally recognised as heir-apparent. At seventeen he was married to Yasodharâ (Ya-shu-da-ra). At eighteen he began to think of leaving home, because he perceived how existence was traversed by the

pains of birth, old age, disease and death. On the seventh day of the second month of his nineteenth year, he entered the forest in order to study the perfect way.

On the seventh day of the second month of his thirtieth year, he awoke to perfect knowledge, while sitting under the Bodhi tree. Buddha had three bodies, viz., 1. Dharma-kâya (Hosshin) or the 'law-body,' which is colourless and formless; 2. Sambhoga-kâya (Hō-shin) or ' the compensation-body,' by which Buddha appears before the Bodhisattvas of the Dasa-bhûmis (Jū-ji) or ten stages; and 3. Nirmâna-kâya (Ō-jin, or Ke-shin) or the 'transformed body,' by which he appears before the Pratyekabuddhas, Srâvakas, Devas and men. This is the reason why Buddha Sâkyamuni was seen differently by the hearers of the Mahâyâna and Hînayâna doctrine during his whole life.

After his enlightenment, Buddha sat for seven days absorbed in meditation, and felt the pleasure of the Law.

In the second week, he preached the Buddhâva-tamsaka-mahâvaipulya-sûtra (Ke-gon-gyō)[1] in nine assemblies held at seven different places. This is called the first period of Ke-gon by Ten-dai Dai-shi.

On the thirtieth day of the second month (i. e. the

---
[1] *Nos.* 87,88.

XIV INTRODUCTION.

4 th week), Buddha converted the Nâgarâga or 'snake king' Makilinda (Mon-rin Ryū-ō). On the seventh day of the third month, he converted Devapâla (? Dai-i-ha-ri). On the following day, he went to Vârânasî, where Kaundinya and others were converted. At the age of thirty-one, he converted the Sreshthin or wealthy merchant Yasas (Ya-sha Chō-ja). Then he went to the kingdom of Magadha and converted Uruvilvâ-kâsyapa and others. Then, going to Râgagriha, he converted King Bimbisâra and his retainers. In the same year, the Sreshthin Kâlya (? Ka-ryō Chō-ja) presented to Buddha the monastery of Venuvana (Chiku-rin-shō-ja) or the 'bamboo grove.' At the age of thirty-two, he converted Nâgas (Ryū) or snakes and Yakshas (? Ki) or demons, at mount Gajasîrsha (Zō-dzu) or the 'elephant's head.' At thirty-three, Sâriputra and Mahâmaudgalyâyana became his disciples. At this time the disciples who attained to Arhatship numbered twelve hundred and fifty. In the same year, Mahâkâsyap became a disciple of Buddha. He presented to Buddha a robe valued at one hundred thousand taels. At thirty-four, Buddha was in Vaisâli and established the rules of morality. After this year, he constantly added to the number of these rules. At thirty-five, the Sreshthin Sudatta (Shudatsu Chō-ja) of Srâvastî together with the Prince Geta, presented to Buddha the Geta-vana Anâtha-

INTRODUCTION.   XV

pi*n*dada-ârâma (Gi–ju Gikko–doku–on) or *G*eta's grove and Anâthapi*n*dada's garden known as the Gi-on-shō-ja. In this year, Buddha went back to Kapilavastu, when his father King *S*uddhodana sent his retainers and subject people to meet him at a distance of forty miles. The king also selected five hundred rich men to wait upon Buddha, so that he was as splendid as a phoenix flying towards Mount Sumeru. At thirty-six, Buddha preached the Pratyutpanna–buddhasa*m*mukhâvasthita–sûtra (Han-ju-kyō),[2] in Godhanya (Ku-ya-ni). At thirty-seven, Ânanda became his disciple, when he was eight years old. In this year, Buddha converted a younger brother of Kinnara–râ*g*a Druma (Jun Shin-da-ra-ō) on Mount Ryū. At thirty-eight, Râhula became his disciple, when he was nine years old. At thirty-nine, Buddha went to Magadha and converted King Pushya (? Hokka-sha-ō). In this year, a 'votive altar' (Kai-dan) was erected on the south-east of the Gi-on. At forty, Buddha preached to Maitreya (Mi-roku) the Abhinishkrama*n*a-sûtra (Hon-gi-kyō).[3] At forty-one, he returned to Kapilavastu a second time and preached the Buddha-dhyâna–samâdhi–sâgara–sûtra (Kwan-butsu-san-mai-kyō),[4] to his father the king. In this year, his aunt Mahâpra*g*âpatî left home and became a Bhikshu*n*î. During the above twelve years, Buddha spoke for the

[2] *No.* 73. [3] *No.* 509. [4] *No.* 430.

XVI INTRODUCTION.

most part the Hînayâna doctrine. This is called the second period of Roku-on (Mriga-dâva or 'deer park') or A-gon (Âgama) by Ten-dai Dai-shi.

At the age of forty two, Buddha preached the Vimala-kîrtti-nirdesa-sûtra (Yui-ma-kitsu-kyō)[5] in the city of Vaisâlî. At forty-three, he preached the Viseshakintâ-brahma-pariprikkhâ-sûtra (Shi-yaku-bon-den-sho-mon-gyō).[6] At forty-four, he preached the Laṅkâvatâra-sûtra (Ryō-ga-kyō)[7] on mount Laṅkâ in the Southern sea. In this year he also spoke the Suvarna-prabhâsa-sûtra (Kon-kō-myō-kyō)[8] and the Srîmâlâ-devî-simhanâda-sûtra (Shō-man-gyō).[9] From the age of forty-five to forty-nine, Buddha preached the Mahâvaipulya-mahâ-samnipâta-sûtra (Dai-hō-dō-dai-shikkyō)[10] to Buddhas and Bodhisattvas assembled from ten different regions, by a great stair-case made between the world of desire and that of form. He also preached to Ânanda the Sûrâm gama-samâdhi-sûtra (Shu-ryō-gon-gyō).[11] The above eight years are called the third period of Hō-dō (Vaipulya) by Ten-dai Dai-shi.

During the next twenty-two years from the age of fifty to seventy-one, Buddha preached the Pragñâ-pâramitâ-sûtra in sixteen assemblies (Jū-roku-e) held

---

[5] Nos. 146, 247, 149. [6] Nos. 189·190. [7] Nos. 175, 176, 177. [8] Nos. 126, 127, 130. [9] No. 59. [10] No. 61. [11] No. 399.

INTRODUCTION. XVII

at four different places, namely, 1. Mount Gridhra-kûta ('vulture's peak'), 2. Anâthapindada's garden in Srâvastî, 3. the Abode of the Paranirmitavasa-vartins (Ta-ke-ji-zai-ten), and 4. the Venuvana ('bamboo-grove').[12] This is called the fourth period of Han-nya (Pragñâ-pâramitâ) by Ten-dai Dai-shi.

During the last eight years from the age of seventy-

---

[12] No. 1, i. e. the Dai-han-nya-ha-ra-mi-ta-kyō. It is the largest of the Chinese translations of the Buddhist sûtras, as it consists of 600 fasciculi or books. The following is a summary of the contents:—

	FASC.	FASC.	CHAPT.	PLACE OF THE SCENE.
(a)	400	(1–400),	79,	Gridhrakûta.
(b)	78	(401–478),	85,	
(c)	59	(479–537),	31,	
(d)	18	(538–555),	29,	
(e)	10	(556–565),	24,	
(f)	8	(566–573),	17,	
(g)	2	(574–575),		Srâvastî.
(h)	1	(576),		
(i)	1	(577),		
(j)	1	(578),		Abode of the Paranir-mita-vasavartins.
(k)	5	(579–583),		
(l)	5	(584–588),		Srâvastî.
(m)	1	(589),		
(n)	1	(590),		
(o)	2	(591–592),		Gridhrakûta.
(p)	8	(593–600),		Venuvana.

XVIII INTRODUCTION.

one to seventy-nine, Buddha preached for the most part the Saddharma-puṇḍarîka-sûtra (Ho-ke-kyō).[13] He also preached the Amitâyur-dhyâna-sûtra (Kwan-mu-ryō-ju-kyō)[14] to Queen Vaidehî in the city of Râgagṛiha. At the age of seventy-five, his father the king deid. At seventy-eight, he spoke the Samantabhadra-bodhisattva-karyâ-dharma-sûtra (Fu-gen-bo-satsu-gyō-bō-kyō)[15] in the city of Vaisâlî. At the age of seventy-nine, that was the fifty-first or fifty-third year of King Boku of the Shū (Chow) dynasty in China, 949 B. C., Buddha ascended to the Trayastriṃsa heaven (Tō-ri-ten) and preached to his mother Queen Mâyâ.[16] Coming down from it, he preached the Nirvâṇa-sûtra (Ne-han-gyō)[17] and the Sukhâvatîvyûha (A-mi-da-kyō),[18] etc. At midnight on the fifteenth day of the second month, he entered Parinirvâṇa, lying down in an avenue of Sâla trees near the city of Kushi. All the Devas and all mankind mourned the departure of their Great Teacher. This is called the fifth period of Hokke and Ne-han by Ten-pai Dai-shi.

Thus we have arranged Buddha's preachings in a chronological order. But this is not at all complete. For the true state of Buddha is not perfectly understood by the Bodhisattvas, Pratyekabuddhas, Srâvakas, Devas and men. The appearance of Buddha in

---

[13] *Nos.* 134. 138. 139. [14] *No.* 198. [15] *No.* 394.
[16] *No.* 153. [17] *Nos.* 113, 114. [18] *No.* 200.

INTRODUCTION.   XIX

the world is free from any ordinary form and speech. Therefore he can put countless Kalpas in one thought, and make his transformed body appear at several different places at the same time, just as the *K*intâma*n*i (Nyo-i-hō-shu) or fabulous gem yields its possessor all desires, and the sun and moon are reflected in the water of rivers, lakes and wells at one and the same time. In short, Buddha leads those who are not yet enlightened, teaching them the doctrine which he has perfectly understood. The dispositions of beings are various, so that the teachings for them are also divided into several manners. Accordingly there are different classes of doctrines, greater and lesser, partial and complete, temporary and true, apparent and hidden. Though there are numerous doctrine, yet the object is only one, that is, to perceive the truth. If they are confused, all beings on the three worlds are ignorant. If enlightened, the ten different worlds are full of nothing but Buddhas.

BUDDHISM IN INDIA.

There were two schools in India after Buddha's entry into Nirvâ*n*a, namely, 1. the Sthaviras (Jō-zabu), and 2. the Mahâsa*m*ghikas (Dai-shu-bu). In the former there were five succeeding teachers, whose names are Kâsyapa, Ânanda, Madyhântika, *S*a*n*avâsa and Upagupta. They are equally revered as patriarchs by the followers of the Hînayâna and Mahâyâna schools. In the Ten-daisect, twenty-

three patriarchs are enumerated, with Kâsyapa as the first. Kâsyapa is also the first of the twenty-eight patriarchs of the Zen sect. At the assembly in which Buddha preached the Nirvâna-sûtra (Ne-han-gyō), Kâsyapa was intrusted with the transmission of the teaching of Buddha's whole life. When the Mahâbrahma-râga-pariprikkhâ-sûtra (Dai-bonnō-mon-butsu-ketsu-gi-kyō) was spoken, the secret of the eye of right Law (see chapter 10) was also intrusted to Kâsyapa.

For a hundred years after Buddha, while the five teachers succeed each other as patriarchs, the two schools were harmonious. After that, they began to quarrel. Two centuries after Buddha, the Mahâsamghikas were divided into nine schools. A century later, the Sthaviras were also divided into eleven schools. These are called the twenty schools of the Hînayâna. Of these, the Sarvâstivâda school was the most flourishing. It depended upon one cheif Sâstra and on its so-called 'six feet.' The latter are: 1. Sâriputra's Samgîti-paryâya-pâda(Shū-i-mon-soku-ron),[19] 2. Mahâmaudgalyâyana's Dharma-skandhapâda (Hō-un-soku-ron),[20] 3. Kâtyâyana's (or Mahâmaudgalyâyana's) Pragñapti-pâda (Shi-setsu-soku-ron),[21] 4. Devasarman's Vigñâna-kâya-pâda (Shiki-shin-soku ron),[22] 5. Vasumitra's Prakarana-

[19] *No.* 1276. [20] *No.* 1396. [21] *No.* 1317. [22] *No.* 1381.

INTRODUCTION.   XXI

pâda (Hon-rui-soku-ron),[23] and 6. Dhâtu-kâya-pâda (Kai-shin-soku-ron).[24] These six *S*âstras are called the 'six feet,' of which the first three were composed during Buddha's life-time; the fourth was produced a century, and the last two, three centuries after Buddha. The chief *S*âstra is Kâtyâyana's *Gñ*âna-prasthâna-*s*âstra (Hot-chi-ron),[25] which also dated from three centuries after Buddha. A century later, five hundred Arhats who were disciples of Kâtyâyana, compiled the Mahâ-vibhâshâ-*s*âstra (Dai-bi-ba-sha-ron).[26] This is a commentary on the last *S*âstra. Nine centuries after Buddha, Vasubandhu (Se-shin) composed the Abhidharma-kosa-*s*âstra (Ku-sha-ron),[27] in which the author sometimes adopts the principles of the Sautrântikas (Kyō-bu). Sa*m*ghabhdra (Shu-gen) then composed the Nyâyânusâra-*s*âstra (Jun-shō-ri-ron)[28] and refuted the last mentioned work. This may show that the flourishing state of the Sarvâstivâda school lasted for some time in India.

Eight hundred and ninety years after Buddha, there was an Indian named Harivarman, who was a disciple of Kumârila-bha*tt*a (?) of the Sarvâstivâda school, and composed the Satya-siddhi-*s*âstra (Jō-jitsu-ron).[29] This book was much studied in India.

The above is an outline of the history of the Hîna-

[23] *No.* 1217. [24] *No.* 1282. [25] *No.* 1275. [26] *No.* 1263.
[27] *Nos.* 1267, 1269. [28] *No.* 1265. [29] *No.* 1274.

INTRODUCTION.

yâna schools in India.

Though the doctrine of the Mahâyâna was transmitted by Kâsyapa and Ânanda, it lost its power, when the doctrine of the Hînayâna became flourishing. Six centuries after Buddha, Asvaghosha (Me-myō) composed the Mahâyâna-sraddhotpâda-sâstra (Dai-jō-ki-shin-ron)[30] and promulgated the Mahâyâna. A century later, Nâgârguna (Ryū-ju) composed the Mahâbhaya-sâstra (Dai-mu-i-ron),[31] the Mahâpragñâ-pâramitâ-sâstra (Dai-chi-do-ron),[32] the Madhyamaka-sâstra (Chū-ron),[33] and other works; with which he explained the apparent doctrine. Finding the iron tower in South India, he also expounded the hidden doctrine.[34] At that time, the Mahâyâna school was as bright as the rising sun. Nine centuries after Buddha, Asamga (Mu-jaku) asked the Bodhisattva Maitreya to discourse the Yogâkârya-bhûmi-sâstra (Yu-ga-ron).[35] He himself composed the Mahâyâna-samparigraha-sâstra (Shō-dai-jō-ron),[36] on which his younger brother Vasubandhu (Se-shin) compiled a commentary.[37] The latter also composed the Amitâyus-sûtropadesa (Jō-do-ron),[38] the Buddha-gotra-sâstra (Bus-shō-ron),[39] the Saddharma-pundarîka-sûtra-sâstra (Hokke-ron),[40] the Nirvâna-sâstra

---

[30] Nos. 1249, 1250. [31] This has not yet been translated into Chinese. [32] No. 1169. [33] No. 1179. [34] See Chapter 8. [35] No. 1170. [36] Nos. 1183, 1184. [37] No. 1171. [38] No. 1204. [39] No. 1220. [40] Nos. 1232, 1233.

INTRODUCTION. XXIII

(Ne-han-ron),[41] the Va*grakkhe*dikâ sûtra-*s*âstra (Kongō-han-nya-ron),[42] and the Da*s*abhûmika-sâstra (Jū-ji-ron).[43] He also composed thirty verses of the Vidyâmâtra-siddhi-tri-da*s*a-*s*âstra (or-trim*s*a*kkh*âstra)-kârikâ (Yui-shiki-san-jū-ju),[44] on which ten *S*âstra-teachers each compiled a commentary.[45] The works of Va*s*ubandhu are said to number one thousand in all. The doctrine of the Mahâyâna has become flourishing, owing to the influence of the two teachers Nâgârguna and Vasubandhu. Therefore every Succeeding generation has looked up to them with deep veneration.

BUDDHISM IN CHINA.

In the tenth year of the Ei-hei period, in the reign of the Emperor Mei (Ming) of the Latter Kan (Han) dynasty, 67 A. D., i. e. one thousand and sixteen years after Buddha, the two Indian priests Kâsyapa Mâtaṅga (Ka-shōMa-tō) and Chiku Hō-ran (Dharmaraksha?) bringing with them an image of Buddha and some sacred books, arrived in Raku-yō, the capital of China. The Emperor then ordered them to live in the Haku-ba-ji, or 'White horse monastery.' This was the first time that Buddhism was known in the Far-East. During the period of the

[41] *No.* 1206. [42] *No.* 1168. [43] *No.* 1194. [44] *No.* 1215.
[45] *No.* 1197, i. e. Jō-yui-shiki-ron, consists of extracts made by the translator Gen-jō from the ten different commentaries.

XXIV INTRODUCTION.

Latter or Eastern Kan dynasty (25-220 A. D.) and of the San-goku or 'Three Kingdoms' (220-265 A. D.), it was not yet very flourishing. After the Western Shin (Tsin, 265-316 A. D.), or the Eastern Shin (317-420 A. D.), the scholars of the Tripitaka (San-zō-hos-shi) came to China from India one after another, and translated the sacred books into Chinese. From that time, the three trainings in the higher morality, thought and learning became greatly prosperous. China is a vast country and its people are numerous; so that we can not minutely here give the history of Buddhism there, except an outline of the following thirteen sects:—

1. The San-ron-shū, or 'Three Śāstra sect' (see chapter 5). In 409 A. D., Kumāragîva finished his translation of the Three Śāstras.[46] His four principal disciples Dō-shō, Sō-jō, Dō-yū and Sō-ei, generally called Shō Jō Yū Ei for brevity, expounded these books. This sect was firmly established by Kichi-zō of the Ka-jō monastery under the Zui (Sui) dynasty, 589-618 A. D.

2. The Jō-jitsu-shū, or 'Satya-siddhi-śāstra-sect' (see chapter 2). Kumāragîva translated the Jō-jitsu-ron,[47] which was extensively taught by the priests of succeeding ages.

3. The Ne-han-shū, or 'Nirvâna-sûtra-sect.' In 423 A. D., Dharmaraksha (Don-mu-sen) translated

[46] Nos. 1179, 1186, 1188. [47] No. 1274.

INTRODUCTION. XXV

the Ne-han-gyō.[4] E-kwan of the Sō (Sung) dynasty (424-453 A. D.) divided the doctrines into five classes with reference to their chronological order, and called the doctrine of the Nirvâna-sûtra the fifth doctrine of permanence.

4. The Ji-ron-shū, or 'Dasa-bhûmika-sâstra-sect.' In 508 A. D., Bodhiruki translated the Jū-ji-ron,[49] which was extensively taught by the priests of succeeding ages.

5. The Jō-do-shū, or 'Pure Land sect' (see chapter 9). Bodhiruki translated the Jō-do-ron or 'Pure Land Sâstra,' i. e. the Amitâyus-sûtropadesa,[50] on which Don-ran of the Gi dynasty (386-534 A. D.) compiled a commentary. At the time of Dō-shaku and Zen-dō (both lived about 600-650 A. D.), this sect was firmly established.

6. The Zen-shū, or 'Dhyâna sect' (see chapter 10). In 520 A. D., the twenty-eighth partriarch Bodhidharma arrived in China, and transmitted the seal of thought to E-ka. It passed throgh Sō-san, Dō-shin- and Kō-nin successively. After Kō-nin, the sect was divided into five schools.

7. The Shō-ron-shū, or 'Mahâyâna-samparigraha-sâstra-sect.' In 563 A. D., Paramârtha (Shin-dai) translated the Shō-dai-jō-ron,[51] which was extensively taught by the priests of succeeding ages.

8. The Ten-dai-shū, or 'Mount Ten-dai sect' (see

[48] *No.* 113· [49] *No.* 1194. [50] *No.* 1204. [51] *No.* 1183.

XXVI INTRODUCTION.

chapter 7). In 551 A. D., E-mon understood the doctrine of Buddha through the Ho-ke-kyō, i. e. Saddharma-pu*nd*arîka-sûtra.[52] He was succeeded by E-shi and Chi-ki. The latter, who is better known by his posthumous title of Chi-sha Dai-shi of Ten-dai (died 597 A. D.), caused this sect to become firmly established.

9. The Ke-gon-shū, or 'Avatamsaka-sūtra-sect' (see chapter 6). In 418 A. D., Buddhabhadra (Kakugen) translated the Ke-gon-gyō[53] in sixty volumes. Under the Chin dynasty, 557–589 A. D., To Jun expounded it and was succeeded by Chi-gon. At the time of Hō-zō (Gen-ju Dai-shi, died 712 A. D.) this sect was firmly established.

10. The Hossō-shū, or 'Dharma-lakshana sect' (see chapter 4). In 645 A. D., Gen-jō (Hiouen-thsang) returned from India to China and translated many Sūtras and *S*âstras. He had three thousand disciples; of whom Ki-ki (Ji-on Dai-shi) was the principal one, and who made this sect flourish in China.

11. The Bi-don-shū, or 'Abhidharma-sect' (see chapter 1). In 391 A. D., Gautama Samghadeva translated the Hosshō-bi-don, i. e. Abhidharma-h*ri*daya-sâstra,[54] which was extensively taught by the priests of succeeding ages. But the flourishing state of this sect dates from the time of Gen-jō (about 650 A. D), when the Ku-sha or Abhidharma-kosa,[55] the

[52] *No.* 134. [53] *No.* 87. [54] *No.* 1288. [55] *No.* 1267.

INTRODUCTION.   XXVII

Ba-sha or Mahâvibhâshâ[56] and other *Sâstras* were translated into Chinese.

12. The Kai-ritsu-shū, or 'Vinaya sect' (see chapter 3). In 410 A. D., Buddhayasas translated the Shi-bun-ritsu, or 'Vinaya of four divisions,' i. e. the Dharmagupta-vinaya.[57] There were three great commentators on this book under the Tō (T'ang) dynasty, 618-907 A. D. Among them, Dō-sen of the Nan-zan or Mount Shū-nan is considered the orthodox teacher of this sect.

13. The Shin-gon-shū, or 'Mantra sect' (see chapter 8). In 716 A. D., *S*ubhakarasimha (Zen-mu-i) arrived in China and greatly promulgated the hidden doctrine. He was succeeded by Va*g*rabodhi (Kon-gō-chi) and Amo*g*hava*g*ra (Fu-kū).

The above thirteen sects are those which existed up to the time of the Tō (T'ang, 618-907 A. D.) and Sō (Sung, 960-1280) dynasties. Since the accession of the Gen (Yuen) dynasty, 1280-1368 A. D, there has been added one sect more, namely, the doctrine of Rāma, or Lâmaism, of Tibet. In 1873, I went to Peking, and ascended Mount Go dai (Wu-tai) in the following year. Two years later I visited Mount Ten-dai (Tien-tai), and also went through Sei-ko, Nanking, Bu-shō and Kan-kō. Thus I examined the religions of the people of that vast country, and found out that there were three, viz., 1.

---
[56] *No.* 1263.   [57] *No.* 1117.   [58] *Mr*. Ogurusu.

XXVIII INTRODUCTION.

Confucianism (Ju), 2. Buddhism (Butsu), and 3. Taoism (Dō).

There are two great divisions of Buddhism in China at present, namely, the Blue robe sect (Sei-i-ha) and the Yellow robe sect (Kō-i-ha). The Emperor Tai-sō (627–649 A. D.) gave one of his daughters called Bun-sei Kō-shu in marriage to Sampu of To-ban or Tibet. Then the whole of Tibet became a field for Buddhist labourers. Afterwards Sampu frequented India and promulgated the doctrine of Buddha. Lâmaism is a part of the hidden doctrine, and its followers in China form the Yellow robe sect.

The Blue robe sect consists of the priests of the old Chinese sects. They have established the names of Shū or principle, Kyō or teaching, and Ritsu or discipline. The Dhyâna or contemplation is their principle, the doctrines of the Ke-gon or Avatamsaka-sûtra and the Hokke or Saddharma-pundarîka-sûtra, etc. are their teachings, and the Vinaya of the Four Divisions or the Dharmagupta-vinaya is their discipline. Therefore each monastery is possessed of these three. The priests in the monasteries on Mount Go-dai belong to the Shō-ryō-shū, i. e. Ke-gon, but they also practise contemplation and discipline. Similarly those on Mount Ten-dai belong to the Chi-sha-shū, i. e. Ten-dai, but they also practise contemplation and discipline. The Chinese

INTRODUCTION. XXIX

Buddhists seem, therefore, to unite all different sects so as to make one harmonious sect.

BUDDHISM IN JAPAN.

The twelve sects treated of in this book include the principal Japanese Buddhist sects, though the number of different schools might be increased, if we were to count minutely the original and secondary divisions. We shall now try to divide the twelve sects into three periods, namely: —

1. The earliest period includes the first six sects. In the thirteenth year of the reign of the Emperor Kim-mei, 552 A. D., i. e. fifteen hundred years after Buddha, the king of Kudara, one of the three ancient divisions of Korea, presented to the Japanese Court an image of Buddha and some sacred books. In 625 A. D., E-kwan came to Japan from Koma, another division of Korea, and became the founder of the Jō-jitsu and San-ron sects (chapter 2 and 5). At that time, the Prince Imperial Shō-toku (died 621 A. D.) had already promulgated the doctrine of Buddha. In 653 A. D., Dō-shō went to China and studied under Gen-jō and transmitted the doctrine of the Hossō sect to Japan (chap. 4). In 658 A. D., Chi-tsū and Chi-tatsu went to China and also became disciples of Gen-jō and transmitted the doctrines of the Hossō and Ku-sha sects (chaps. 1 and 4). In 703 A. D., Chi-hō and Chi-ran went to China, and so did Gen-bōin 716 A. D. They all transmitted the doctrine of

the Hossō sect. Thus there are four different dates of this transmission. In 736 A. D., a Chinese priest named Dō-sen came to Japan and established the Kegon sect (chap. 6). In 754 A. D., another Chinese priest named Gan-jin arrived in Japan and became the founder of the Ritsu sect (chap. 3). The above may be called the ancient sects, being called the six sects of the Nan-to or Southern Capital, i. e. Nara, where they were established in the earliest period. They are generally enumerated in the order of Ku-sha, Jō-jitsu, Ritsu, Hossō, San-ron and Kegon.

2. The mediæval sects are two, namely, the Tendai (chap. 7) and the Shin-gon (chap. 8). These are called the two sects of Kyō-to. In 804 A. D., Saichō and Kū-kai went to China. Having returned to Japan, the former established the Ten-dai sect on Mount Hi-ei; and the latter founded the Shingon sect on mount Kō-ya. In these sects there have been many eminent priests.

3. The modern sects are the remaining four. In 1174 (or 1175) A. D, Gen-kū founded the Jō-do-shū (chap. 9). In 1191 A. D., Ei-sai established the Zen-shū (chap. 10). In 1224 A. D., Shin-ran founded the Shin-shū (chap. 11). In 1253 A. D., Nichi-ren founded the Nichi-ren-shū (chap. 12).

It seems to me that as the ancient sects were flourishing in the ancient period only, so were those

of the Middle Ages and of modern times in their respective periods. If we want to restore the older sects to their flourishing state and also to increase the power of the later ones, we must rely on the activity of the determined scholars of all the sects. Is it not true that nations in ancient times were as far from each other as the utmost verge of the heavens or the ends of the earth; so that it was almost impossible to go to and fro? But nations in the present time are not so, as it is very easy to travel through all different countries in a short time, as if the world had become small comparatively.

It is said in the Jō-do-ron, or 'Pure Land *S*âstra:
> 'In any world where there is not known
> The Law of Buddha, which is the pearl of good qualities,
> There I pray that all (Bodhisattvas) shall be born
> And show (the people) the Law of Buddha, just like Buddha himself.'

Must the determined scholars and the men of virtue not examine themselves on this point and become ardent in the pursuit of promulgating the Law?

A SHORT HISTORY OF THE TWELVE JAPANESE BUDDHIST SECTS.

CHAPTER I.

The Ku-sha-shū, or Abhidharma-kosa-sâstra-sect.
1. A history of the sect.

The term Ku-sha is a transliteration of the Sanskrit word Kosa or 'store,' in the title of the principal book of this sect or school, the Abhidharma-kosa-sâstra,'[1] or the 'Book of the treasury of metaphysics.' It was composed by Vasubandhu (Se-shin), who lived in India about nine centuries after Buddha. The Sâstra is divided into nine chapters, in which the author refers not only to the principal books of the Sarvâstivâdins, one of eighteen schools of the Hînayâna doctrine, but also makes a selection of different views of other schools. The composition is so excellent that it is said to have been praised in India as an 'Intelligence-making Sâstra' (Sō-mei-ron).

[1] No. 1267 in the Min-zō-moku-roku, or Catalogue of the Chinese Translation of the Buddhist Tripitaka, by Bunyiu Nanjio, Oxford, 1883. Similar numbers hereafter refer to those in the same Catalogue.

Although the names of eighteen schools of the Hînayâna are mentioned in the sacred books, yet the doctrines of two of them only are handed down to us at present as subjects of study. These two schools are the Sautrântikas (Kyō-bu) and the Sarvâstivâdins (U-bu). The former is somewhat approximated to by the jō-jitsu-shū, and the latter is represented by the Ku-sha-shū. The character of the Abhidharma-kosa-sâstra is, however, very impartial, including the best of all the doctrinal views of the other schools. The doctrine of this Sâstra is free from inclination to either the peculiar views of the Sarvâstivâdins or those of the Sautrântikas.

The Sarvâstivâdins have many books which belong to the Abhidharma-pitaka (Ron-zō), the last division of the Tripitaka, or the three collections of the sacred books. Among them there are one chief and six secondary works in the following order:—

1. Gñâna-prasthâna-sâstra (Hot-chi-ron),[2] by Kâtyâyana. This is the chief book, and the following six works are called the Shatpâda or the 'six feet' of the chief book.

2. Dharma-skandha-pâda (Hō-un-soku-ron),[3] by Mahâmaudgalyâyana.

3. Samgîti-paryâya-sâstra (Shū-i-mon-soku-ron),[4] by Sâriputra.

4. Vigñâna-kâya-pâda (Shiki-shin-soku-ron),[5] by

---
[2] No. 1275. [3] No. 1296. [4] No. 1276.

KU-SHA-SHŪ.

Devasarman.

5. Prag*ñ*apti-pâda (Shi-setsu-soku-ron),[6] by Mahâmaudgalyâyana.

6. Praka*r*a*n*a-pâda (Hon-rui-soku-ron),[7] by Vasumitra.

7. Dhâtu-kâya-pâda (Kai-shin-soku-ron),[8] by the same as before.

Besides these, there is a work entitled Mahâ-vibhâshâ-sâstra (Dai-bi-ba-sha-ron),[9] which was compiled by five hundred Arhats, and is a commentary on Kâtyâyana's G*ñ*âna-prasthâna-sâstra.

In 563 A. D. an Indian named Paramârtha (Shindai) translated Vasubandhu's *S*âstra into Chinese (A-bi-datsu-ma-ku-sha-shaku-ron),[10] Afterwards, in 654 A. D. under the Tō (T'ang) dynasty, Gen-jō (known as Hiouen-thsang in Europe), made another and better translation (A-bi-datsu-ma-ku-sha-ron).[11] His disciples Fu-kō and Hō-hō each compiled a commentary on the *S*âstra. Besides them, Jin-dai and En-ki also compiled a commentary.

In 658 A. D., two Japanese priests, Chi-tsū and Chi-tatsu, went to Chiña, became disciples of Gen-jō, and brought his new translation of the Kosa or Kusha over to Japan. Thus this *S*âstra was first known in the Empire. Though they did in fact never form an independent sect, being themselves members of

---

[5] *No.* 1281. [6] *No.* 1317. [7] *No.* 1277. [8] *No.* 1282.
[9] *No.* 1263. [10] *No.* 1269. [11] *No.* 1267.

4 KU-SHA-SHŪ.

the Hossō sect, the doctrine taught in the Sâstra has always been studied by the learners of all the Buddhist sects in Japan till the present day.

II. The doctrine of the sect.

In the Abhidharma-kosa-sâstra, there are many technical terms, such as the five Skandhas (Un) or 'collections,' the twelve Âyatanas (sho) or 'places,' the eighteen Dhâtus (Kai) or 'elements,' and the seventy-five Dharmas (Hō) or 'things.' All these terms are used for explaining things, both Samskrita (U-i) or 'compounded,' and Asamskrita (Mu-i) or 'immaterial.' There are also the terms of the four Satyas (Tai) or 'truths,' and the twelve Pratîtya-samutpâdas (En-gi) or 'chains of causation,' and so forth.

Now, let us see what the seventy-five Dharmas are, and how they are grouped together.

1. Samskrita-dharmas (U-i-hō) or 'compounded things.' These are the first seventy-two, the remaining three being Asamskrita (Mu-i) or 'immaterial.' The 72 compounded things are grouped under the following four heads.

(1) Rûpas (Shiki) or 'forms,' eleven in number, viz;

    1. Kakshus (Gen) or the 'eye,' that sees;
    2. Srotra (Ni) or the 'ear,' that hears;
    3. Ghrâna (Bi) or the 'nose,' that smells;
    4. Gihvâ (Zetsu) or the 'tongue,' that tastes; and

KU-SHA-SHŪ.

5. Kâya (Shin) or the 'body,' that touches objects.

These five are the Indriyas (Kon) or 'organs of sense,' which have an eminent and vigorous actions.

6. Rûpa (Shiki) or 'form,'
7. *S*abda (Shō) or 'sound,'
8. Gandha (Kō) or 'smell,'
9. Rasa (Mi) or 'taste,' and
10. Spar*s*a (Soku) or 'touch.'

These five are called the Vishayas (Kyō) or 'objects of sense,' on which the organs of sense act.

11. Avi*ñ*apti-rûpa (Mu-hyō-shiki) or 'unapparent form.' This is a peculiar one. Though it is in reality formless, yet it is called form; because its character has some reference to speech and deed, but not to thought. When an action either good or bad is apparent, something will follow it within the actor, which is nevertheless quite unapparent. Hence this object is made distinct.

(2) *K*itta (Shin) or 'mind,' also called Manas (I) or 'thought' and Vi*gñ*âna (Shiki) or 'knowledge.' The Manas is explained by comparison to the pith of a tree, which unites all the branches, leaves, flowers and fruits in one body. If it follows the five organs of sense and thought, it is accounted to be of six kinds. But the *K*itta itself is only one, so that it cannot appear in two or more different places at one

and the same moment. Therefore the Abhidharma-kosa-sâstra speaks of the subject as only one, yet with the names of six different kinds of Vig*ñ*âna (Shiki) or 'knowledge,' namely;

    1. *K*akshuṙ-vig*ñ*âna (Gen-shiki) or 'eye knowledge,'

    2. *S*rotra-vig*ñ*âna (Ni-shiki) or 'ear knowledge,'

    3. Ghrâ*n*a-vig*ñ*âna (Bi-shiki) or 'nose knowledge,'

    4. *G*ihvâ-vig*ñ*âna (Zetsu-shiki) or 'tongue knowledge,'

    5. Kâya-vig*ñ*âna (Shin-shiki) or 'body knowledge,' and

    6. Mano-vig*ñ*âna (I-shiki), or 'mind knowledge,' It is also called the Mano-râ*g*a (Shinnō) or 'mind-king,' because it thinks of every object which appears before it, just as a monarch has the supreme control of every kind of affairs, though the mind or thought itself is also after all one of the seventy-five Dharmas without Âtman or self.

    (3) *K*aitta-dharmas (Shin-jo-u-hō) or 'mental qualities.' There are forty-six different qualities, which are again grouped under six heads.

    (a) Mahâ-bhûmika-dharmas (Dai-ji-hō) or 'qualities of great ground.' These are ten in number, which always accompany the 'mind' or 'thought.'

    1. Vedanâ (Ju) or 'perception,'

    2. Sa*m*g*ñ*â (Sō) or 'name,'

3. *K*etanâ (Shi) or 'intention,'
4. Sparsa (Soku) or 'touching,'
5. *Kh*anda (Yoku) or 'desire,'
6. Mati (E) or 'intelligence,'
7. Sm*r*iti (Nen) or 'memory,'
8. Manaskara (Sa-i) or 'attention,'
9. Adhimoksha (Shō-ge) or 'determination, and
10. Samâdhi (San-ma-ji) or 'self-concentration.'

(b) Kusala-mahâbhûmika-dharmas (Dai-zen-ji-hō) or 'qualities of great ground of goodness.' There are ten in number, which always accompany the mind when it is good.

1. *S*raddhâ (Shin) or 'calmness of mind,'
2. Apramâda (Fu-hō-itsu) or 'carefulness,'
3. Pra*s*rabdhi (Kyō-an) or 'confidence,'
4. Upekshâ (Sha) or 'equanimity,'
5. Hrî (Zan) or 'shame,'
6. Apatrapâ (Gi) or 'bashfulness,'
7. Alobha (Mu-ton) or 'absence of covetousness,'
8. Advesha (Mu-shin) or 'absence of anger,'
9. Ahi*m*sâ (Fu-gai) or 'not hurting,' and
10. Vîrya (Gon) or 'effort.'

Besides these ten, two more are added in the Vibhâ-shâ-sâstra, namely, wish (Gon) and dislike (En). But, as they do not exist at the same moment, so they are now left out here.

(c) Klesa-mahâbhûmika-dharmas (Dai-bon-nō-ji-hō) or 'qualities of great ground of passions.' There

are six in number, which always accompany the mind when it is not pure.
1. Moha (Mu-myō) or 'ignorance,'
2. Pramâda (Hō-itsu) or 'carelessness,'
3. Kausîdya (Ke-dai) or 'indolence,'
4. Asrâddhya (Fu-shin) or 'unbelief,'
5. Styâna (Kon-jin) or 'idleness,' and
6. Auddhatya (Jō-ko) or 'arrogance.'

(d) Akusala-mahâbhûmika-dharmas (Dai-fu-zen-ji-hō) or 'qualities of great ground of badness.' These are two in number, which always accompany the mind when it is not good.
1. Ahrîkatâ (Mu-zan) or 'absence of shame,' and
2. Anapatrapâ (Mu-gi) or 'absence of bashfulness.'

(e) Upaklesa-bhûmika-dharmas (Shō-bon-nō-ji-hō) or 'qualities of ground of secondary passions.' These are ten in number, which do not accompany the mind altogether at one and the same moment like ignorance, etc., but only one after another; so that they are called 'secondary passions.'
1. Krodha (Fun) or 'anger,'
2. Mraksha (Fuku) or 'hypocrisy,'
3. Mâtsarya (Ken) or 'selfishness,'
4. Îrshyâ (Shitsu) or 'envy,'
5. Pradâsa (Nō) or 'vexation,'
6. Vihimsâ (Gai) or 'hurting,'
7. Upanâha (Kon) or 'enmity,'

KU-SHA-SHŪ.

8. Mâyâ (Ten) or 'deceit,'
9. Sâ*th*ya (Ō) or 'dishonesty,' and,
10. Mada (Kyō) or 'vanity.'

(f) Aniyata-bhûmika-dharmas (Fu-jō-ji-hō) or 'qualities of uncertain ground.' These are eight in number, which accompany the mind at any time.

1. Vitarka (Jin) or 'reflection,'
2. Vi*k*âra (Shi) or 'investigation,'
3. Kau*k*r*i*tya (Aku-sa) or 'repentance,'
4. Middha (Sui-men) or 'somnolence,'
5. Râga (Ton) or 'greediness,'
6. Pratigha (Shin) or 'anger,'
7. Mâna (Man) or 'pride,' and
8. Vi*k*ikitsâ (Gi) or 'doubt.'

The above forty-six are mental qualities (Shin-jo).

(4) *K*itta-viprayukta-sa*m*skâras (Shin-fu-sō-ō-bō) or 'conceptions separated from the mind.' There are fourteen in all.

1. Prâpti (Toku) or 'attainment,'
2. Aprâpti (Hi-toku) or 'non-attainment,'
3. Sabhâgatâ (Dō-bun) or 'commonness,' i. e. that which makes living beings equal;
4. Asa*m*g*ñ*ika (Mu-sō-kwa) or 'namelessness,' i. e. the state of one who is born in the Asa*m*g*ñ*ika heaven, where his mind and mental faculties are in rest during a hundred great kalpas or periods;
5. Asa*m*g*ñ*i-samâpatti (Mu-sō-jō) or 'attainment

of namelessness' by the venerable men,
6. Nirodha-samâpatti (Metsu-jin-jō) or 'attainment of destruction' by the heretics,
7. Gîvita (Myō-kon) or 'life,'
8. Gâti (Shō) or 'birth,'
9. Sthiti (Jū) or 'exisetnce,'
10. Garâ (I) or 'decay,'
11. Anityatâ (Metsu) or 'non-eternity,' i. e. deat a

The above four (8-11) are called the four forms of the compounded things (Shi-u-i-sō).

12. Nâma-kâya (Myō-shin) or 'name,'
13. Pada-kâya (Ku-shin) or 'word,' and
14. Vyañgana-kâya (Mon-shin) or 'letter.'

Thus there are seventy-two compounded things, all of which belong to the five Skandhas or collections. The following three complete number of the seventy-five Dharmas explained in the Abhidharma-koshsâstra. They are not included in the five collections, being immaterial in their nature.

II. Asamskrita-dharmas (Mu-i-hō) or 'immaterial things.'

    1. Pratisamkhyâ-nirodha (Chaku-metsu) or 'conscious cessafion of existence.'
    2. Apratisamkhyâ-nirodha (Hi-chaku-metsu) or 'unconscious cessation of existence.'
    3. Âkâsa (Ko-ku) or 'space.'

The above seventy-five Dharmas are, as we have seen, divided into two classes, compounded things

KU-SHA-SHŪ.

and immaterial things. The former include all things that proceed from a cause. This cause is Karma, to which every existing thing is due, Space (Âkâsa) and Nirvâna (Nirodha) alone excepted. Again, of the three immaterial things, the last two are not subjects to be understood by the wisdom not free from frailty. Therefore the 'conscious cessation of existence' is considered as the goal of all the effort by him who longs for deliverance from misery

According to the doctrine of the Abhidharma-kosa-sâstra, there is a division into three Yânas or vehicles of the Srâvakas (Shō-mon), Pratyekabuddhas (Engaku) and Bodhisattvas (Bo-satsu), which help to destroy doubt and make the truth understood. The Srâvakas meditate on the cause and effect of every thing. If they are acute in understanding, they become free from confusion after three different births. But, if they are dull, they pass sixty kalpas, before they attain to the state of enlightenment. The Pratyekabuddhas meditate on the twelve chains of causation (Jū-ni-innen), or understand the non-eternity of the world, while gazing upon the falling flowers and leaves. Thus they become enlightened, either after passing through four different births, or after a hundred kalpas according to their ability. The Bodhisattvas practise the six Pâramitâs (Rokudo) or 'perfections' and become Buddhas, after three Asamkhya or 'countless' kalpas. The six Pâramitâs

are the perfect exersice of the same number of principal virtues by a Bodhisattva, as a preliminary to, and indeed a condition of, his attaining Buddhahood. They are as follow : 1. Dâna-pâramitâ, or 'perfect practice of almsgiving,' 2. Sîla-, or 'morality,' 3. Kshânti-, or 'patience,' 4. Vîrya-, or 'energy,' 5. Dhyâna-, or 'meditation,' and 6. Pragñâ-, or 'wisdom.'

The reason why all things are so minutely explained in this Sâstra is to drive away the idea of self (Âtman), and to show the truth, in order to make living beings reach Nirvâna.

Those who may wish to know more of this doctrine, should study the Abhidharma-kosa-sâstra, by the help of the two Chinese commentaries of Fu-kō and Hō-hō. After that, they might study the other Sâstras of the Sarvâstivâdins, which we have already mentioned.

CHAPTER II.

The Jō-jitsu-shū, or Satya-siddhi-sâstra-sect.
I. The doctrine of the sect.

The principal book of this sect is entitled the Jō-jistu-ron, or Satya-siddhi-sâstra,[1] literally meaning the 'Book of the perfection of the truth.' This book contains selections from and explanations of the true meaning of the Tripiṭaka, or Three Baskets (San-zō) of the Hînayâna doctrine preached by the Tathâgata.

It is the work of an Indian named Harivarman ('lion armour'), a disciple of Kumârila-bha*tt*a (? Ku-ma-ra-da), who was a scholar of the Sarvâstivâda school (U-bu), and lived about nine centuries after Buddha.

Harivarman not satisfied with the narrow views of his teacher, made selections of the best and broadest interpretations current in the several different schools of the Hînayâna. Therefore it is not certain to which school he originally belonged. Some say that it was the Bahu-srutikas (Ta-mon-bu), ohers that it was the Sautrântikas (Kyō-bu). others again say that it was the Dharmaguptas, (Don-mu-toku-bu), or the Mahîsâsakas (Ke-ji-bu). All these different versions are equally without proof. It is therefore better to consider the book indepently as simply eclectic and owning to unite all that was best in each of the Hînayâna schools.

---
[1] *No.* 1274.

Again Ten-dai, Ka-jō and Kumâra*g*îva (Ra-jū) agreed in taking the *S*âstra of this sect as that of the Hînayâna; and Hō-un, Chi-zō and Mon-bin, who were called the three great teachers of the Ryō dynasty (502–557 A. D.), took it as that of the Mahâyâna. These opinions are still one sided. The Vinaya teacher Nan-zan, however, said that the doctrine of the *S*âstra is the Hînayâna, but that its explanations are applicable to the Mahâyâna also.

This opinion would perhaps be right. The knowledge of the author of the *S*âstra was so clear, that he was able to explain the deep meaning of the Tripi*t*aka, and express the unreal character of all human knowledge as taught in the Mahâyâna.

What is the best meaning of all the schools of the Hînayâna, selected in the Satya-siddhi-sâstra? It is of two kinds of emptiness or unreality, in which as many kinds of meditation are established. The first is the Meditation on emptiness or unreality.

As an empty jar, there is not anything to be called Âtman or self in the five Skandhas or collections (which constitute what we should call the consciousness of an intelligent subject). This is therefore the Meditation on the emptiness or unreality of Âtman or self. The second is the Meditation on unselfishness. As the nature of the jar itself is unreal, all things in the five Skandhas are names only. This is the Meditation on Dharmas or things. Thus the

JŌ-JITSU-SHŪ.

two kinds of unreality are explained, so that the meaning of the Śāstra are the best of all those of the Hînayâna schools. But as to the way of dispelling doubts for enlightenment, the most minute ones technically known as the Sho-chi-shō, or the 'obstacles of those which are to be known,' or of the want of knowledge, are not removed. Only the obstacles of seeing and thinking, known as the Bon-nō-shō, or the 'obstacles of passions,' are removed. These are the distinctions between the Mahâyâna and Hînayâna.

In the Sarvâstivâda school (U-bu), the Âtman or self is said to be unreal, but the Dharmas or things real. Therefore in the doctrine of that school, the three states of existence are real, and the nature of the Dharmas or things are constantly in existence. But the doctrine of the Satya-siddhi-sâstra explains the emptiness of the Âtman and Dharma. It asserts that the past and future are without reality, but the present state of things only stands as if it were real. That is to say, the true state of things is constantly changing, being produced and destroyed each Kshaṇa (Setsu-na) or 'moment.' Yet it seems as if the state of things were existing, even as a circle of fire seen when a rope-match is turned round very quickly. This is called the 'temporariness continued' (Sō-zoku-ke). Those which are produced by certain causes and combinations of circumstances are called the

'temporariness done by causes' (In-jō-ke). The names of things are made temporarily by the comparison of this and that. This is called the 'temporariness of comparison.' Thus all things are temporary like bubbles, so that they are empty and fleeting. To look upon living beings with the view of the above enumerated three kinds of temporariness is called the 'emptiness of being or self.' This is not the same as the opinion of the Abhidharma school on this subject; because in that school, self is denied on the Skandhas only. Ignorant people and heretics do not know these two kinds of emptiness of the Âtman and Dharma, and have the false idea of seeing and thinking, by which they suffer the misery of transmigration. If one understands the meaning of the two kinds of emptiness, and practises the meditation on them, al his passions will be cured.

This emptiness of the two kinds is not that of nature itself, but that by breaking or destroying the Âtman or self and Dharma or thing. This is one of the differences between the Mahâyâna and the Hînayâna. Again it is said in the Sâstra that 'one can obtain enlightenment by one Satya (Tai) or 'truth' only, which is the Nirodha (Metsu), or 'destruction of pain.' This is the third of the four holy truths (Shi-shō-tai). It differs from the views of the Abhidharma school, which says that those of the three Yânas or vehicles of the Srâvakas, Pratyekabuddhas

JŌ-JITSU-SHŪ.

and Bodhisattvas, see the truth in the same way, and that they attain to the Path by understanding the four truths. Accordingly there are two ways of explaining the title of the Satya-siddhi-sâstra (Jō-jitsu-ron), or 'Book of the perfection of truth.' The first is that it is called so, because it explains perfectly the true meaning of the two kinds of emptiness. The second is that it expounds the reality of the four truths.

This is only an outline of this doctrine.

II. A history of the sect.

According to the Kai-gen-roku,[2] a Catalogue of the Buddhist Books compiled in the Kai-gen period, 730 A. D., Kumâra*g*îva translated the *S*âstra of this school, under the Shin dynasty of the Yō family, in 411-412 A. D. But the Nai-den-roku,[3] another and earlier catalogue, compiled about 667 A. D. puts the date of the translation five years earlier, 406 A. D. The *S*âstra is divided into sixteen or twenty volumes and two hundred and two chapters. When the translation was made, Kumâra*g*îva ordered his-disciple Sō-ei to lecture on it; and all his disciples three thousand in number studied and expounded it.

In the period of the Sō dynasty, 420-479 A. D., Sō-dō and Dō-kō each compiled a commentary, and the three great teachers already alluded to taught the doctrine of this school under the Ryō dynasty,

[2] *No.* 1485. [3] *No.* 1483.

502-557. Hō-kei compiled another commentary on the Sâstra in twenty volumes, under the Chin dynasty, 557-589, and was flourishing under the Zui dynasty, 589-618, and in the earliest period of the Tō dynasty, 618-907. But after Gen-jō's return to China from his famous journey to India, 629-645, the doctrines of the Ku-sha and Ho-ssō schools became more flourishing in China.

Buddhism was first introduced into Japan from Korea in 552 A. D. Thirty years later, the Prince Inperial Shō-toku was born, who, when grown up, became a great promulgator of Buddhism. He studied the doctrines of the San-ron and Jō-jitsu schools, under the instruction of the Korean priests E-ji, E-sō and Kwan-roku. Therefore, in his commentaries on the three Sûtras Saddharma-puṇḍarîka (Hokke[4]), Srîmâlâ (Shō-man[5]), and Vimalakîrtti-nirdesa (Yui-ma[6]), the Prince Imperial depends on the explanations of Kō-taku, who was a teacher of the Jō-jitsu school, and also a promulgator of the Mahâyâna doctrine. In 625, E-kwan came to Japan from Korea. Like Kwan-roku who had already been in Japan, he was a scholar of the San-ron school. Before he left korea for Japan, he went to China and became a pupil of Ka-jō, the founder of that school. The doctrine of the Jō-jitsu school was therefore made known in Japan at the same time as that of the

[4] *No.* 134. [5] *No.* 59. [6] *No.* 146.

JŌ-JITSU-SHŪ.

San-ron by Kwan-roku and E-kwan. For this reason, the Jō-jitsu school was hereafter always a branch of the San-ron. The scholars of this school always used a great commentary on the *S*âstra compiled by the Korean priest Dō-zō in sixteen volumes. Besides this there are two other commentaries, the Jō-jitsu-gi-sho in 23 volumes, and the Jō-jitsu-gi-rin in 2 volumes. The reason why the scholars of the San-ron especially studied the Jō-jitsu-ron is this, that Ka-jō, the founder of the San-ron school, constantly refutes the doctrine of the *S*âstra in his works, in order to make the teaching of the Mahâyâna on emptiness or unreality clear.

The two schools of the Ku-sha and Jō-jitsu have never become independent, the former being a branch of the Hossō, and the latter of the San-ron. Kū-kai, Kō-bō Dai-shi of the Shin-gon sect, said in his last instructions that his followers should study the doctrines of the Hossō and San-ron. If so, they ought also to know the doctrine of the Jō-jitsu. At present, however, the San-ron school is already almost extinct; how much less could the Jō-jitsu school continue to exist? It is hoped that there may be a person, who thinks of this and renews the study of it, in order to understand more clearly the distinctions of the Mahâyâna and Hînayâna.

CHAPTER III.

The Ris-shū, or Vinaya sect.
I. The doctrine of this sect.

This sect was founded by the Chinese priest Dō-sen, Chō-shō Dai-shi, who lived on Mount Shū-nan at the beginning of the T'ang or Tō dynasty (618-907 A.D.). He was well acquainted with the Tripitaka, and especially versed in the Vinaya, or discipline. He himself practised the Vinaya, of the Dharmagupta school, according to the Shi-bun-ritsu[1], or Vinaya of Four Divisions, and taught others by it. There is a work entitled Kyō-kai-gi, or 'Rules of Instruction,' written by him for novices. In the preface to it, he says: 'If man does not practise the Dhyâna and Samâdhi (Zen-na and San-mai), i.e. meditation and contemplation, he cannot understand the truth. If he does not keep all the good precepts, he cannot accomplish his excellent practice.' This shows that the wisdom of meditation is produced by keeping the moral precepts.

Moreover the power of Vinaya or precepts also causes the Law of Buddha to exist long in this world. If Buddha's doctrine continues to exist, there will be no calamity in the country, where the people can therefore get salvation. It is the root of all good things. Not only the men of the Hînayâna keep it,

---
[1] *No.* 1117.

but also those of the mahâyâna do so without any distinction. Accordingly it is called the learning of the Mahâyâna in the *S*rîmâlâ-sûtra (Shō-man-gyō),² In the Mahâpra*gñ*â-pâramitâ-*s*âstra (Dai-chi-do-ron),³ eighty parts (of the Vinaya recited by Upâli on as many occasions in three months of the summer immediately following Buddha's Nirvâ*n*a) are called the *S*îla-pâramitâ, or 'perfection of morality.' There is no separate Sa*m*gha, or priesthood, consisting of Bodhisattvas, in the doctrine of *S*âkyamuni. Those who are ignorant of the meaning of the doctrine do not practise the precepts kept by the Hînayâna, saying that they are men of the Mahâyâna. This is extremely wrong. Dō-sen refuted this view in his works. In the Gō-sho, or 'Work on Action' (Karman), he establishes three doctrinal divisions, viz.

1. The School of True Dharma (Jippō [Jitsu-hō]-shū) i. e. the Sarvâstivâda school, by which Rûpa (Shiki), or form, is considered as the substance of *S*îla, or morality.

2. The School of Temporary Name (Ke-myō-shū), i. e. the Dharmagupta school, by which the substance of the *S*îla is considered neither to be form nor thought. The latter is therefore deeper in meaning than the former.

3. The School of Complete Doctrine (En-gyō-shū),

² *No.* 59. ³ *No.* 1169.

i. e. the meaning of the two Sûtras Saddharma-puṇdarîka (Hokke)[4] and the Mahâparinirvâṇa (Ne-han),[5] by which the temporary vehicle, such as the Hînayâna, is determinately understood as the means to approach the true path. In the two Sûtras above mentioned, the three Yânas or vehicles are admitted, yet they are after all altogether put into one vehicle, i. e. the Mahâyâna. This is technically called Kai-e, literally, 'opening or admitting and uniting.' Dōsen depended on this principle, and led his disciples to the Complete Doctrine. This is the characteristic of the Vinaya expounded by him, and it is the teaching of the Vinaya sect in Japan.

Although the Dharmagupta-vinaya (Shi-bun-ritsu) of the Hînayâna is used by the sect, the doctrine itself is complete and sudden (En-don) in its character, without any distinction between the larger and smaller vehicles, as well as the three learnings (San-gaku) of morality, meditation and wisdom. It is very high and very deep being the same as the true nature (Jissō) explained in the Saddharma-puṇḍarîka-sûtra (Hokke),[4] or permanence (Jō-jū) as explained in the Mahâparinirvâṇa-sûtra (Ne-han),[5] and the Dharma-dhâtu (Hokkai), or 'state of things,' in the Avataṃsaka-sûtra (Ke-gon).[6]

The Vinaya of all the different schools may equally be said to have the meaning of Kai-e already

[4] No. 134. [5] Nos. 113, 114. [6] Nos. 87, 88.

explained. Why did Dō-sen select the Dharmagupta-vinaya only, in asserting that meaning? Because this Vinaya has been always used by the Chinese Buddhists from olden times. It is the Vinaya of the School of the Temporary Name (Ke-myō), surpassing that of the School of True Dharma (Jippō). Moreover there is a convinience in establishing the doctrine which unites both vehicles, as this Vinaya is equally applicable to the Mahâyana, though it originally belongs to the Hînayâna. For this reason, Dō-sen taught the excellent morality of the one vehicle of completion, without separating it from the Dharmagupta-vinaya.

The three doctrinal divisions above enumerated are made chiefly in connection with morality, but at the same time include the doctrines of meditation and wisdom. Besides these, Dō-sen divided the whole doctrine of the Tathâgata (Nyo-rai, i. e. Buddha) into three parts, namely:

1. The Doctrine of the Emptiness of Nature (Shō-kū-kyō), which includes all the Hînayâna teachings.

2. The Doctrine of the Emptiness of Form (Sō-kū-kyō), which includes all the shallower teachings of the Mahâyâna.

3. The Doctrine of the Completion of the Only Knowledge (Yui-shiki-en-gyō), which includes all the deeper teachings of the Mahâyâna.

These divisions are made in connection with the

doctrines of meditation and wisdom, including the morality taught by Buddha during his whole life.

Now the Vinaya of the Four Divisions (Shi-bun-ritsu) is a part of the Doctrine of the Emptiness of Nature. But Dō-sen judged it from his own thought as the Doctrine of the Completion of the Only Knowledge, because the three learnings of morality, meditation and wisdom (Kai-jō-e san-gaku) are in fact completly reconciled to each other (Ennyū-mu-ge). Though he made these several divisions, yet he took nothing but completion and quickness as the principle of his doctrine. This is his excellent view.

Moreover, if the learning of Sîla or morality of the Doctrine of Completion is spoken of with regard to reason, any Sîla includes the Three Collective Pure Sîlas (San-ju-jō-kai), viz., 1. the Sîla of good behaviour, 2. the Sîla of collecting or holding good deeds, 3. the Sîla of benevolence towards living beings. But, if it is spoken of with regard to form, there are two ways of receiving it, viz. thoroughly and partially Receiving it thoroughly (Tsū-ju) is to receive the There Collections above enumerated. Receiving it partially (Betsu-ju) is to receive only the first of the Three, viz., the Sîla of good behaviour. Now the doctrine of Sîla of Completion in Meaning (En-i-kai) established by Dō-sen, is the latter kind of receiving by a Bodhisattva. In this doctrine, there is an action called Byaku-shi-kom-ma, or Ichi-byaku-

san-kom-ma, literally, 'once stating (his wish and) thrice (repeating) an action or karman.' That is to say, one who wishes to receive *S*íla has to state his wish bepore a chapter of monks, and then three times he repeats the karmava*k*ana, or ritual, which his teacher teaches him. After that, he receives the *S*íla of the Bodhisattva. This is what is called 'Receiving thoroughly.'

At present, therefore, the learners of the Vinaya sect prepare both forms of Receiving thoroughly and partially upon the ceremonial platform (Dan-jō), and keep the *S*íla, according to the Vinaya of the Four Divisions (the Hînayâna-vinaya) and the Brahma-*g*âla-sûtra (Bon-mō-kyō, i. e. the Mahâyâna-vinaya).[7] The terms 'Receiving thoroughly and partially' originated in the Hossō sect, and they were adopted by Dō-sen in the most active sense. Who could have thus established his doctrine, unless he were a holy person? Boku-sō, an Emperor of the T"ang or Tō dynasty, who reigned from 821 to 824 A. D., praised him with a verse. The Devas and Spiritual Leaders (such as Vai*s*rama*n*a or Bi-sha-mon) are said to have always guarded and praised him and offered him heavenly food; so that if he had a doubt about any thing, the heavenly beings answerd his questions. Last of all, the holy Bhikshu Pindola (Bin-dzu-ru) appeared before

---

[7] *No.* 1087.

him and praised him, saying that Dō-sen was the best man who had promulgated the Vinaya after Buddha. He is therfore worthy to be honoured and to be believed in by the learners of his doctrine.

II. A history of the sect.

During fifty years, the Tathâgata Sâkyamuni preached the Vinaya, whenever any circumstance required a rule of discipline After Buddha's entering Nirvâṇa, his disciple Upâli, sitting upon a high seat, collected or recited the Vinaya-piṭaka, which is called the Vinaya of Eighty Recitations (Hachi-jū-ju-ritsu).[8] In the first century after Buddha, there were five teachers in succession without any different views. Their names are Mahâkâsyapa (Ma-ka-ka-shō), Ânanda (A-nan), Madhyântika (Ma-den-ji), Saṇavâsa (Shō-na-wa-shu), and Upagupta (U-ba-kiku-ta) After the first century, the faithful diverged into two, five, and twenty different schools each possessing the text of the Tripiṭaka. Among the Vinaya-piṭaka of the twenty schools, four Vinayas and five Sâstras only were transmitted or translated into Chinese. The Vinaya of the Four Divisions (Shi-bun-ritsu),[9] one of the four Vinayas, is the text of the Dharmagupta school, and has been translated into Chinese in sixty volumes (Kwan). This work was first recited by the Arhat Dharmagupta, one of the five disciples of Upagupta. The

[8] *No.* 1115. [9] *No.* 1117.

names of the five disciples (or rather of their schools) are Dharmagupta (Don-mu-toku), Sarvâstivâda (Sappa-ta), Kâsyapîya (Ka-shō-bi), Mahî-sâsaka (Mi-sha-soku), and Vâstîputrîya (Ba-so-fu-ra).

In the period of the Gi dynasty of the Sō family, 220-265 A. D., Dharmakâla, or Hō-ji, began to teach the Vinaya in China; and in 405, Buddhayasas, or Kaku-myō, first translated the full Vinaya (Shibun-ritsu),[10] under the Shin dynasty of the Yō family. These are the dates of the transmission of the Vinaya in China. Sixty years later, there was a Chinese Vinaya-teacher named Hō-sō, who was well acquainted with the Mahâsamghîka-vinaya (Ma-ka-sō-gi-ritsu).[11] But this Vinaya was not in harmony with that of the Dharmagupta school, which had been adopted in China ever since Dharmakâla; so that he began to teach the Vinaya of the Four Divisions instead of that of the Mahâsamghikas. From this time down to the Tō (or T'ang) dynasty which lasted from 618 to 907 A. D., the Chinese Buddhists unanimously followed the Vinaya of the Dharmagupta school. This may have been the result of the labours of Hō-sō.

But Dō-sen Nan-zan Dai-shi was the founder of the Vinaya sect in China. Among his works, there are the so called Three Great Books of Vinaya (Ritsu-san-dai-bu), viz., 1. Kai-sho, or Commentary on the Sîla or Morality, in eight volumes; 2. Gossho,

---
[10] *No.* 1117. [11] *No.* 1119

or Commentary on the Karman or Action, in eight volumes; 3. Gyō-ji-shō, or Record of the Daily Practice, in twelve volumes. There is a catalogue of his works compiled by the Vinaya teacher Gwan-jō.

Dō-sen was succeeded by the second patriarch named Shū, whose successor was Dō-kō. The fifteenth patriarch was Gwan-jō, who was accorded the laudatory name of Dai-chi ('great wisdom'). He was a very learned man, and compiled a commentary on each of the Three Great Books of this sect. Thus the doctrine of Dō-sen was greatly promulgated by him, so that he may be called the re-founder of the Vinaya sect.

Buddhism was introduced into Japan in 552 A. D. But two centuries passed before the doctrine of Vinaya was fully known in this country. In the reign of Shō-mu (724-748), two Japanese priests, Ei-ei and Fu-shō, went to China, and saw the Upâdhyâya (Wa-jō, or Kwa-shō, i. e. teacher) Gan-jin in the Daimyō monastery of Gō-shū. The latter then consented to their request to promulgate the Vinaya in the East. Gan-jin together with Shō-gen and others eighty in number, promised to come to Japan. They arrived here in 753, having unsuccessfully attempted the journey five times, and having spent twelve years on the sea without approaching Japan. In the following year, the Empress Kō-ken invited him to live in the Eastern Great Monastery (Tō-dai-ji) in Nara,

the capital of Japan at that time, and intrusted him with the ordination service, teaching the *S*îla or moral precepts, according to the Vinaya.

Before this, the ex-Emperor Shō-mu, while still on the throne, had by the advice of the venerable Rō-ben, caused a bronze image of Vairo*k*ana Buddha (Bi-ru-sha-na Butsu), the lord of the *S*îla-pâramitâ, or perfection of morality, to be made, one hundred and sixty feet in height, and to be installed in the Eastern Great Monastery. After Gan-jin's arrival, both the ex-Emperor and his daughter, the reigning Empress, took the vow to practise the *S*îla of the Bodhisattvas (Bo-satsu-kai), ascending the Kai-dan, or '*S*îla-terrace,' built of earth before the temple of Vairo*k*ana. The Empress consort and the Prince Imperial as well as many hundreds of priests all followed their example. Afterwards, a separate building of the '*S*îla terrace' (Kai-dan-in) was built, to the west of the temple. The earth with which this high terrace was formed, was that which had been used for the terrace of the Emperor; and this earth is said to be that of the *G*eta-vana-vihâra (Gi-on-shō-ja) in India, and of Mount Shū-na*n* in China. The three stories of the '*S*îla terrace' represent the Three Collective Pure *S*îlas (San-ju-jō-kai). There is placed a tower above it, in which the images of *S*âkyamuni and Prabhûtaratna (Ta-hō) are enshrined; because the excellent meaning of the one vehicle and

the deep sense of the secret Dharma-dhâtu are included in this doctrine. Therefore, if one takes the vow to practise the moral precepts on this terrace, he is said to keep the *S*îla of all the hidden and apparent doctrines.

In 759, the Empress Kō-ken ordered Gan-jin to found a monastery called Tō-shō-dai-ji. The '*S*îla terrace' was built therein, where the Empress took the vow. After this, both priests and laymen continually follow her example.

In 762, the following resolution was carried out by Imperial order: — A '*S*îla terrace' was built in two monasteries, Yaku-shi-ji in the province of Shimotsuke and Kwanon-ji in Chiku-zen. The former was the place of taking the vow to practise the *S*îla for the people of the ten eastern provinces; and the latter, for those of the nine western provinces. Both Places, being in remote regions from the capital, a chapter of five monks was held in the ceremony.
The people of all the other provinces received instruction in the *S*îla-at the '*S*îla-terrace' within the Eastern Great Monastery in Nara. A chapter of ten monks was regularly held there. There were these three Kai-dan, or '*S*îla terraces,' in Japan. This shows that how greatly the Imperial care was exercise for the sake of the people's religion.

Gan-jin was a successor of two lines of patriarchs, called the lines of Nan-zan and Sō-bu. In the form-

er, he succeeded Gu-kei, who was the successor of Dō-sen, Nan-zan Dai-shi. In the latter, the patriarchs were Hō-rei, Dō-jō, Man-i, Dai-ryō and Gan-jin in succession. Gan-jin was, however, the first patriarch of the Japanese Vinaya sect. He belonged properly to the Nan-zan school, though he was equally a succesor of the Sō-bu; because he received instruction in the full *S*îla from Gu-kei, who did so from Dō-sen.

CHAPTER IV.

The Hossō-shū, or Dharma-lakshana-sect, i. e. the sect or school that studies the nature of Dharmas or things (i. e. the Yoga school).

I. A history of the sect.

The Tathâgata (Nyo-rai) Sâkyamuni preached the clear meaning of the truth of the 'middle path' of the Vidyâ mâtra (Yui-shiki) or the 'only knowledge' —the principle of the doctrine of this sect—in six Sûtras, such as the Avatamsaka-sûtra (Ke-gon-gyō),[1] Sandhi-nirmokana-sûtra (Ge-jin-mitsu-kyō)[2] and others. Nine centuries after Buddha, Maitreya (Mi-roku or Ji-shi) came down from the Tushita heaven to the lecture hall in the kingdom of Ayodhya (A-yu-sha) in Central India, at the request of the Bodhisattva Asamga (Mu-jaku), and discoursed five Sâstras (1. Yogâkârya-bhûmi-sâstra (Yu-ga-shi-ji-ron),[3] 2. Vibhâga-yoga (?)-sâstra (Fun-betsu-yu-ga-ron),[4] 3. Mahâyânâlankâra-or Sûtrâlankâra-sâstra (Dai-jō-shō-gon-ron),[5] 4. Madhyânta-vibhâga-sâstra or -grantha (Ben-chū-ben-ron),[6] and 5. Vagrakkhedikâ-pragñâpâramitâ-sâstra (Kon-gō-han-nya-ron).[7] After that, the two great Sâstra-teachers Asamga and Vasubandhu (Se-shin), who were brothers, composed

---

[1] No. 87. [2] No. 247. [3] 1170. [4] This has not yet been translated into Chinese [5] No. 1190? [6] No. 1244, or No. 1245? [7] No. 1231?

HOSSŌ-SHŪ. 33

many *S*âstras (Ron) and cleared up the meaning of the Mahâyâna. Especially the Vidyâ-mâtra-siddhi-sâstra-kârikâ (Jō-yui-shiki-ron)[8] is the last and most careful work of Vasubandhu, as it is perfect in composition and meaning. There were ten great teachers beginning with Dharmapâla (Go-hō), each of whom compiled a commentary. But Dharmapâla's commentary is considered to contain the right meaning of the doctrine. His disciple *S*îlabhadra (Kaigen) lived in the Nâlanda monastery in Magadha in Central India. He was the greatest master of his day, being well versed in the secret meaning of the *S*âstras Yoga and Vidyâ-mâtra (Yui-shiki), as well as in those of the Hetu-vidyâ (In-myō) or 'science of cause,' i. e. the Indian logic or rhetoric, and the *S*abda-vidyâ (Shō-myō) or 'science of sound,' i. e. grammar. This is the history of the doctrine of this sect in India.

In 629 A. D., when he was in his twenty-ninth year, the famous Chinese pilgrim Gen-jō (Hiouen-thsang) went to India and studied the several *S*âstras and Sciences above alluded to, under the instruction of *S*îlabhadra. Having mastered all these subjects, he came back to China in 645. Five months later, he began his great work of translation under the imperial order, in the monastery of Gu-fuku-ji. He continued the work for nineteen years. Thus he

---
[8] *No.* 1215.

HOSSŌ-SHŪ.

greatly promulgated the doctrine of this sect in China. His principal disciple was Ki-ki, who was very clever and wise. He is said to be the author of a hundred commentaries on several Sûtras and Sâstras, and was called Ji-on Dai-shi, or the 'great teacher of the Ji-on monastery.' In his works, he generally gives what he had learned by oral instruction from his master Gen-jō. Therefore, most of his works are called Jukki, or 'Records of transmission.' Ki-ki had a disciple named E-shō, (Shi-jū Dai-shi), whose disciple was Chi-shū, (Boku-yō Dai-shi). They each wrote some works and made the doctrine of this sect known in China.

There are four different dates of transmission of this doctrine into Japan, of which the following two dates are clearer and called the Northern and Southern transmission. In 653 A. D., a Japanese priest named Dō-shō of Gwan-gō-ji went to China and became a fellow-disciple of Ki-ki, receiving the instruction from Gen-jō. When he reterned to Japan, he transmitted the doctrine to Gyō-gi. This is the transmission of the so-called Northern monastery, Gwan-gō-ji, being at Asuka in the province of Yamato. Afterwards, in 712 A. D., Gen-bō went to China and studied the doctrine of the Hossō sect, following Chi-shū. Having come back, Gen-bō transmitted it to Zen-ju. This is the transmission of the Northern monastery, Kō-buku-ji, in Nara on the north of Asuka. Since

that time, the doctrine has been successively handed down by various learned men.

II. The doctrine of the sect.

(a) The doctrinal division.

According to the Sandhi-nirmo*k*ana-sûtra (Ge-jin-mitsu-kyō), this sect divides the whole preachings of the Tathâgata *S*âkyamuni into the three periods of 'existence' (U), 'emptiness' (Kū), and the 'middle path' (Chū-dō). All the doctrines of the Mahâyâna and Hînayâna, to the number of eighty thousand, are included in these three divisions. In the first period, ignorant people falsely believed in the existence of their own Âtman (Ga) or 'self,' and were accordingly sunk in the sea of transmigration. For such people, the first division of the doctrine of existence was taught by Buddha on purpose, to the effect that every living being was unreal, but that the Dharmas or things were existing. The doctrine preached in the four Âgamas (A-gon)[9] and other Sûtras of the Hînayâna

[9] These are, 1. Madhyamâgama (Ma*gghi*ma-nikâya), Chū-a-gon, collection of middle sûtras, *No.* 542.

2. Ekottarâgama (Aṅguttara-nikâya) Zō-ichi-a-gon, miscellaneous Sûtras in divisions the length of which increases by one, *No.* 543.

3. Sa*m*yuktâgama (Sa*m*yutta-nikâya), Zō-a-gon, collection of joined Sûtras, *No.* 544.

4. Dîrghâgama (Dîgha-nikâya), Jō-a-gon, collection of long Sûtras, *No.* 545.

is of this character.

In the second period, though people of small intellect could destroy the false idea of the existence of 'self,' and escape from continual re-births, following the doctrine of the first period; yet they still believed in the 'real existence of Dharmas or things.' Thus they were not able to see the truth. The second division of the doctrine of the 'emptiness of all things was then taught by Buddha still on purpose in the Mahâ-pragñâ-pâramitâ-sûtra and similar works. By this doctrine, the false idea of the 'existence of things' was removed, but it caused man to believe in the 'real emptiness of all things.' Thus there were two kinds of people, one of whom believed in the 'existence or reality of things,' and the other, in the 'emptiness or unreality.'

In order to destroy their false ideas, Buddha in the third period preached the middle path, neither existence nor emptiness. The doctrine of this period shows that the Parikalpita-lakshana (Hen-ge-sho-shū-shō) or the 'invented nature' is unreal, but that the Paratantra-lakshana (E-ta-ki-shō) or the 'subservient nature,' and the Parinishpanna-lakshana (En-jō-jitsu-shō) or the 'completed nature,' are both real. In the Avataṃsaka-sûtra (Ke-gon-gyō) and the Sandhi-nirmokana-sûtra (Ge-jin-mitsu-kyō), there are given several technical expressions, such as San-gai-yui-shin, or Three worlds (of Kâma [Yoku] or 'desire,' Rûpa

HOSSŌ-SHŪ. 37

[Shiki] or 'form,' and Arûpa [Mu-shiki] or 'formless') are the only mind; and the eight Vig*ñ*ânas (Shiki) or 'knowledges,' and the three Laksha*n*as (Shō) or 'natures.'

However, the doctrine is in fact of one and the same tendency, without much difference between the three periods. The human beings are of three classes, viz, those of the highest, those of middle, and those of the lowest intelect, for whom the systems of teaching are necessarily of as many kinds. Those of the highest intellect can understand the true nature of the middle path, which is neither 'existence' nor 'emptiness.' But those of the middle and lowest intellect are unable to understand it at once, only knowing the one side of 'existence' or 'emptiness.' They are called the Bodhisattvas of gradual or slow understanding.
At first they know only the existence of things, then the emptiness of them, and finally enter the middle path of 'true emptiness and wonderful existence' (Shin-kū-myō-u).

The three periods are explained in the following two ways. If the three periods are spoken with regard to those of gradual understanding, they are in the order of time. The three words Sho or 'beginning,' Shaku or 'formerly,' and Kon or 'now,' are respectively used for these three periods in the Sandhi-nirmo*k*ana-sûtra. But if the division of all teachings of Buddha is made according to the meaning of 'ex-

istence, emptiness and the middle path,' then the three periods are the collections of similar meaning : thus the Avatamsaka-sûtra (Ke-gon-gyō) is put in the third period as it explains the middle path, though it is the first preaching of Buddha; while the Sûtra of the Last Instruction (Yui-kyō-gyō) [10] is included in the first period from its character.

(b) An outline of the doctrine.

This school explains the five ranks or groups of a hundred Dharmas, according to the middle path of the Vidyâ-mâtra-siddhi-sâstra (Jō-yui-shiki-ron). They are, 1. *K*itta-râ*g*as (Shinnō) or 'mind-kings,' 2. *K*aitta-dharmas (Shin-jo-hō) or 'mental qualities,' 3. Rûpa-dharmas (Shiki-hō) or 'things having form,' 4. *K*itta-viprayukta-dharmas (Shin-fu-sō-ō-bō) or 'things separated from the mind,' and 5. A*sam*skrita-dharmas (Mu-i-hō) or 'immaterial things.' Though these five groups are enumerated, there is nothing but the *K*itta (Shin) or mind only. There are eight *K*itta-râ*g*as or 'mind-kings,' namely, 1. *K*akshur-vi*gñ*âna (Gen-shiki) or 'eye-knowledge,' 2. *S*rotra-vi*gñ*âna (Ni-shiki) or 'ear-knowledge,' 3. Ghrâ*n*a-vi*gñ*âna (Bi-shiki) or 'nose-knowledge,' 4. *G*ihvâ-vi*gñ*âna (Zetsu-shiki) or 'tongue-knowledge,' 5. Kâya vi*gñ*âna (Shin-shiki) or 'body-knowledge,' 6. Mano-vi*gñ*âna (I-shiki) or 'mind-knowledge,' 7. Klish*t*a-mano-vi*gñ*âna (Zenna-i-shiki or Ma-na-shiki)

---

[10] *No.*122.

HOSSŌ-SHŪ. 39

or 'soiled-mind-knowledge,' and 8. Ālaya-vijñāna (A-ra-ya-shiki) or 'receptacle (like)-knowledge.' The eighth has three senses, viz., active (Nō-zō), passive (Sho-zō) and being the object of the false belief (Shū-zō).

In the active sense, it holds the seeds of all things. In the passive, it continues, while receiving the influence of all things. As to the third meaning, it is taken as the inner self or soul by beings. It is called the principal knowledge, because it holds the seeds of all things, which are produced from it accordingly. The first seven kinds of knowledge arise depending upon the eighth. The seventh knowledge takes the 'division of seeing' (Ken-bun) or perception (?) of the eighth as its object. The first five kinds of knowledge take a part of the material world within the 'division of forming' (Sō-bun) or imagination (?) of the eighth as their object. For the sixth, mind-knowledge, all things are its objects.

Therefore all things are made to appear by these eight kinds of knowledge, without which there is nothing whatever. The mental qualities (Shin-jo) are in accordance with, dependent on, and not separated from knowledge. The things that have form (Shiki-hō) are all in the 'division of forms' (Sō-bun) made to appear by the mind and mental qualities, so that they have no separate nature. The 'things separated from the mind' (Shin-fu-sō ō-bō) have no

real nature, being formed temporarily upon the part of the mind, mental qualities and forms. The 'immaterial things' (Mu-i-hō) are not any thing made to appear by the mind, being the abstract reason free from birth and death. But they are not separated from the mind, being the true nature of it.

That is to say, things which suffer constant changes of birth and death, or production and destruction, appear according to causes and combination of circumstances; but the abstract reason of the true nature of things itself is permanent and not apparent only. But, if there is no reason, no compounded things ever come to exist. In other words, if there is the reason of production and destruction, then things appear. Therfore Asamskrita-dharmas, or 'immaterial things,' are those on which Samskrita-dharmas, or 'compounded things' depend. Yet they are, of course, not separated from each other, so that the 'only knowledge' (Yui-shiki) includes all compounded and immaterial things.

A hundred Dharmas enumerated in the Śâstra of this sect are subdivisions of the five ranks as already mentioned. They are the eight Kitta-râgas, or 'mind-kings,' the fifty-one Kaitta-dharmas, or 'mental qualities,' the eleven Rûpa-dharmas, or 'things that have form,' the twenty-four Kitta-viprayukta-dharmas, or 'things separated from the mind,' and the six Asamskrita-dharmas, or 'immaterial

things.' These are the hundred Dharmas of the Vidyâ-mâtra-siddhi-sâstra(Jō-yui-shiki-ron), in which they are also called the two Dharmas of 'matter or thing' (Ji) and 'reason' (Ri). Again, they are altogether inclusively called the 'only mind' (Yui-shin). In the Yoga-sâstra, there are six hundred and sixty Dharmas enumerated.

(c) The doctrine of meditation (Kwan-mon).

In explaining this doctrine, we have to investigate the nature of the object and subject of meditation. In the first place, the object of meditation includes all things compounded and immaterial, and of three different natures. There are five technical expressions on this point, viz.:

1. Ken-ko-zon-jitsu-shiki, or the 'knowledge of rejecting untruth and preserving truth,' is to reject the 'invented nature' (Hen-ge-sho-shū-shō) as emptiness, and to preserve the 'subserveint (E-ta-ki) and completed (En-jō-jitsu) natures' as existing or real.

2. Sha-ran-ru-jun-shiki, or the 'knowledge of rejecting confusedness and preserving pureness,' is to reject objects which may be confused as being both internal and external, and to preserve the mind only that is purely internal.

3. Shō-matsu-ki-hon-shiki, or the 'knowledge of putting away the end, and arriving at the beginning,' is to put away the 'divisions of forming and seeing' (Sō-bun and Ken-bun, i. e. imagination and per-

ception?) as the end, and to arrive at their beginning, the 'division of understanding' (Ji-tai-bun, or Ji-shō-bun).

4. On-retsu-ken-shō-shiki, or the 'knowledge of concealing inferiority and showing superiority,' is to conceal mental qualities (Shin-jo) as inferior to the mind-king (Shinnō) which is superior.

5. Ken-sō-shō-shō-shiki, or the knowledge of rejecting forms and understanding the nature,' is to reject the matters or things (Ji) as forms, and to seek to understand the abstract reason that is the nature. This nature is called the Ji-shō-shō-jō-shin, or 'Self (-existing) natural pure mind,' in the Srîmâla-sûtra (Shō-man-gyō). The above five terms explain the object of meditation.

Now the nature of the subject of meditation is Pragñâ (E) or 'wisdom,' one of the mental qualities of a group called the different states' (Betsu-kyō). This is the wisdom which appears in the meditation.

At what time after passing stages and destroying passions, can one who practises the meditation on the 'only knowledge' (Yui-shiki-kwan), attain the state of Buddha? Since first raising his thoughts towards Bodhi or 'enlightenment' deeply and firmly, according to the powers of certain causes and the advice of good friends, he has to pass three great Asamkhya or 'countless' kalpas, constantly practising this meditation. Thus, passing through several

HOSSŌ-SHŪ.

stages and destroying the two obstacles of passions and cognisable things (Klesa-âvaraṇa and Gñeya-âvaraṇa, or Bon-nō-shō and Sho-chi-shō), he obtains four kinds of wisdom, and truly attains to the perfect enlightenment (Parinirvâṇa). The full explanations of this doctrin are given in the principal Śâstra of this sect, the Jō-yui-shiki-ron.

CHAPTER V.

The San-ron-shū, or Three Sâstra sect (i. e. the Madhyamika school).

I. A history of the sect.

The principal books of this sect are three, viz., 1. the Madhyamaka-sâstra (Chū-ron) or 'Middle Book,'[1] 2. the Sata-sâstra (Hyaku-ron) or 'Hundred Books,'[2] and 3. the Dvâdasa-nikâya (or-mukha)-sâstra (Jū-ni-mon-ron) or 'Book of Twelve Gates.'[3] Hence the name of San-ron-shū. These Sâstras explain thoroughly the teachings of Buddha's whole life.

The sect is therefore, also called Ichi-dai-kyō-shū, or 'Sect of the Teachings of Buddha's Whole Life.' Accordingly it differs much from all other sects which latter are founded on a certain Sûtra or other sacred books. Those who select a Sûtra are liable to become narrow in opinion, and speak about the comparative excellence of other Mahâyâna doctrines; thus the Avatamsaka-sûtra (Ke-gon-gyō)[4] is regarded by one sect as the principal Sûtra, looking at all the other Sûtras as its branches, while the Saddharmapundarîka-sûtra (Ho-ke-kyō)[5] is revered by another sect just in the same way.

This arises from ignorance of Buddha's original thought, which was to make others understand the

---

[1] No. 1179. [2] No. 1188. [3] No. 1186. [4] Nos. 87,88. [5] No. 134.

SAN-RON-SHŪ. 45

truth. As the dispositions of living beings are of several kinds, the system of teaching for them is also necessarily various. All the doctrines of Mahâyâna have, however, one and the same object without any difference, that is, to cause beings to attain to the middle path. So, any Sûtra or doctrine which suits hearers may be preached to them with advantage.

A physician gives his patient a medicine, for the purpose of curing the disease. Who then disputes about the comparative excellence of drugs? The Mahâyâna doctrines are altogether Sâkya's principal teachings, which are thoroughly explained by the three Sâstras of this sect.

There are two lines of transmission of the doctrine of this sect, viz., the line of Ka-jō and of Gen-ju.

The former is as follows: The first patriarch in India was the Boddisattva Nâgârguna (Ryū-ju), the author of the Chū-ron and Jū-ni-mon-ron, two of the three Sâstras. He transmitted the doctrine to the Bodhisattva Deva (Dai-ba), the author of the Hyaku-ron. He was succeeded by Râhula (Ra-gora), whose successor was Nîlanetra (Shō-moku, lit. 'blue eye'). After this, there was a prince of the country of Kharakar (Ki-ji), Sûryasoma by name, who was well versed in the Three Sâstras and taught the doctrine to Kumâragîva (Ra-jū). In his sixty-third year, Kumâragîva arrived in China, and reached Chō-an, the capital, when he was eighty-one years

old. There he translated the Three Sâstras into Chinese and became the founder of this sect in China. His disciples numbered three thousand, of whom the four greatest (Shi-tetsu) were Dō-shō, Sō-jō, Dō-yū and Sō-ei. Dō-shō transmitted the doctrine to Donsai, Dō-rō, Sū-rō, Hō-rō, and Kichi-zō of the mona-s tery of Ka-jō-ji successively. This last named made the doctrine of this sect perfect.

His disciple E-kwan came from Korea to Japan in 625 A. D., and was appointed to Gwan-gō-ji. He once lectured on the Three Sâstras as prayers to procure rain with success, and was appointed Sō-jō or Bishop. He is considered to be the first patriarch of this sect in Japan. He transmitted the doctrine to Fuku-ryō, who come from Go in China. Fuku-ryō transmitted it to Chi-zō, who went over to China and became a disciple of Kichi-zō, known as Ka-jō Daishi. After that, Dō-ji, Zen-gi, Gon-sō and An-chō, etc. successively transmitted this doctrine, and made it flourish in this country.

The other line is that of Nîlanetra (Shō-moku) Bhavaviveka (Shō-ben), Gñânaprabha (Chi-kō) and Divâkara (Nichi-shō), who were all Indians. Divâkara transmitted the doctrine to Hō-zō, better known by his posthumous title of Gen-ju Dai-shi, who died in 712 A. D. Af terHō-zō, there was no successor in China.

Of the above two lines of transmission, the Ka-jō

SAN-RON-SHŪ.

school is considered the orthodox one.

II. The doctrine of the sect.

During his whole life, Buddha preached two kinds of truth (Ni-tai), to remove the confused ideas of the people who were either Astikas, i. e. those who believed in the existence of every thing, or Nâstikas, i. e. those who believed in the emptiness of every thing. These ideas caused them to suffer from endless transmigration, so that they are called the original confusion (Hon-mei). The two kinds of truth are true by general consent (Zoku-tai), and true or absolute truth (Shin-dai). These are not the subjects on which Buddha meditated, but only the differences of the style of his preaching. It is said in the Madhyamaka-sâstra, that Buddhas preach the Law to the beings according to the two kinds of truth.

But after Buddha's entry into Nirvâna, people mistook his words and again became either Astikas or Nâstikas. These mistakes are called the later confusion (Matsu-mei). The Three Sâstras of this sect were then composed by the Bodhisattvas Nâgârguna and Deva, for the purpose of destroying this confusion.

The full title of Chū-ron (Madhyamaka-sâstra) is Chū-kwan-ron, or 'Book on the middle meditation.' The word Chū means the middle path of 'not obtaining' (Mu-toku). To contemplate on this middle path is the right meditation. The book contains

the words which come out from this right meditation. The words themselves are the two kinds of truth. Truth by general consent (Zoku-tai) is explained for the Nâstikas, who believe that there is nothing. The true truth (Shin-dai) is expounded for the Astikas who believe that there is something. Thus they are equally made to understand the middle path. There are twenty-seven chapters in the Madhyamaka-sâstra. The first twenty-five chapters refute the confused ideas of the learners of the Mahâyâna doctrine; and the last two, those of the Hînayâna.

The Dvâdasa-nikâya-sâstra (Jū-ni-mon-ron) is divided into twelve parts and refutes the confusion of the men of the Mahâyâna. Generally speaking, this Sâstra also consists of the words of the two kinds of truth, by which the later confusion is refuted.

The two Sâstras, Madhyamaka and Dvâdasa-nikâya, are the works of Nâgârguna. Did Indians ever believe his works? They did indeel. The people of the sixteen great provinces into which India was formerly divided, unanimously called Nâgârguna 'Buddha without his charactersistic marks' (Mu-sō-gō-butsu), and respected his works as if they had been the Sûtras of Buddha's own words. This respect of the people perhaps originated in the prophecy spoken by Buddha in the Laṅkâvatâra-sûtra (Ryō-ga-kyō),[6] which is as follows:

[6] *Nos.* 175, 176, 177.

SAN-RON-SHŪ.

'After the Nirvâna of the Tathâgata,
There will be a man in the future,
Listen to me carefully, O Mahâmati (Dai-e),
A man who will hold my Law.
In the great country of South,
There will be a venerable Bhikshu,
The Bodhisattva Nâgârguna by name,
Who will destroy the views of Astikas and Nâstikas,
Who will preach unto men my Yâna ('vehicle'),
The highest Law of the Mahâyâna,
And will attain to the Pramuditâ-bhûmi ('stage of joy'),
And go to be born in the country of Sukhâvatî.'

Now there may be a man who asserts the following opinion. The Laṅkâvatâra is one of the Mahâyâna-sûtras, and these Sûtras are not Buddha's words, but come from the hands of men of later periods. Buddha enterd Nirvâna on the fifteenth day of the second month, and two months after, on the fifteenth day of the fourth month, Mahâkâsyapa collected the Tripitaka at the Sapta-parna ('seven leaves') cave. Besides this collection, there are not any other Sûtras containing Buddha's words. None of the Mahâyâna-sûtras are genuine, so that they are said to have been discovered either in the dragon palace beneath the sea, or in the iron tower in India, etc. Thus they are not worth while to be believed in.

We shall now answer him, so as to make him understand clearly, just as the obstinate clouds are blown away by the strong wind. The Indians who doubted about the genuineness of the Mahâyâna doctrine were of two kinds. Some entertained the doubt, not being free from vulgar and rude customs. The others know the invincibleness of the Mahâyâna doctrine, yet obstinately uttered these disrespectful words against it.

In ancient times, there were four divisions of people in India (i. e. the four castes). They were 1. Kshatriyas (Setsu-tei-ri), or the royal race, 2. Brâhmanas (Ba-ra-mon), or the military class, 3 Vaisya (Bi-sha), or the merchants, and 4. Sûdras (Shu-da), or the husbandmen.[7] Besides them, there was a mixed tribe called Kandâlas. The men of a higher class looked upon those of a lower, as on the lower animals. For the purpose of destroying this rude custom, Buddha showed them the great path or doctrine, by which they could freely attain to Buddhahood, because they were equally possessed of the nature of enlightenment. But, after Buddha entered Nirvâna, he people still did not quite forget their old rude

---

[7] According to the Manu, the four castes are Brâhmanas, or the priestly class; Kshatriyas, or the military class; Vaisya, or men whose business was agriculture and trade; and Sûdras, or the servile tribe.

SAN-RON-SHŪ

customs, and believed only that they might attain to the state of Srâvakas or Pratyekabuddhas, but not to Buddhahood, which latter would be reached only by a person like Sâkyamuni in this universe. So that they doubted about the Mahâyâna doctrine, which taught that all beings would become Buddhas. It is just as a Preta (Ga-ki), or departed spirit, cannot see the water but only sees the fire while looking at the real water.

There were three different collections of the Tripitaka made after Buddha's entery into Nirvâna. The first was the collection made within the cave of seven leaves near Râgagriha, the capital of Magadha. This is called the Tripitaka of the Sthavira school (Jō-za-bu). The second was that made without the cave. This is the Tripitaka of the Mahâsamghika school (Dai-shu-bu). The third was the collection made by Mañgusrî and Maitreya. This is the collection of the Mahâyâna books. Though it is as clear or bright as the sun at midday, yet the men of the Hînayâna are not ashamed at their inability to know them, and speak evil of them instead, just as the Confucianists call Buddhism a law of barbarians, without reading the Buddhist books at all.

There was an event to add some Mahâyâna-sûtras to the Tripitaka of the Hînayâna one hundred and sixteen years after Buddha's Nirvâna. If there were no Mahâyâna-sûtras, whence were they brought then?

Moreover, two centuries after Buddha, the following Sûtras were also added to the Tripitaka, namely the Avatamsaka (Ke-gon),[8] Nirvâna (Ne-han),[9] Srîmâlâ-devî-simhanâda (Shō-man),[10] Vimalakîrtti-nirdesa (Yui-ma),[11] Suvarna-prabhâsa(Kon-kō-myō),[12] Pragñâ-pâramitâ (Han-nya),[13] and others. At that time, neither Asvaghosha (Me-myō) nor Nâgârguna (Ryū-ju) was yet born in India. Who can then still say that the Avatamsaka-sútra (Ke-gon-gyō) is a work of Nâgârguna?

At that period, the Ekavyahârika school (Ichi-setsu-bu) of the Hînayâna believed in the Mahâyâna doctrine, but the Lokottaravâda school (Shus-se-bu) did not. In the former school, there were perhaps very old men who had heard Buddha's preaching, so that their school was faithful to the Mahâyâna. Two centuries after Buddha's Nirvâna, Shi-he-e (?) came down from the Himâlaya mountains, and Mahâkâtyâyana (Dai-ka-sennen) from the Anavatapta lake (A-nuku-tat-chi). They both were old Sramanas (Sha-mon), being Buddha's immediate disciples, and somewhat united the Mahâyâna with the Hînayâna. Their schools were called Bahusrutika (Ta-mon) and Bahusrutika-vibhagya (Ta-mon-fun-betsu). It will be seen that some men of the Hînayâna did not abuse the Mahâyâna.

[8] *Nos.* 87,88. [9] *Nos.* 113,114. [10] *No.* 59. [11] *Nos.* 146,147,149. [12] *Nos.* 126,127,130. [13] *Nos.* 1-15 *or* 22.

SAN-RON-SHŪ.

We shall now give a clear proof in order to show the genuineness of the Mahâyâna doctrine from the Mâyâ-sûtra, one of the Hînayâna-sûtras, which are not doubted by the men of the latter school. It reads as follows:—

'The correct Law of the Tathâgata will last for five centuries. In the first century, Upagupta will preach the Law and teach the people. In the second century, the Bhikshu Sîlananda will do the same. In the third century, the Bhikshu Nîlapadmanetra (Shō-ren-ge-gen, lit. 'blue-lotus-flower-eye') will do so. In the fourth century, the Bhikshu Gomukha (Go-ku, lit. 'cow-mouth') will preach the doctrine. In the fifth century, the Bhikshu Ratnadeva (Hō-ten, lit. 'gem-god') will preach the Law and convert the people to Buddhism. Then the correct Law will come to an end. In the sixth century, heretical views, as many as ninety-six different kinds, will arise and endeavour to destroy the Law of Buddha. But the Bhikshu Asvaghosha (Me-myō) will smash these heretics to atoms. In the seventh century, there will be a Bhikshu named Nâgârguna (Ryū-ju), who will preach the Law with good means, light the torch of the correct Law, and destroy the banner of the unjust views.'

Thus in the Hînayâna-sûtra, Buddha clearly foretold the actions of Nâgârguna seven centuries after him. Who can doubt it? Even an ordinary

person is ashamed of making a counterfeit thing. How much less would a great man like Nâgârguna do such a thing? Moreover there is no reason to prophesy a man of such a low character in the sûtras of the both Yânas. After all some Indians perhaps produced a false report, which was then exaggerated by jealous and abusive men. But the true Buddhists do not believe in such a thing.

We shall now examine the origin of the Sata-sâstra (Hyaku-ron). At the time of the Bodhisattva Deva, a king of South India, who governed many countries, believed in a heretical doctrine and not in Buddhism. Deva said: 'If the root of the tree is not cut off, its branches will not be bent; so, if a king is not converted, the doctrine will not be heard everywhere.' Thus saying, he became a guard of the palace. Holding a spear he commanded the soldiers, regulated the ranks of the army, and made the words of command clear and short. So all the soldiers gladly obeyed him, and the king was very pleased and asked him what to wish to do. Deva said: 'I am a man of all knowing, who want to debate with several scholars of all directions in the presence of Your Majesty.' The king granted his petition. Thereupon Deva caused a high seat to be spread at a crossroad and proposed his theme with the following words:—

'Among all the holy men,

The holy Buddha is the best;
Among all the laws,
The Law of Buddha is the best
Among all those who save the world,
The Buddhist Samgha (priesthood) is the best.

'If any scholar can overcome these words, I am willing to forfeit my head.'

Then many scholars assembled and Swore saying: 'If we are overcome, we will forfeit our heads.' Deva said: 'The principle of our doctrine is to let the beings live out of compassion, so that we would not want your heads. But if you are overcome, you should shave your heads and become my disciples.'

Thus making an agreement, they began a debate. All the scholars were overcome by Deva, either at once or after two or three days. Three months after, more than a million of people all became his follwers. Deva then retired to a forest and recorded what was going on in the debate. This record is the *Sata*-sâstra, which is divided into ten chapters. It refutes chiefly the heretics and sometimes the false belief of the Buddhists also.

If the doctrine of this sect refutes both the Mahâyâna and Hînayâna as well as the heretics, what is the principle of it? Those who keep in mind the difference between our own doctrine and others, and also believe in the variety of the Mahâyâna and Hînayâna, are said to commit errors. The

truth is nothing but the state where thoughts come to an end. The right meditation is to perceive this truth. He who has obtained this meditation is called Buddha. This is the doctrine of the San-ron sect.

CHAPTER VI.

The Ke-gon-shū, or Avata*m*saka-sûtra sect.
I. A history of the sect.
(a) The translation of the principal Sûtra.

This sect depends on the Ke-gon-gyō, or Avata*m*saka-sûtra,[1] so that it is called the Ke-gon-shū. There are said to be six different texts of the Sûtra. The first is called the Gō-hon, or 'Constant text,' and the second, the Dai-hon, or 'Great text.' These two texts have been kept by the power of the Dhara*n*î or 'holding' of the great Bodhisattvas, and not written down upon palm-leaves. The third is the Jō-hon, or 'Highest or longest text,' and the fourth, the Chū-hon, or 'Middle text.' These two are secretely preserved in the 'dragon palace' (Ryū-gu) under the sea, and not kept by the men of *G*ambudvîpa (En-bu-dai), this world. The fifth is the Ge-hon, or 'Lowest or shortest text,' which is said to contain a hundred thousand verses or as many words in thirty-eight chapters. The Bodhisattva Nâgâr*g*una (Ryū-ju) obtained it from the dragon palace and transmitted it in India.

The sixth is the Ryaku-hon, or the 'Abridged text,' which has been translated into Chinese. Under the Eastern Shin dynasty, 317-420 A. D., Buddhabhadra translated thirty-six thousand verses of the former

---
[1] *Nos.* 87,88,89.

KE-GON-SHŪ.

part of the fifth text in sixty volumes.² Afterwards, in the period (695-699) of the Tō (T'ang) dynasty (618-907), *S*ikshânanda translated forty-five thousand verses of the former part of the same text as before in eighty volumes.³ At the same time, Pra*gñ*a made a separate translation of one chapter entitled Dharma-dhâtvavatâra (Nyū-hō-kai). It consists of forty volumes.⁴

What is the 'Constant text,' that is not to be written down? Even at the point of one grain of dust of immeasurable and unlimited worlds, there are innumerable Buddhas, who are constantly preaching the Ke-gon-gyō, throughout the three states of existence, past, present and future; so that the preaching is not at all to be collected. The one thought of *S*âkyamuni is nothing but the truth (Shin-nyo). This truth fills up all the ten directions throughout the three states of existence. The one thought that is not separated from the truth also fills up the same sphere. While remaining in this one thought, *S*âkyamuni preaches his doctrine, so much so that all things in the ten directions throughout the three states of existence do preach at the same time. Even one Buddha does so. How much more all Buddhas constantly do the same. So, there is no means to collect their preachings completly.

(b) The transmission of the doctrine.

---
² *No.* 87. ³ *No.* 88. ⁴ *No.* 89.

KE-GON-SHŪ. 59

The first patriarch Asvaghosha (Me-myō) composed the Mahâyâna sraddhotpâda-sâstra (Dai-jō-ki-shin-ron),[5] or 'book on raising faith in the Mahâyâna.'

The second patriarch Nâgârguna (Ryū-ju) composed the Mahâkintya-sâstra (Dai-fu-shi-gi-ron), or 'book on the great inconceivableness.' There is now a translation of one part of this book, with the title of Dasabhâmi-vibhâshâ-sâstra (Jū-jū-bi-ba-sha-ron),[6] or 'book on the ten stages fully explained.'

The above two patriarchs were the Indian Bodhisattvas, and the following five were the great Chinese teachers.

The third, To-jun Dai-shi; whose family name was To and his personal name Hō-jun, first established the terms of the 'five doctrines' (Go-kyō), and wrote two works, the Go-kyō-shi-kwan and the Hō-kai-kwan-mon.[7]

The fourth, Shi-sō Dai-shi, whose family name was Chō and his personal name Chi-gon, produced the Sō-gen-ki and the Ku-moku-shō.

The fifth, Gen-ju Dai-shi, whose family name was Kō and his personal name Hōzō, wrote the Go-kyō-sho, Tan-gen-ki, and some other works, and perfected the doctrine of this sect. When he lectured on the sûtra, there rained some wonderful heavenly flowers; and rays of white light came

---
[5] *Nos.* 1249, 1250. [6] *No.* 1180. [7] *No.* 1596.

out from his month. The Empress Soku-ten of the Tō dynasty (reigned 684-705 A. D.) gave him the posthumous title of Gen-ju Bosatsu.

The sixth, Shō-ryō Dai-shi, whose family name was Ka-kō and his personal name Chō-kwan, lived on Mount Go-dai and compiled the Dai-sho-shō,[8] a great commentaly on the Ke-gon-gyō in eighty volumes.

The seventh, Kei-hō Zen-ji, whose family name was Ka and his personal name Shu-mitsu, lived in the Sō-dō monastery on Mount Shū-nan and promulgated the doctrine.

In 136 A. D., a Chinese Vinaya teacher, Dō sen, came to Japan, and first brought the works of this sect. Four years later, Ryō-ben reported to the Emperor Shō-mu, and caused a Korean priest Shin-shō to lecture on the Ke-gon-gyō of sixty volumes, in the Kon-shō ('golden bell') hall of the Tō-dai ji, or the 'Eastern great monastery.' On the opening day, there was seen a cloud of purple colour, which the Emperor admired very much. The lecturer went through twenty volumes a year, and thus completed his task at the end of three yeas. After that, lecturing on the Sûtra has become one of the yearly services of the Tō-dai-ji.

II. The doctrine of the Sect.

(a) The time of Buddha's preaching the

---
[8] *Nos.* 1589,1890.

KE-GON-SHŪ. 61

Ke-gon-gyō and its title.

After *S*âkyamani attained to Buddhahood, he was silent for seven days. During that period, he meditated on the doctrine which he understood, and also contemplated upon the dispositions of beings, and upon the law to be preached to them. This is called the Sâgara-mudrâ-samâdhi (Kai-in-san-mai), or 'sea-seal-meditation.' As the four troops of the Asuras ('evil spirits') appear upon the great sea, as if it were sealed, so all things including the doctrines and beings appeared upon the wisdom of Buddha, the perfectly enlightened one He preached his doctrine just as it had appeared in the first meditation, but in accordance with the dispositions of hearers. These preachings numbered more than three hundred 'assemblies' or times, which are characterized as the five doctrines of 'smallness (Shō), beginning (Shi), end (Jū), Suddenness (Ton), and completion' (En).

In the second week after his enlightenment, Buddha preached the Ke-gon-gyō, which was therefore the beginning of the preachings of his whole life. This preaching took place at seven different places, where eight assemblies were held, two of which were in the same room. Three of the seven places were in the human world, but the rest in the heavens. It is, however, not to be thought of, that he actually went to so many different places and meetings to discourse. He did not rise from the Jaku-metsu-dō-jō (the place

where he became Buddhs), yet he preached in those seven places; because he spoke the doctrine of non-impediment of every thing and endlessness of degrees. Again some might doubt that this Sûtra would not have been preached by Buddha as early as the second week after his attainment; because in the eighth assembly, the *S*râvakas such as *S*âriputra (Sha-ri-hotsu) and Mahâmaudgalyâyana (Dai-moku-ken-ren) who became Buddha's disciples sometime later, were present. But this was done so by the power of the Dhâranî or holding of Buddha. It is said in the Sûtra, that 'all Kalpas of the past are placed in the future, and those of the future are turned to the past.' Therefore it was the power of Buddha's Dhâranî, which caused *S*âriputra and Maudgalyâyana, the later converts, to appear in the assembly of the second week.

The Ke-gon-gyō is the orginal sûtra of Buddha's teachings of his whole life. All his teachings, therefore, sprang from this sûtra. If we attribute, all the branches to the origin, we may say that there is no teaching of Buddha for his whole life, except this sûtra. Now, we shall explain the title of the sûtra in the easiest way, in order to show the outline of the whole work, as the title is said to be a sign of the book. The title of the sûtra in question consists of the seven characters, Dai-hō-kō-butsu-ke-gon-gyō, i. e. Buddhâvatamsaka (Butsu-ke-gon)-mahâ (Dai)-vaiplya (hō-kō)-sûtra (kyō). The first

KE-GON-SHŪ. 63

six characters of Dai-hō-kō-butsu-ke-gon, lit 'great-square-wide-Buddha-flower-adornment,' explain the law taught, and the last Kyō or sûtra means the teaching. Again, among the first six characters, the four of Dai-hō-kō-butsu mean the law or thing compared, while the two of Ke-gon mean a comparison. Among the first four characters, the three of Dai-hō-kō mean the reason understood, and the one of Butsu or Buddha the wisdom of understanding. The whole sûtra is nothing but the reason and wisdom. The reason is Samantabhadra (Fu-gen), and the wisdom, Mañgusrî (Mon-ju). The state where the reason and wisdom cease to be two, is called Vairo-kana's Dharma-kâya (Bi-ru-sha-na-hosshin), or the 'Body of the law of the Great Enlightened,' i. e. Buddha.

The word Dai or 'great' means to contain in; Hō, or 'square,' means rules; Kō or 'wide,' means to extend to. The one and true Dharma-kâya ('law-body') lengthwise contains in it the three states of existence, and crosswise extends to the ten directions. It is free from untruth, so that it is called Dai-hō-kō, 'great-square-wide,' i. e. Mahâ-vaipulya, or 'great largeness.' Buddha understood this truth, by his wisdom and preached it just as he knew. This is the Ke-gon-gyō, or the 'flower-adornment-sûtra,' i. e. Avatamsaka-sûtra, or 'garland-book.' The Ke-gon or 'garland' is a comparison. The thirty-four

chapters preached in the seven places and eight assemblies contain nothing but those in which Buddha became enlightened, just as a garland is made up beautiful by collecting immeasurably excellent flowers. Therefore the Sûtra is called the Dai-hō-kō-butsu-ke-gon-gyō, i. e. the 'Sûtra of Buddha's garland of great largeness.'

(b) The division of the Five Doctrines (Go-kyō).

As we have seen already, Buddha preached the perfect Sûtra in the second week after his enlightenment. But those of weak intellect, such as Sâriputra and Maudgalyâyana were like deaf and dumb people, and unable to understand even a word. Accordingly Buddha preached the doctrine of Hînayâna ('small vehicle') with good means. He explained the four truths (Shi-tai) to the Srâvakas (Shōmon), and the twelve chains of causation (Jū-ni-innen) to the Pratyekabuddhas (En-gaku). He also spoke of a long practice for three Asamkhya or 'countless' kalpas to the Bodhisattvas (Bo-satsu) of small intellect. This is only the means of calling in those of weak understanding, just as if it were to make a mirage appear in the space of three hundred Yoganas in order to attract the people to one's own purpose. This is the first of the five doctrines, characterised as 'smallness.'

The second doctrine is described as 'the beginning' (Shi). This is the doctrine which Buddha taught

KE-GON-SHŪ. 65

to those who had just entered the Mahâyâna, coming out from the Hînayâna. There are two kinds of this doctrine, namely, that of 'emptiness' (Kū) and of 'form' (Sō). The former (Kū-shi-kyō) is the teaching in which all things are said to be empty or unreal, in order to destroy the false idea of the existence of things (Hō or Dharma) of the Hînayâna. This is the doctrine related in the Pragñâ-sûtra (Han-nya-kyō), the three Śâstras (San-ron), and similar works. The other (Sō-shi-kyō) is the doctrine which teaches to practise disciplines profitable both for oneself and others, for attaining to Buddhahood. It increases the six kinds of Vigñâna or knowledge of the Hînayâna into eight, and also the seventy-five Dharmas into a hundred. (For these, see Chapters 1 and 4, i. e. the Ku-sha-shū and Hossō-shū.) This is the doctrine of the Sandhi-nirmoḱana-sûtra (Ge-jin-mitsu-kyō), the Yogâḱârya–bhûmi–śâstra (Yu-ga-ron), and the like.

The third doctrine is called 'the end' (Jū), that is to say, the extremity of the Mahâyâna. This doctrine speaks of the causation from the Tathâgata-garbha (Nyo-rai-zō) or the 'Tathâgata's womb;' but not of the Bhûta-tathatâ (Shin-nyo) or the 'true suchness' or truth. It also asserts that all can become Buddhas but not that men are of five different kinds in their nature (the latter views being those of the Hossō sect). It is the doctrine that is expounded

in the Laṅkâvatâra-sûtra (Ryō-ga-kyō),[9] the Mahâyâna-sraddhotpâda-sâstra (Ki-shin-ron), and other works.

The fourth doctrine is characterised as 'Suddenness.' It teaches that when a thought does not rise, it is called Buddha. The nature or truth is not to be explained in words. If a false thought be cut off, then the true nature appears, the state of which is called Buddha. Therefore in this doctrine, there is neither division nor rank. At the one thought of his great understanding, one becomes Buddha in the present body as quickly as an image appears in a mirror. From the older times, this doctrine is compared to the Contemplative sect (Zen-shū) founded by Bodhidharma.

The fifth and last doctrine is described as 'completion.' It is called so, because 'one and many are mutually joined, free and without any obstacles.' The fouth doctrine of 'Suddenness' speaks of becoming Buddha at one thought, but it does not yet know the meaning of the non-impediment of every thing of the state of Buddha. In the whole preachings of Buddha, the Ke-gon Sûtra only expounds the doctrine of 'completion.'

There are two kinds in the Ekayâna (Ichi-jō) or the 'one vehicle.' The one is the 'one vehicle of a special doctrine (Betsu-kyō-ichi-jō), that is the Ke-gon Sûtra.

---

[9] *Nos.* 175,176,177.

KE-GON-SHŪ.

The other is the 'one vehicle of a similar doctrine' (Dō-kyō-ichi-jō), which includes the Saddharma-pundarîka-sûtra (Ho-ke-kyō) also. So, the name of 'one vehicle' is equally given to the Hokke Sûtra, but that of the 'doctrine of completion' is limited to the Ke-gon Sûtra only.

In short, all the virtues of the state of Buddha are not to be shown, without this doctrine. It says that one destruction is equal to that of all. So, if one cuts off one portion of passions, he is said to cut off all. It also says that one practice is equal to that of all. So, if one practises one practice, he is said to accomplish all. Again, it says that one thought equals immeasurable kalpas. Therefore, one passes over the three Asamkhya or countless kalpas within one thought, and becomes Buddha. Thus, in the 'doctrinal division of practice and arrangement' (Gyō-fu-mon), it speaks of the attainment of Buddhahood after passing three different births.

But, in the 'division of completion and circulation' (Ennyū-mon), it asserts that when one first raises his thoughts towards the perfect knowledge, he at once becomes fully enlightened. This is the principle of the doctrine of this sect.

CHAPTER VII.

The Ten-dai-shū, or the sect founded on Mount Tendai in China.

I. The doctrine of the sect.

The doctrine of this sect is to encourage all men, whether quick or slow in understanding, to exercise the principle of 'Completion and Suddenness' (Endon), with four doctrinal divisions; one or all of which are taught to men, according to their ability. The object of the doctrine is to make men get an excellent understanding, practise the good discipline, and attain to the great fruit of enlightened. Thus they can become a benefit to their country.

The principle of Completion and Suddenness is the meditation on the middle path. This path is called the inconceivable state. If one understands this principle, all things are in completion. Though beings were originally in the state of completion, they once sank into confusion and began to suffer miseries of existence, without knowing truth. Out of compassion, therefore, Buddha appeared in the world, and preached the truth in several doctrines according to the circumstances of time and place.

There are the four doctrinal divisions of 'Conpletion (En), Secrecy (Mitsu), Meditation (Zen), and Moral Precept (Kai);' which are the means of knowing the principle of Completion.

The following is the regular order of the four doctrinal divisions: 1. The Moral Precept of Completion and Suddenness (En-don-kai), 2. the Action of Meditation (Shi-kwan-gō), 3. the Action of Vairoḳana (Sha-na-gō), and 4. the Transmission of the Law of Bodhidharma (Daru-ma-fu-hō).

First, the Moral Precept of Completion and Suddenness is the general character of this sect. So instruction is given on this point as soon as a person enters the sect. Then there is no fixed order as to which of the two Actions should be first undertaken. The Law transmitted from Bodhidharma is again quite a different transmission. It is independent of the order of time, as it is taught to a competent man with a special ceremony.

The Moral Precept of Completion and Suddenness is to receive the perfect and good qualities of Buddha. This is called Ju-kai, or 'receiving the moral precepts,' which are known as the Trividha-sîla (San-ju-jō-kai), or 'threefold pure precepts.'

The first is the Sambhâra-sîla (Shō-ritsu-gi-kai), or 'Precept of good behaviour,' which prohibits evil. There is no evil that is not destroyed by this precept. When ignorance and passion come to an end by keeping this precept, the state of the Dharma-kâya (Hosshin) or 'spiritual body' of Buddha is attained to. This is called the virtue of destruction (Dantoku).

The second is the Kusala-samgrâha-sîla (Shō-zen-bō-kai), or 'precept of collecting or holding good deeds,' which causes men to practise good workes. There is no good that is not collected in it. This is explained as signifying to raise wisdom, to practise all good works both worldly and religious, neither to take nor to abandon several practices such as the six Pâramitâs or 'perfections,' and to practies good devices (Hō-ben). Then the Sambhoga-kâya (Hō-shin) or 'compensation-body' of Buddha is attained to. This is called the virtue of wisdom (Chi-toku).

The third is the Sattvârtha-kriyâ-sîla (Shō-shujō-kai), or 'precept by benevolence towards beings,' which profits beings. There is no being that is not saved by this precept. When all living beings were led to the path of Buddha (or made to follow the doctrine of Buddha), the Nirmâna-kâya (Ō-jin, or Ke-shin) or 'transformed body' is attained to. This is called the virtue of benevolence (On-doku).

These three precepts are the three kinds of the seeds or causes of Buddha. All the Dharmas or 'things' are comprehended in these. Buddha has accomplished all the three, so that he is possessed of perfectly good qualities. These qualities were collected by him for the purpose of giving them to beings.

Therefore it is said in a Sûtra that if beings receive the precepts of Buddha, they at the same time

TEN-DAI-SHŪ. 71

enter the state of Buddhahood. The order of the above three precepts is not fixed. But so far as practice is concerned, the Sambhâra-sîla, or 'precept of good behaviour,' is to be kept first; because it is necessary for all who follow the doctrine of this sect.

Secondly, the Action of Meditation is to practise the excellent contemplation on the middle path, in order to understand the principle of Completion and Suddenness. All the teachings of Buddha in the five periods of his life are comprehended herein. This action belongs to the teaching of completion, so that it is briefly called the Completion (En).

There are also eight divisions of Buddha's doctrine, according to its characteristics suitable to various classes of listners. The 'five periods' (Go-ji) and 'eight divisions of teaching' (Hakkyō) are called the 'doctrine and meditation' (Kyō-kwan) of the Ten-dai sect. The five deriods are called after the titles of the principal Sûtras, namely: 1. The Ke-gon,[1] or Avataṃsaka; 2. the A-gon,[2] or Âgama; 3. the Hō-dō,[3] or Vaipulya; 4. the Han-nya,[4] or Pragñâ-pâramitâ; and 5. the Hokke,[5] or Saddharma-puṇḍarîka; and 6. the Ne-han,[6] or Nirvâṇa. The eight divisions of teaching are (1) The sudden (Ton), (2)

[1] *Nos.* 87–112. [2] *Nos.* 542–781 etc. [3] *Nos.* 23–86 and many others. [4] *Nos.* 1–22. [5] *Nos.* 133–139.
[6] *Nos.* 113–125.

The gradual (Zen), (3) The secret (Hi-mitsu), (4) The indeterminate (Fu-jō), (5) Collection (Zō), (6) Progress (Tsū), (7) Distinction (Betsu), and (8) Completion (En).

Thirdly, the Action of Vairokana is the doctrine of the highest Yâna or vehicle of the Yoga or union. Those who practise the great doctrine of secrecy of the form and reason, perfect the Siddhi (Shitsu-ji) or 'success,' and benefit the country, are accomplishers of this Law.

This action is the secret performance practised in accordance with the ability of votaries, who wish to understand the perfect way quickly. Therefore it is called the Ji-mitsu or 'secret of matters or forms.' If they understand the meaning of the secrecy of both the form and reason, and reach the state of enlightenment, at the stage of agreement of reason and wisdom, they are quite certain to attain to Buddhahood in the present life.

Fourthly, the Transmission of the Law of Bodhidharma requires only one thought and three rules. Those who begin this practice have to enter at once the spiritual world, and cultivate their mind, wishing to obtain the highest active power of wisdom. Finally, if they were considered to be competent men for the transmission, they are given a sealed diploma in the special ceremony.

II. A history of the sect.

TEN-DAI-SHŪ. 73

First, the transmission of the Moral Precept of Completion and Suddenness was first received by Śâkyamuni from Vairoḱana (Dai-nichi) Buddha, by whom in turn it was given to the Bodhisattva A*gi*ta (A-it-ta, i. e. Maitreya or Mi-roku). Thus it passed through more than twenty Bodhisattvas. Kumâra*gî*va arrived in China on the twentieth day of the twelfth month of the year corresponding to 401 A. D., and transmitted this doctrine to his Chinese disciples. Afterwards E-shi of Nan-gaku and Chi-ki of Ten-dai, whose posthumous title is Chi-sha Dai-shi, greatly revered it, both receiving the secret transmission, called the Tō-chū-sō-jō, or 'transmission within the tower.' The successor of Chi-sha was Kwan-jō of Shō-an. Some generations after, there was the Upâdhyâya (Wa-jō) or 'teacher' Dō-sui of Rō-ya. At his time, Sai-chō (Den-gyō Dai-shi) and Gi-shin (Shu-zen Dai-shi) went to China from Japan. In 805 A. D., they together with twenty others received the transmission of this doctrine from Dō-sui, and returned to Japan.

Sai-chō transmitted it to En-nin (Ji-kaku Dai-shi). This is the origin of the transmission of the Sam-mon or En-ryaku-ji (Hi-ei-zan). Gi-shin transmitted it to En-chin (Chi-shō Dai-shi). This is the origin of the transmission of the Ji-mon or On-jō-ji (Mi-i-dera). After these, it was widely spread over the whole country, and divided into many different schools.

Secondly, the transmission of the Action of Medi-

tation passed through twenty-three patriarchs in India after *S*âkyamuni. In China, E-mon (550 A. D.) followed the views of the Bodhisattva Nâgârguna (Ryū-ju), the thirteenth Indian patriarch, and understood the doctrine of the 'One thought and Three kinds of meditation' (Isshin-San-gwan). He was succeeded by E-shi (Nan-gaku Dai-shi, who died 577 A. D.) and Chi-ki (Ten-dai or Chi-sha Dai-shi, who died 597 A. D.). The latter greatly expounded the doctrine, and it is called ihe transmission of the Spiritual mountain (Ryō-zen, i. e. the Gridhra-ku*t*a (Gi-sha-kutsu) in India, where *S*âkyamuni preached the Saddharma-pu*n*darîka, the principal Sûtra of this sect). Then it passed through five teachers, from Shō-an Dai-shi to Kei-kei Dai-shi.

In 804 A. D., Den-gyō Dai-shi went to China by Imperial order, and received the transmission of this doctrine from Dō-sui, who was the principal disciple of Kei-kei. After his return to this country, Den-gyō Dai-shi taught it specially to En-chō (Jak-kō Dai-shi) and En-nin (Ji-kaku Dai-shi). This is the transmission of the Sam-mon. In 851 A. D., Chi-shō Dai-shi went to China by Imperial order, and learned the hidden meaning of the doctrine of this sect, under the instruction of Ryō-sho, a successor of Ten-dai Daishi in the ninth generation. When he came back to Japan, Chi-shō Dai-shi taught it to Ryō-yū, and completed the system of the doctrine. Since that

TEN-DAI-SHŪ. 75

time, it has been continually handed down. This is the transmission of the Ji-mon.

Thirdly, the Action of Vairo*k*ana, or the great doctrine of the highest vehicle of the secret union, was transmitted in India from the oral intruction of Vairo*k*ana to Va*g*rasattva (Kon-gō-satta), and so on. In China, *S*ubhakarasi*m*ha (Zen-mu-i) arrived there from Central India in 716 A. D., and handed the doctrine down to Gi-rin Dai-shi. Soon after, Va*g*rabodhi (Kon-gō-chi) also came to China from India; and his disciple Amoghava*g*ra (Fu-kū) went back to India from China and again returned to the latter country. They both transmitted this doctrine to the Chinese Buddhists.

In 805 A. D., Den-gyō Dai-shi met the Â*k*ârya (A-ja-ri) Jun-kyō, a disciple of Gi-rin Dai-shi, and received instruction in this doctrine, and then came home to Japan. In 808, he first practised the secret rite of the Abhisheka (Kwan-jō), or 'sprinkling water on the head,' by Imperial order, in the Takao monastery on Mount Kiyo-taki, on the north-west of Kyōto. Shu-en, Gon-sō, En-chō and some others were then the receivers. This was the day on which this ceremony of Kwan-jō was first performed in Japan.

In 838, Ji-kaku Dai-shi went to China and received instruction in the doctrine of Completion (En), Secrecy (Mitsu), and Meditation (Zen), and also in the

TEN-DAI-SHŪ.

Siddha (Shit-tan) or Sanskrit alphabet, and made clear what had not been known clearly. More especially was he initiated into the secret rites of the great doctrine of Yoga or union. He followed Hō-zen, Gwan-jō and Gi-shin, who were the disciples of the Indian teacher Zen-mu-i's pupil, and received the doctrinal rank of Dai-kyō-ō, or 'great doctrinal king.' In 847, A. D. he came back to this country and became the founder of the Tai-mitsu, i. e. 'secret (Mitsu) doctrine transmitted by the Ten-dai sect.' In some respects, it is far superior to the similar doctrine handed down by the two great teachers (Dai-shi) Den-gyō and Kō-bō. In 854, A. D. it was transmitted to Anne and others. It has since diverged into several schools. This is the transmission of the Sam-mon,

In 853, A. D. Chi-shō Dai-shi went to China, and became the disciple of Hō-zen, and was given two things, viz., a pestle, or a kind of brass mace (Sho or Kine), and a bell (Rei or Suzu), in token of his complete acquirement of the teachings of all the Buddhas. He brought back with him several books and other things. Especially was he granted permission by the Emperor to promulgate the 'meditation according to true words' (Shin-gon-shi-kwan). Thus he perfected the meaning of complete secrecy (En-mitsu). Though their genealogical line so far as the Indian and Chinese patriarchs are concerned is the

TEN-DAI-SHŪ. 77

same, Chi-shō Dai-shi was the disciple, in all the three great Laws, of the Âkârya Hō-zen, who praised him greatly and taught him all that was most important. After he came back to Japan, he handed the Laws down to Shū-ei, Kō-sai and others. There is also a school of the transmission of the Siddhi or Sanskrit letters, and some others which belong to the doctrine of Yoga.

Fourthly, the line of the Transmission of the Law of Bodhidharma passed through twenty-eight Indian and seven Chinese patiarchs. In 736, A. D., Dō-sen came to Japan from China and transmitted this Law to Gyō-hyō, who in turn handed it down to Dengyō. In 804, Den-gyō again received instruction in this Law from Shō-nen in China, and taught it to Ji-kaku, who transmitted it to Chō-i, and so on. There are not any different lines in the transmission of this Law among the Sam-mon and Ji-mon.

CHAPTER VIII.

The Shin-gon-shū, or True Word (Mantra) sect.

1. A history of the sect.

The doctrine of this sect is a great secret law. It teaches us that we can attain to the state of the 'Great Enlightened,' that is the state of 'Buddha,' while in the present physical body which was born of our parents (and which consists of six elements, Earth, Water, Fire, Wind, Ether and Knowledge), if we follow the three great secret laws regarding Body, Speech and Thought.

The Tathâgata Mahâvairokana (Dai-nichi Nyorai) in the state of his Dharma-kâya or 'spiritual body,' preached the doctrine of the secret Mantras or true words (Shin-gon) to his own subjects, in order to show the truth understood by him. This doctrine is recorded in the sûtras such as the Mahâvairokanâbhisambodhi-sûtra (Dai-nichi-kyō,)[1] and the Vagrasekhara-sûtra (Kon-gō-chō-kyō),[2] etc. Although there are numerous words in these sûtras, yet the essential point is nothing but the Mandala or the 'circle' of the Two Parts (Ryō-bu) of Vagra-dhâtu (Kon-gō-kai) and Garbha-dhâtu (Tai-zō-kai). The Mandala is, therefore, the body or substance of the doctrine of this sect. In the assembly called Ji-shō-e ('self-nature-assembly') in which Buddha preached the law, Vagrasattva (Kon-

---

[1] *No.* 530. [2] *No.* 534.

SHIN-GON-SHŪ.

gō-satta) received the secret Abhisheka (Kwan-jō), i. e. the initiation by sprinkling water upon the head, as the sign of the successor in the Law.

Afterwards the great-minded Nâgârguna (Ryū-myō) saw Vagrasattva in the iron tower in South India, and received the secret doctrine from him, concerning the Two Parts of Vagra and Garbha-dhâtu. Nâgârguna transmitted the Law to his disciple Nâgabodhi (? Ryū-chi), who transmitted it to Vagrabodhi (Kon-gō-chi). Vagrabodhi was a man very learned with regard to many doctrines of Buddhism and other religions, and was expecially well acquainted with the deepest meaning of the doctrine of this sect, which he taught in India for a considerable time.

This is an outline of the transmission of this doctrine in India.

In 720 A. D. Vagrabodhi bringing his disciple Amoghavagra (Fu-kū-kon-gō) arrived in Chō-an, the capital of China. The Emperor Gen-sō of the T'ang or Tō dynasty was then greatly delighted, and ordered him to translate the work called the Yu-ga-nen-ju-hō, or the 'Law of reading and recital in the Yoga doctrine.' He is considered the founder of the secret doctrine of Buddhism in China. After his death, Amoghavagra went back to India, in order to make further researches in his doctrin. In 746 A. D., he came back to China and translated the sacred books, to the number of seventy-seven in all. Kei-kwa of

SHIN-GON-SHŪ.

the Sei-ryū-ji was his disciple, who like his master was a very learned man, well versed in the Tripi*t*aka and the Two Parts. Thus he propagated this doctrine throughout the Chinese empire.

In 804 A. D., Kū-kai, better known by his posthumous title Kō-bō Dai-shi, went to China from Japan, and became the disciple of Kei-kwa. The latter was very pleased to see him, and said: 'I have waited for yous coming here a long time.' During two months after his arrival there, Kū-kai received secret instruction concerning the Two Parts. In the fourth month, Kei kwa gave him the Abhisheka, or 'sprinkling water on the head' (Kwan-jō), as the sign of successorship, and said: 'The Bhagavat, or the Blessed one, gave the secret key to the truth to Va*g*rasattva, who transmitted it to Nâgâr*g*una, and so on till myself. Now, because I see you are indeed a man well qualified for this learning, I give you the key to the secret great doctrine of the Two Parts. You should propagate it in your native country.' In 806 A. D., he came back to Japan. The Emperor Hei-zei received him cordially, and ordered him to teach it to the people at large.

Thus, from the Tathâgata Mahâvairo*k*ana to Ku-kai, there were eight patriarchs who were the successors in the Law. Besides them there is another series of so-called eight patriarchs who transmitted

SHIN-GON-SHŪ. 81

the Law. Their names are Nâgârguna (Ryū-myō), Nâgabodhi (Ryū-chi), Vagrabodhi (Kon-gō-chi), Subhakarasimha (Zen-mu-i), Amoghavagra (Fu-kū-kon-gō), Kei-kwa, Ichi-gyō and Kū-kai.

Kū-kai had ten great disciples, but two of them were the true successors, namely, Jichi-e and Shin-ga. Gen-nin succeeded them and transmitted the Law to Yaku-shin and Shō-bō. Shō-bō was the founder of the O-no school; and Yaku-shin, of the Hiro-sawa school.

A genealogical table of the succeeding Patriarchs.

India.

1. Mahâvairokana (Dai-nichi), 'Sâkyamuni's self and inner enlightened body' (Sha-ka-ji-nai-shō-shin).
2. Vagrasattva (Kon-gō-satta).
3. Nâgârguna,
4. Nâgabodhi.

China.

5. Vagrabodhi.
6. Amoghavagra.
7. Kei-kwa.

Japan.

8. Ku-kai, Kō-bō Dai-shi.
   Jichi-e and Shin-ga.
   Yaku-shin, of the Hiro-sawa school.
   Shō-bō, of the O-no school.

SHIN-GON-SHŪ.

II. The doctrine of the sect.
(a) The doctrinal divisions.

According to this sect, there are two ways of classifying all the doctrines of Buddha. First, as the 'Ten Stages of Thoughts' (Jū-jū-shin), when the doctrines are tabulated and considered consecutively, or lengthwise, of the table. Secondly, as two doctrines, hidden and apparent (Ken-mitsu Ni-kyō), a division which cuts the table across the middle. In the latter divission, all the Laws preached by Sâkyamun are called apparent doctrine (Ken-gyō); and those delivered by the Dharmakâya (Hosshin), or the spiritual body, hidden or secret doctrine (Mitsu-kyō). The Dharmakâya is the inner enlightened body of Buddha. It is considered by the adharents of the apparent doctrine formless and speechless; but in the hidden doctrine, the Dharmakâya is said to have a form and to preach the Law. The apparent doctrine is that which is adapted to the hearers, like formal conversation with honoured guests. The hidden doctrine, on the other hand, is the Law understood secretly by Buddha and given to his own disciples, like familiar conversation among relatives. This division is, therefore, used to explain the differences of depth and shallowness of the doctrines of this sect and four others, viz., the Hossō, San-ron, Ten-dai and Ke-gon.

The Ten Stages of Thoughts are originally enumerated in the Chapter on the 'Stages of Thoughts,'

SHIN-GON-SHŪ.

in the Dai-nichi-kyō. They are the names used to illustrate ten different stages of the thoughts of living beings. Kū-kai however wisely took them to illustrate the difference of sects. There are also two ways of explaining these thoughts 'crosswise' and 'lengthwise.' 'Crosswise,' they explain the different sorts of objects in the Dharmalhâtu-mandala (Hō-kai-man-da-ra), or the 'circle of the state of things,' and include the meaning of all the doctrines of Buddha. 'Lengthwise,' they explain the gradual improvement of the thoughts of those who practise the doctrine of this sect, from the first moment of their good thought, till the final perfect enlightenment.

The Ten Stages of Thoughts are as follow:—

1. The I-shō-tei-yō-shin, (lit 'different-birth-ram-sheep-thought') is the characteristic of the three evil states of Nârakas or dwellers in hell, Pretas or departed spirits, and Tiryagyonigata-sattvas or lower animals. The I-shō means ignorant people who are 'different in birth' from the wise men. They are maddened with passions, and can not distinguish good and bad, nor comprehend the reason of cause and effect; but only long for the satisfaction of their appetite and lust, just as a ram. This animal is very low and stupid in nature, and knows nothing but appetite and lust; so that a man who is ignorant of the doctrine of cause and effect is, in India, compared to a ram.

This first Stage of Thought is the gradual cause of pure thought; and when this is once got rid of, the good thought in the second stage is to be substituted.

2. The Gu-dō-ji-sai-shin (lit. 'stupid-boy-holding-fasting-thought') is the characteristic of mankind. The darkness of ignorance of common people is compared with the state of mind of a stupid boy. The fasting is a *S*îla, or moral precept, to keep the body and speech from disorder. If a man keeps the moral precept, according to the instruction of the teacher and friends, and cultivates his good thought, his state is as the flourishing state of trees and grasses in the spring time. Again, in the case of the practiser of the Shin-gon sect, this is the first state of the Samaya, or meditation, in which he performs the practice of the Three Secrets, regarding Body, Speech and Thought. The five cardinal virtues and the five relationships of Confucianism, and the five precepts of Buddhism are included in this Stage of thought.

3. The Ei-dō-mu-i-shin(lit.'infant-boy-without-fear-thought') is the characteristic of the heavenly state. The weakness of ignorant people is compared with that of an infant. When they meet good friend, hear the excellent Law, and practise the ten precepts, they will be free from the pains of the three evil states for a time. Hence the name 'mu-i' or 'without

SHIN-GON-SHŪ.   85

fear.' In the practiser of the Shin-gon sect, it is the state of gradual advance in his practice of the Three Secrets. The opinions of Brahmanism and the ten precepts of Buddhism are included in this Stage of Thought.

4. The Yui-un-mu-ga-shin (lit. 'only-collection-without-self-thought') is the characteristic of the *S*râvakas (Shō-mon), or hearers. There is no self that possesses the supreme power within a living being, which consists of the five Skandhas (Go-un), or collections, namely, Rûpa (Shiki) or form, Vedanâ (Ju) or perception, Samgñâ (Sō) or name, Samskâra (Gyō) or conception, and Vigñâna (Shiki) or knowledge. The Tripitaka of the Hînayâna is altogeher included in this Stage of Thought; and it is the meaning of the doctrine of the Ku-sha sect.

5. The Batsu-gō-in-shu-shin (lit. 'extracting-action-cause-seed-thought') is the characteristic of the Pratyekabuddhas (En-gaku, or Doku-kaku), or 'singly enlightened.' The 'Gō' or action in the term is passion, the 'In' or cause means the twelve causes, and the 'Shu' or seed is the Avidyâ or darkness. From this seed of darkness, passion is raised and an action follows, so that the twelve causes are produced as a link. The Pratyekabuddhas contemplate on these causes and become enlightened, hence the name of 'extracting the seeds or causes of actions.' If these fourth and fifth Stages of Thought are reached,

the practiser of the Shin-gon sect is in the state of meditation, in which any object is contemplated as having no nature, like an image in a mirror, or the reflection of the moon in the water.

6. The Ta-en-dai-jō-shin (lit. 'other-relation-great-vehicle-thought') is the characteristic of the Hossō sect. Having understood the truth that there is nothing but thought, one raises an unlimited compassion, and transfers beings to the other shore of Nirvâna.

7. The Kaku-shin-fu-shō-shin (lit. 'understanding-thought-without-production-thought') is the sharacteristic of the San-ron sect. The Kaku-chin,' or understanding thought,' means to know that the impure thought of passion itself is originally pure. The 'Fu-shō,' or without production,' is the first of eight negative terms to explain the middle path. Taking the first, the other seven are understood. It is said that if the cloud of the false idea of eight confusions is blown away by the wind of the excellent reason explained by eight negations, then the sky of the middle path or truth is clear and calm. If these sixth and seventh stages of Thoughts are reached, the practiser of the Shin-gon sect is in the state of freedom of thought in the meditation of Yoga or union.

8. The Ichi-dō-mu-i-shin (lit.' one-path-without-

doing-thought') is the characteristic of the Tendai sect. The ' Ichi-dō,' or ' one path,' is even and equal, and called ' Ichi-nyo,' or 'one suchness' in the Ten-dai sect. The mu-i (Asamskrita), or 'without doing,' is natural, being called 'Jis-sō or 'true form' in that sect.

9. The Goku-mu-ji-shō-shin (lit. 'extreme-without-self-nature-thought') is the characteristic of the Ke-gon sect. The word 'Goku' means extreme or best. In the apparent doctrine (Kengyō), the Ke-gon sûtra, or Buddhâvatamsaka-mahâvaipulya-sûtra, is the best of all; and in that sûtra, the truth is explained in accordance with relation and does not keep the so-called 'self-nature.'

10. The Hi-mitsu-shō-gon-shin (lit. ' secret-hiddengrave-adornment-thought') is the characteristic of the hidden doctrine. The ' Hi-mitsu,' or 'secret,' is the hidden practice of the Three Secrets of the Tathâgata or Buddha, which adorns the good qualities.

Kū-kai said: 'The apparent doctrine drives away the outer dust, and the Shin-gon, or True Word opens the store (or, shows the inner truth).' Thus the first nine Stages or Thoughts are only the means of stopping passions and driving away the false belief. When he reaches the tenth and last Stage of Thought, the practiser first under-

stands the source and bottom of his own thought, and knows the secret of becoming Buddha by the present body. This is called the true meaning of showing virtue.

(b) The Two Parts of the Vajra-dhâtu and Garbhadhâtu.

The mandala, or circle,' of the Two Parts represents the nature of the reason and wisdom of Buddhas, and also the truth of the from and thought of living beings. The reason why the mandala is estabished in this sect is to show that the form and thought of Buddhas and of other living beings, who are not enlightened, equally consist of six elements. In the term Vajra-dhâtu, or Kon-gō-kai (lit. 'diamond element'), the word Vajra has the two senses of hardness and utility. In the former sense it is understood to be compared with the secret truth which is always in existence and not to be broken. In the latter sense, it implies the power of wisdom of the enlightened that destroys the obstacles of passions. The Garbha-dhâtu, or Tai-zō-kai (lit. 'womb element.'), means to take hold of. It is compared with the state of things that are taken hold of within the original body of beings, just as a child is within the body of his mother. These two divisions of the Dhâtus are representations of the nature of form and thought, the

SHIN-GON-SHŪ. 89

one from reason and the other from wisdom, being the principles of this sect. They are, therefore, never to be sought outside of the thought of beings, within which they are really in existence. The important object of the Two Parts of the Vajra and Garbha-dhātu is to know truly the origin or bottom of one's own thought, and understand the measure or constituents of one's own body.

Although the Two Parts are originally one, yet they are so divided according to the treatment of reason and wisdom. Then the Vajra-dhātu is the wisdom not separated from reason, and it is that which benefits one's own self. The Garbha-dhātu is the reason not separated from wisdom, and it is that which benefits others. Again the Garbha-dhātu consists of the three things of the great meditation, wisdom and compassion, which are Buddha, Vajra and Padma or lotus respectively. These three are technically called Tathāgtânubhâva (Butsu-bu) or Buddha class,' Vajrânubhâva (Kon-gō-bu) or diamond class,' and Padmânubhâva Ren-ge-bu or lotus flower class. The Buddha class corresponds to the Tathāgata Mahāvairokana, (Dai-nichi Nyorai), meaning the perfection of enlightenment. The Vajra class represents the wisdom possessed by Vajra-sattva, which wisdom, being firm in nature can destroy all passions

even though it has been sunken in the mud of transmigration for a very long time. The Padma class represents the compassion of Avalokitesvara, showing that there is the pure thought within all living beings, which is neither destroyed nor defiled throughout the transmigration in six states of existence, like a lotus flower in mud.

The Vagra-dhâtu explains the five kinds of wisdom (see below), and consists of five classes. These are the Ratnânubhâva (Hō-bu) or 'gem-class' and Karmânubhâva Katsu-ma-bu or 'action class, together with the three classes of the Garbha-dhâtu. The Karma class means to accomplish all the actions, and the Ratna class shows the unlimitedness of virtue and happiness within the perfection of Buddha's enlightenment.

Moreover there is the Mandala or circle of nine assemblies in the Vagra-dhâtu, which circle means the perfectness. This Mandala is of four kinds, namely, 1. Mahâmandala, the bodies of all the objects worshipped; 2. Samaya-mandala, the sword and other things held by the worthies; 3. Dharma-mandala, their Vîga, (Shu-ji) or 'seed' i. e. the mystical letter or syllable forming the essential part of a Mantra, and 4. Karma-mandala, their actions.

The Mandala of nine assemblies of the Vagra-dhâtu is as follows:—

5 Katur-mudrâ-parshad 5	4 Eka-mudrâ-parshad 6	3 Buddhi-gati(?)-parshad 7
6 Pûgâ-parshad 4	9 Karma-parshad 1	2 Trailokya-vigaya-karma-parshad 8
7 Sûkshma (?)-parshad 3	8 Samaya-parshad 2	1 Trailokya-vigaya-samaya-parshad 9

1. The Karmad-parshad, (Katsuma-e) or 'action assembly' represents the dignified forms and actions of the objects worshipped. This assembly corresponds to the first of the four Ma*n*dalas. If we minutely count them, there are altogether 1061 worshies therin, but generally they are reduced into 37 according to the number of their good qualities, as the 37 Bodhy-aṅgas, or divisions of the perfect knowledge. The 37 worthies of the Karma assembly, the first of the nine assemblies in the Vagra-dhatu, are in the following order:—

SHIN-GON-SHŪ.

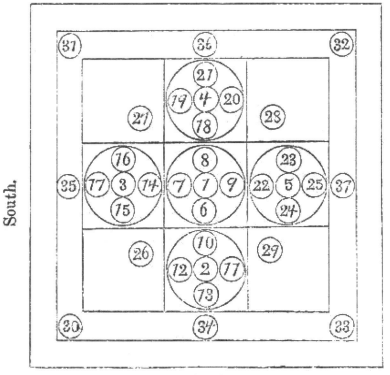

No. 1. Mahâvairoḱana, or Dai-nichi ('great sun'), who holds the Mudrâ or seal of the fist of wisdom.

No. 2. Akshobhya, or Ashuku ('immoveable'), who represents the firmness of the thought of Bodhi or perfect wisdom.

No. 3. Ratnasambhava, or Hō-shō ('gem-birth'), who governs virtues and happiness.

No. 4 Amitâbha, or Amida ('immeasurable light'), who rules over the act of preaching the Law and destroying doubts.

No. 5. Amoghasiddhi, or Fu-kū-jō-ju ('unfailing completion'), i. e. Sâkyamuni, who rules over the accomplishment of the action of Nirvâna.

The above five are Buddhas, and the following are Bodhisattvas.

Nos. 6. Sattva-vagra (' being diamond'), 7. Ratna-vagra('gem d.), 8 Dharma-vagra ('law d.'), 9. Karma-vagra ('action d.'); 10. Vagra-sattva ('diamond being'), 11. Vagra-râga ('d. king'), 12. Vagra-râga ('d. affection'), 13. Vagra-sâdhu ('d. pleasing'); 14. Vagra-ratna ('d. gem'), 15. Vagra-tegas ('d. light'). 16. Vagra-ketu ('d. banner'), 17. Vagra-hâsa ('d. laughing'); 18. Vagra, dharma ('d. law'), 19. Vagra-tîkshna ('d. sharp (thing)'), 20. Vagra-hetu ('d. cause'), 21. Vagra-vâk ('d. speech'); 22. Vagra-karma ('d. action), 23. Vagra-raksha ('d. protection'), 24. Vagra-yaksha ('d. tooth (?)'), 25. Vagra-sandhi ('d. firt (?)'); 26. Vagra-lâsa ('d. sport'), 27. Vagra-mâli ('d. garland'), 28. Vagra-gîti (' d. song'), 29. Vagra-nriti ('d. dancing'); 30. Vagra-dhûpa ('d. incense'), 31. vagra-pushpa ('d. flower'). 32. Vagrâ-loka (d. light,), 33. Vagra-gandhi ('d. smearing perfume'); 34. Vagrânkusa ('d. hook'), 35. Vagra-bandha (d. tie'), 36.

Va*gra*-spho*t*a ('d. chain'), and 37. Va*gra*-gha*nt*â ('d. bell').

In the above list, Nos. 10-25 are called the sixteen worthies of wisdom, and Nos. 6-9 and 26-37 are those of meditation.

2. The Samaya-parshad, (San-mai-ya-e) or 'agreement assembly' corresponds to the Samaya-ma*n*dala. The worthies of this assembly, make the appearance of weapons and Mudrâs or seals, etc., according to their original vow.

3. The Sûkshma (?)-parshad, (Mi-sai-e) or ' minute assembly' corresdonds to the Dharma-ma*n*dala. This represents the minute virtues such as five kinds of wisdom of the worthies.

4. The Mahapûgâ-parshad, (Dai-ku-jō-e) or 'great-worshipping-assembly' corresponds to the Karma-ma*n*dala. In this assembly each of the worthies worships mahâvairo*k*ana with gem diadem and wreath, etc. .

In each of the above three assemblies (2-4) there are 73 worthies.

5. The *K*atur-mudrâ-parshad, (Shi-in-e) or four 'seal-assembly' shows the four Ma*n*dalas together in this one assembly, in which there are 13 worthies.

In the above five assemblies mahâvairo*k*ana (Dai-nichi) is placed in the middle, showing that the cause itself is the effect.

SHIN-GON-SHŪ. 95

6. The Eka-mudra-parshad, (Ichi-in-e) or 'one-seal-assembly' shows the one seal of mahâvairo*k*ana and there is only one worthy, viz, mahâvairo*k*ana.

7. The Buddhigati (?) -parshad (Ri-shu-e) or 'reason-state-assembly' has 17 worthies, Va*g*rasattva being placed in the middle. Mahâvairo*k*ana of the above six assemblies manifests himself as Va*g*rasattva in this assembly and benefits living beings. This shows that the effect itself is the cause.

8. The Trailokya-vi*g*aya-karma-parshad (Gō-san-ze-katsu-ma-e) or 'three-world-subduing-action assembly' has 77 worthies. It shows the state of the Mahâ-krodha-kâya ('great-anger-body') manifested by Va*g*rasattva to destroy the enemies of the three worlds, viz. covetousness, anger and foolishness.

9. The Trailokya-vi*g*aya-samaya-parshad (Gō-san-ze-san-mai-ya-e) or 'three-world-subduing-agreement-assembly' has 73 worthies. It shows the state of the form of Samaya, or agreement of Va*g*rasattva, who holds the bow and arrow, to warn living beings.

The order of the above nine assemblies is of two kinds. The order given above is from root to completion. If we speak of becoming Buddha, then the Trailokya-vi*g*aya-samaya-parshad is the

SHIN-GON-SHŪ.

first, and the Karma-parshad is the end. The former order is from the self-enlightenment to subjugation, and the latter from subjugation to the self-enlightenment.

Thus 437 worthies are counted in the Vagradhâtu. But in fact there are innumerable objects worshipped, which are all omitted.

Next the Garbha-dhâtu ('womb element') is called 13 great enclosures (Mahâ-vritis?) The following Mandala, however, omits the shi-dai-go-in ('four-great-protection-enclosure'); so that there are twelve enclosures only:—

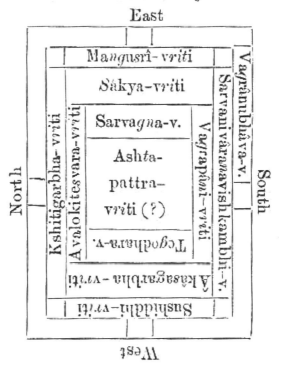

SHIN-GON-SHŪ.

1. The middle Ash*t*a-pattra-v*r*iti, (Hachi-yōin) or 'eight-leaf-enclosure' is like the following:—

This represents H*r*idaya, or 'heart,' of beings. If they meditate on the lotus flower of their heart, eight petals of the flower are burst open and five Buddhas and four Bodhisattvas appear on them, Mahâvairo*k*ana being in the middle. Thus in the middle 'eight-leaf-enclosure,' there

are 9 worthies.

2. The Sarvagña-vriti (Hen-chi-in) or 'all-knowing-enclosure' on the top contains 7 worthies.

3. The Avalokitesvara-vriti (Kwan-on-in) or 'looking-on-sound-enclosure' on the north contains 37 worthies.

4. The Vagrapâni-vriti (Kon-gō-shu-in) or 'diamond-hand-enclosure' on the south also contains 37 worthies.

5. The Tegodhara-vriti (Ji-miyō-in) or 'holding-light-enclosure' on the bottom contains 5 worthies.

6. The Sâkya-vriti (Sha-ka-in) or 'able-one-enclosure' on the top contains 39 worthies.

7. The Mangusrî-vriti (Mon-ju-in) or 'lucky-enclosure' on the top contains 35 worthies.

8. The Sarvanivâranavishkambhi-vriti (Jo-gai-shō-in or 'removing-covering-obstacle-enclosure' on the south contains 9 worthies.

9. Ths Kshitigarbha-vriti (Ji-zō-in) or 'earth-womb-enclosure' on the north contains 9 worthies.

10. The Âkâsagarbha-vriti (Ko-ku-zō-in) or 'sky-womb-enclosure' on the bottom contains 28 worthies.

11. The Susiddhi-vriti (So-shitsu-ji-in) or 'well-perfection-enclosure' on the bottom contains 8 worthies.

12. The outside Vagrânubhâva-vriti (Kon-gō-bu-in) or 'diamond-class-enclosure' on the four sides contains altogether 205 worthies.

SNIN-GON-SHŪ.   99

The total number of the worthies in the above twelve enclosures is 428. Again there are altogether 865 worthies in the Two Parts; but in reality there are endless objects worshipped in the state of things throughout the ten directions, which are all included in these Two Parts. Even if we should know that one Buddha exists within our own body, our merit would be immeasurable. How much more there exist originally unlimited worthies within the heart of all living beings equally. This is truly the extreme secret.

(c) The unimpeded state of six elements

The sha*n*-mahâbhûtas (Roku-dai) or 'six great elements' are earth, water, fire, air, ether, and knowledge. These six exist everywhere, so that they are called Mahâbhûtas, or great elements. If they are divided among the Two Parts, the first five are reason, corresponding to the Garbha-dhâtu, or Tai-zō-kai; and the last is wisdom, being the Va*gr*a-dhâtu, or Kon-gō-kai. However, the reason and wisdom are originally not two; so that there is no knowledge besides the first five elements, and vice versâ. So, if the sixth element vi*gñ*âna, or knowledge, is divided into five elements, these are as many kinds of wisdom, technically called Go-chi, or ' five-wisdom.' They are as follow: — 1. The Dharma-dhâtu-prak*ri*t-*gñ*âna, or Hō-kai-tai-shō-chi ('thing-element-substance-nature-wisdom'), corresponds to

the element ether, being the wisdom to become the substance of things. 2. The Âdarsana-*gñ*âna, or Dai-en-kyō-chi ('great-round-mirror-wisdom'), corresponds to the element earth, manifesting the images of all things just as in the mirror. 3. The Samatâ-*gñ*âna, or Byō-dō-shō-chi('even-equal-nature-wisdom') corresponds to the element fire, making no distinction between this and that, while looking at the things. 4. The Praty-avekshan̄a-*gñ*âna, or Myō-kwan-zatsu-chi ('well-looking-considering-wisdom')corresponds to the element water, being the wisdom that governs the act of preaching the Law and destroying doubts, and that distinguishes clearly what is right or wrong. 5. The Kr̥ityânusht͟hâna-*gñ*âna, or Jō-sho-sa-chi ('wisdom of accomplishing what is to be done') corresponds to the element air, being the wisdom of completing the good action of helping both one's own self and others. This comparison is however not permanent.

The unimpeded state of these elements one with another is compared with the rays of light of many different lamps. The six elements of Buddha are not hindered by those of unenlightened beings. Therfore there is no being besides Buddha, and no Buddha besides being. Such is the unimpeded state of the six elements.

 (d) The Yoga or union of the three secrets (San-mitsu-sō-ō).

SNIN-GON-SHŪ.

The three secrets are the three actions of body, speech and thought. These are originally even and equal. Body is equal to speech, and speech is equal to thought. They all exist everywhere in the Dharma-dhâtu, or element of things, and are called the three secrets even and equal to all Buddhas. Speaking briefly of the form of the Dharma-dhâtu, the apparent form of all things is that of the five elements; and it is the secret of body. This form or body produces sound, and it is the secret of speech. This form has the power (Kō-nō) and it is the secret of thought. These three secrets exist in things both animate and inanimate. Therefore if the wind blows trees, waves beat rocks, and a man raises hands, moves feet, speaks and keeps silence, all are in the three secrets. But these are the states understood by Buddha only, and not approached by an ordinary man; so that they are called secrets. Buddha taught us the rules of Mudrâs or seals and Mantras or True Words, etc., in order to cause ignorant people unite with the state of Buddha. This is the meaning of union (Yoga). It makes no difference between the 'equal' three secrets of Buddha and the 'distinct' three secrets of beings. The three secrets are originally equal without distinction, but ignorant people make distinction of them falsely. Therefore Buddha adds his three secrets to those of beings. This addition is however not that of two

different things. The nature of the secrets of beings are originally not different from those of Buddha's. But ignorant people do not know it. So Buddha teaches them to understand and meditate on this. Such meditation and understanding are those of Buddha, so that there is the meaning of adding the three secrets of Buddha to the three actions of beings. If our practice is ripe in imitating the action of Buddha and becomes equal to the three secrets of Buddha, then there is the meaning of union (Yoga). It is said: San-mitsu-sō-ō-soku-shin-jō, or 'Three secrets united, the present body becomes (Buddha).'

(e) The attainment to the state of Buddha by the present body (Soku-shin-jō-butsu).

There are three kinds of explaining this subject, viz, Ri-gu ('reason-completed'), Ka-ji ('adding-holding'), and Ken-toku ('apparent-obtaining'). The first is explained in the following word: The true form of body and thought of all living beings is the Ma*n*dala, or circle, of the Two Parts of Va*g*ra and Garbha-dhâtu. The flesh body is the reason of the first five elements, and it is th Garbha-dhâtu; while the thought is the wisdom of the sixth element, knowledge, and it is the Va*g*ra-dhâtu. These wisdom and reason are originally completed in all living beings. This is technically called Ri-gu-soku-shin-jō-butsu, or 'the attainment of Buddhahood by the present body completed in reason.'

SHIN-GON-SHŪ.

The second is to make the originally completed Ma*n*dala or circle opened and manisfested by the power of 'adding and holding' (Ka-ji) of the three secrets.

The third is to reach the origin of one's own thought, obtain the Ma*n*dala, and attain to the final state of perfect enlightenment, after completing the practice of the three secrets.

These three kinds of becoming Buddha are only difference in explanation, and in reality they are one and no distinction.

The virtue completed in one's self and not obtained from others is the character of the first (Ri-gu). The ignorant people do not know it, but can perceive it by the power of 'adding and holding' of the Three Secrets. This is the second (Ka-ji). The third is to complete the practice and become the perfectly enlightened (Ken-toku).

The above sketch is only an outline of the doctrine of this sect. If one wants to examine it more minutely, he has to read the three principal Sûtras, Dai-nichi-kyō,[4] So-shitsu-ji-kyō,[5] and Kon-gō-chō-kyō,[6] and also many works called Gi-ki, or 'ceremonial rules.' Besides them, there are several works written by Kû-kai, Kō-bō Dai-shi, who established this Shin-gon sect in Japan.

---

[4] *No.* 530. [5] *No.* 533. [6] *No.* 534.

CHAPTER IX.

The Jō-do-shū, or Pure Land sect.

1. A history of the sect.

Buddhism was first introduced into China from India, in 67 A. D. In 252 A. D., an indian scholar of the Tripitaka, Samghavarman (Kō Sō-gai) by name, came to China and translated the great Amitâyus-sûtra (Mu-ryō-ju-kyō)[1] or Larger Sukhâvatî-vyûha in two volumes. This is the first and longest of the three sacred books of this sect. This Sûtra gives a history of the Tathâgata Amstâbha from the first spiritual impulses which led him to the attainment of Buddhahood in remote Kalpas down to the present time when he dwells in the western world called Sukhâvatî (Goku-raku, or 'happy'), where he receives all living beings from every direction, helping them to turn away from confusion and to become enlightened.

In 400 A. D., Kumâragîva (Ra-jū) came to China from the kingdom of Kharachar (Ki-ji) and produced a translation of the small Amitâyus-sûtra (A-mi-da-kyō)[2] or Smaller Sukhâvatîvyûha in one volume. This is the shortest of the three sacred books. It is taught in this Sûtra that if man keeps in his memory the name of Buddha Amitâbha one day or seven days, the Buddha together with Bodhisattvas will come

[1] No. 27. [2] No. 200.

JŌ-DO-SHŪ. 105

and meet him at the moment of his death in order to let him be born in the Pure Land Sukhâvatî; and that this matter has equally been approved by all other Buddhas of ten different directions.

In 424 A. D., Kâlayasas (Kyō-ryō-ya-sha) arrived in China from India and translated the Amitâyus-dhyâna-sûtra (Kwan-mu-ryō-ju-kyō)[3] in one volume. This is the second longest of the three sacred books. An outline of this sûtra is as follows: Vaidehî, consort of king Bimbisâra of Magadha, seeing the wicked actions of her son A*g*âtasatru, began to feel weary of this world Sahâ (Sha-ba, or 'enduring'). *S*âkyamuni then taught her how to be born in the Pure Land Sukhâvatî instructing her in the method of being born in that world, enumerating three kinds of good actions. The first is worldly goodness, which includes good actions in general, such as filial piety, respect for elders, loyalty, faithfulness, etc. The second is the goodness of *S*îla or morality, in which there are differences between the priesthood and the laity. In short, however, all that do not oppose the general rule of reproving wickedness and exhorting to the practice of virtue are included in this goodness. The third is the goodness of practice, which includes that of the four Satyas or truths and the six Pâramitâs or perfections. Besides these all other pure and good actions such as the reading and recital of the Mahâ-

---
[3] *No.* 198.

yâna-sûtras, persuading others to hear the Law, and thirteen kinds of goodness to be practised by fixed thought are comprised in this. Towards the end of the Sûtra Buddha says: 'Let not one's voice cease, but ten times complete the thought, and repeat Namo'mitâbhâya Buddhâya (Na-mu-a-mi-da-butsu), or adoration to Amitâbha Buddha.' This practice is the most excellent of all.

Buddha teaches us in his doctrine the truth of cause and effect from his right wisdom and understanding. Bad seed produces bad fruit, and good seed produces good fruit, just as red pepper is pungent and sugar-cane sweet according to their own seeds. This is quite natural. No one doubts about it. Therefore the Sûtra is quite true when it says that the right cause of the three kinds of goodness gains the right fruit of nine different stages in the Pure Land Sukhâvatî.

Depending on the three Sûtras above mentioned, there were three patriarchs in India, who preached the doctrine of the Pure Land. They were Asvaghosha (Me-myō), Nâgârguna (Ryū-ju) and Vasubandhu (Se-shin), who were born in India six, seven and nine hundred years after Buddha respectively.

In China, E-on (died 416 A. D.) of the Shin dynasty, Don-ran (d. 542) of the Gi dynasty, and Dōshaku and Zen-dō (both lived about 600-650) of the Tō (T'ang) dynasty chiefly taught this doctrine.

JŌ-DO-SHŪ.   107

Especially Zen-dō used his whole power for the Kwan-mu-ryō-ju-kyō, and wrote a new commentary on it in four volumes. He understood thoroughly the thought of Buddha, and clearly explained the text. In this way, he really excelled his predecessors, such as Jō-yō, Ten-dai, Ka-jō and others. He said himself that he had laid a rule for all ages. This is not at all an exaggsration.

Afterwards Hosshō went to Mount Go-dai, where he worshipped Mañgusrî, and wrote a number of verses, collectively called Go-e-san, or 'verses for five assemblies.' Another teacher named Shō-kō is said to have seen light coming out from the books left by Zen-dō in the temple of Haku-ba-ji, or 'white horse temple.' All these were the benefits left by Zen-dō after his death. During his life-time, the influence of his teaching was so great that the most people abstained from fish or flesh and the market meat of the capital was not sold much. This is the reason why he is generally considered as the greatest master of this doctrine in China.

About five centuries after Zen-dō, in 1133 A. D., a boy was born in the Uruma family of the province of Mimasaka in Japan. This boy's name was Sei-shi-maru. In his ninth year, he was converted by his father's dying words, and when he was fourteen years old, he went up to mount Hi-ei where in the following year, he shaved his head and receiv-

ed the precepts. Then his name was changed to Gen-ku. In his eighteenth year he retired to Kurodani, and five times read through the five thousand volumes of the Tripitaka. He did this for the purpose of finding out the way for the ordinary and ignorant people of the present day to escape from misery. Taking this opportunity he studied Zen-do's commentary already alluded to. He repeated his examination altogether eight times. At last he noticed a passage in it, beginning with the words 'Chiefly remember or repeat the name of Amitâbha with a whole and undivided heart' (Is-shin-sen-nen-mi-da-myō-gō), etc. Then he at once understood the thought of Zen-dō, who taught in his work that whoever at any time practises to remember Buddha or calls his name only once, will gain the right effect of going to be born in the Pure Land after death. Gen-kū then abandoned all sorts of practices, which he had hitherto followed for years; and began to repeat the name of Buddha Amitâbha sixty thousand times a day. This event occurred in 1175 A.D., when Gen-kū was in his forty-third year. The name of Jō-do-shū or Pure Land sect was first known in Japan in this year. This account is given in the Choku-shu-den, or Life of Gen-kū compiled by Imperial Order, and the Sen-jaku-shū, that is Gen-kū's own work.

Gen-kū was very famous in his life-time. He

JŌ-DO-SHŪ. 109

became the spiritual preceptor of the three Emperors Taka-kura, Go Shira-kawa, and Go To-ba. After his death, his biography was compiled in forty-eight volumes, by Imperial Order. It was copied by three other Emperors Fushi-mi, Go Fushi-mi, and Go Ni-jō.

Before Gen-kū, there were eminent priests in Japan, such as Kū-ya, Ei-kwan, and E-shin also called Gen-shin, who all preached this doctrine, but had no successors. Gen-ku had hundreds of disciples. Among them, Shō-kō of Chin-zei and Zenne of Sei-zan were the principal ones. At present there are myriads of monasteries and priests of this sect in the Empire.

II. The doctrine of the sect.

Dō-shaku says in his work, the An-raku-shū, that there are two divisions in the teaching of Śākyamuni, namely, Mahâyâna (Dai-jō) and Hînayâna (Shō-jō). In the former again, there are two gates, viz., the Holy Path (Shō-dō) and the Pure Land (Jō-do). The Hînayâna is the doctrine by which the immediate disciples of Buddha, and those of the period of five hundred years after Buddha, practised the three Śikshâs (San-gaku) or trainings of Adhiśîla (Kai) or 'higher morality,' Adhiḵitta (Jō) or 'higher thought,' and Adhipragñâ (E) or 'higher learning,' and obtained in their present life the four holy fruits of Srota-âpanna, Sakrid-âgâmin, Anâgâmin, and

Arhat. The gate of the Mahâyâna is also the doctrine by which man practises the three trainings above mentioned; and in his present life, he understands the three virtues of Dharma-kâya (Hosshin) or 'spiritual body,' Pragñâ (Han-nya) or 'wisdom,' and Moksha (Ge-datsu) or 'deliverance.' The man who is able to do this is no ordinary one, but has natural vigour, and is supposed to possess merit produced from good actions performed in a former state of existence. The firmness of this man's heart is as hard as a rock, and his fearlessness of any obstacles is like a brave soldier's crushing his enemy. The doctrine which causes man to do so, is called the gate of the Holy Path, and the man is called one who enters the holy state in this world. During fifteen hundred years after Buddha, there were such personages in the world from time to time. The flourishing state of Buddhism at that period and the lives of those eminent priests are to be seen from several compilations of their memoirs.

Now, as the present time belongs to the Latter Day of the Law (Mappō), people become insincere, their covetousness and anger daily increase, and their contentions yearly arise. The three trainings already alluded to are the correct causes of deliverance; but if people think them as useless as last year's almanac, when can they complete their deliverance? Gen-kū, therefore, deeply thinking of this, shut up the gate of

JŌ-DO-SHŪ. 111

the Holy Path and opened that of the Pure Land. For in the former the effect of deliverance is expected in this world by the three trainings of morality, thought and learning; and in the latter the great fruit of going to be born in the Pure Land after death is expected through the sole practice of repeating Buddha's name. Moreover it is not easy to accomplish the cause and effect of the Holy Path. But those of the doctrine of the Pure Land are both very easy to be completed. This difference is compared with going by land and water in Ryū-ju's work. Both the gates of the Holy Path and Pure Land, being the docrine of Mahâyâna, have the same object to attain to the state of Buddhahood. As the time and people for the two gates are not the same, the dotrines are necessarily different, just as one uses a carriage on the land, while another employs a ship upon the water.

The doctrines preached by *S*âkyamuni are altogether eighty-four-thousand in number; that is to say, he taught one kind of people one doctrine such as the Holy Path, and another, as that of the Pure Land. The doctrine of the Pure Land was not only shown by Gen-kū, but also by Zen-dō in his great work. Again this was not only pointed out by Zen-dō, but it was derived from the Sûtra preached by the great teacher *S*âkyamuni. It is said that when Zen-dō was writing his commentary, he prayed for a

wonderful exhibition of supernatural power. Then there appeared to him in a dream every night a dignified priest, who gave him instruction on the division of the text in his first volume. Therefore the author (Zen-dō) treats his own work, as if it were the work of Buddha; and says that no one is allowed either to add or take away even a word or sentence of the book. This is the reason why Gen-kū quotes the three Sûtras and Zen-dō's commentary as the texts in his own work, the Sen-jaku-shū.

If one wants to know the doctrine of the Pure Land, he must believe in the words of Buddha. Sâkyamuni was the sage who perceived the three times, past, present and future, which are just as yesterday, to-day and to-morrow. Among the Indian heretics, there were some who spoke of the future, but their account of it was not accurate; and there was none who spoke of the past. Now the modern people speak of the present life only, and do not know the past and future. Buddha alone knows the three without any mistakes.

The Pure Land is the western world where Buddha Amitâbha lives. It is perfectly pure and free from faults. Therefore it is called the Pure Land. Those who wish to go there, will certainly be born there; but otherwise they will not. This world Sahâ (Shaba), on the contrary, is the effect of the actions of all beings, so that even those who do not wish to be born

JŌ-DO-SHŪ. 113

here, are also obliged to come. This world is called the path of pain, because it is full of all sorts of pains, such as birth, old age, disease, death, etc. This is therefore a world not to be attached to, but to be disgusted with and separated from. One who is disgusted with this world Sahâ and who is filled with desire for that world Sukhâvatî will after death be forn there. Not to doubt about these words of Buddha even in the slightest degree is called the deep faith; but if one entertains any doubts, he will not be born there. For this reason, Ryū-ju said: 'In the great sea of the Law of Buddha, faith is the only means to enter.' This is an outline of the doctrine of this sect.

CHAPTER X.

The Zen-shū or Contemplative sect.

I. A doctrine of the sect.

The word Zen is a shortened form of the term Zen-na, which is a transliteration of the Sanskrit word Dhyâna, or contemplation.

The general character of the doctrine of this sect is briefly explained by the eight Chinese words, Kyō-ge-betsu-den-fu-ryū-mon-ji, or Special transmission independent of a common teaching and not established on any letter or word. Besides all the doctrines of the Mahâyâna and Hînayâna, whether hidden or apparent, there is, therefore, one distinct line of transmission of a secret doctrine, which is not subject to any utterance at all. According to this doctrine, one is directly to see the so-called key to the thought of Buddha or the nature of Buddha, by his own thought, being free from the multitude of different doctrines, the number of which is said to reach eighty-four thousand. In short, it is the truth made apparent by one's own thought.

II. A history of the sect.

(a) The transmission of the doctrine.

When the Bhagavat (Se-son, or 'Blessed') Sâkyamuni was at the assembly on Mount Gridhrakûta (Ryō-zen) or 'vulture's peak,' there came the heavenly king Mahâbrahman (Dai-bon), who offered Buddha

ZEN-SHŪ. 115

a flower of a golden colour, and asked him to preach the Law. The Blessed one only took the flower and held it in his hand, but said no word. No one in the whole assembly could understand what he meant. The venerable Mahâkâsyapa alone smiled. Then the Blessed one said to him: 'I have the wonderful thought of Nirvâna (Ne-han), the eye of the right law, which I shall now give to you.' (See the Dai-bon-tennō-mon-butsu-ketsu-gi-kyō, or 'Sûtra on the Great Bramnan king's questioning Buddha to dispel a doubt.') This is called the doctrine of thought transmitted by thought.

Kâsyapa gave it to Ânanda, who gave it in turn to Sanavâsa, and so on till Bodhidharma, the twenty-eighth patriarch. The following is a list of the names of these patriarchs:—

1. Mahâkâsyapa (Ma-ka-ka-shō).
2. Ânanda (A-nan-da).
3. Sanavâsa (Shō-na-wa-shu)
4. Upagupta (U-ba-kiku-ta)
5. Dhritaka (Dai-ta-ka).
6. Mikkhaka (Mi-sha-ka).
7. Vasumitra (Ba-shu-mtisu).
8. Buddhanandi (Butsu-da-nan-dai).
9. Buddhamitra (Fu-da-mi-ta).
10. Pârsva (Ha-ri-shu-ba).
11. Punyayasas (Fu-na-ya-sha).
12. Asvaghosha (A-na-bo-tei).

13. Kapimala (Ka-bi-mo-ra).
14. Nâgârguna (Na-gya-a-ra-ju-na).
15. Kânadeva (Ka-na-dai-ba).
16. Râhulata (Ra-go-ra-ta).
17. Samghanandi (Sō-gya-nan-dai).
18. Samghayasas (Ka-ya-sha-ta).
19. Kumârata (Ku-mo-ra-ta).
20. Gayata (Sha-ya-ta).
21. Vasubandhu (Ba-shu-han-dzu).
22. Manura (Ma-do-ra).
23. Haklenayasas (Kaku-roku-na).
24. Simha (Shi-shi).
25. Vasasuta (Ba-sha-shi ta).
26. Punyamitra (Fu-nyo-mit-ta).
27. Pragñâtara (Han nya-ta-ra).
28. Bodhidharma (Bo-dai-daru-ma).

Bodhidharma was the third son of a king of the Kâshis, in South India. Thinking that the time of teaching his doctrine of contemplation in the East had come, he arrived in China, in the first year of the Fu-tsū period under the Ryō dynasty, 520 A. D. Bodhidharma then taught the Emperor Bu the secret key of Buddha's thought, who was, however, not yet able to understand it. So leaving there, he crossed the river Yō-shi, and entered the dominion of the Northern Gi. In the Shō-rin-ji (the name of a monastery) on Mount Sū he sat down cross-legged in meditation, with his face to a wall, for nine

ZEN-SHŪ.

years. During that period, people did not know him, and called him simply the Wall-gazing Brâhmana.

Afterwards he had a number of disciples, but they had different views, that are called the transmission of either skin, flesh, or bone of the teacher. Only one of them, E-ka by name, got the whole body of his teaching. The fifth patriarch from Bodhidharma was Kō-nin. Among his disciples, there were two worthy men, E-nō and Jin-shū. The latter taught the doctrine to his followers in the northern part of China, and established the Northern sect. E-nō did so in the southern part, founding the Southern sect.

The Southern sect was soon divided into five schools known as Rin-zai, Gi-gō, Sō-tō, Un-mon and Hō-gen. In the first school Rin-zai, there were two subdivisions, namely, Yō-gi and O-ryū. All these are collectively called the five houses and seven schools of the Southern sect. There was no division of the Northern sect.

As to the propagation of this doctrine in Japan, Dō-sen, a disciple of one of Jin-shū's pupils, came over from China to this country, in 729 A. D. He lived in the Dai-an-ji, and handed down the doctrine of the Northern Contemplation to Gyō-hyō, who transmitted it to Sai-chō, the establisher of the Tendai sect in Japan.

The Southern branch of the Contemplative sect was first transferred to Japan by Ei-sai, of the Ken-nin-ji. He went to China in 1168 A. D., and became the disciple of Kyo-an, of the Man-nen-ji. By him the Rin-zai sect was first established in the Empire. After that, the successors of the Rin-zai school became numerous. Shō-ichi of the Tō-fuku-ji and But-kō of the En-gaku-ji were both the disciples of Yō-gi's ninth generation. Shō-ichi had a disciple named Dai myō, who had the Nan-zen-ji built. Mu-sō of the Ten-ryū-ji was taught by a pupil of But-kō. Dai-kaku of the Ken-chō-ji was a disciple in the tenth generation of Yō-gi, and Dai-tō of the Dai-toku-ji, the eleventh. The latter had an active disciple named Kwan-zan, who founded the Myō-shin-ji.

Thus the Ken-nin-ji, Tō-fuku-ji, En-gaku-ji, Nan-zen-ji, Ten-ryū-ji, Ken-chō-ji, Dai-toku-ji, Myō-shin-ji, together with the Sō-koku-ji, are called the nine principal monasteries of the Rin-zai sect.

The Sō-tō sect was established here by Dō gen of the Ei-hei-ji, who went to China in 1223 A. D., and became a disciple of Nyo-jō of Ten-dō. When he returned to Japan, the Emperor Go-Sa-ga paid great respect to him, gave him a purple robe as a gift, and addressed him by the title of Buppō Zen-ji, or the Teacher of Contemplation in the Law of Buddha.

ZEN-SHŪ. 119

Shō-kin of the Sō-ji-ji was a disciple in the fourth generation of Dō gen. The Emperor Go Dai-go gave him a purple robe, and called his monastery as the principal one of the sect. The Emperor Go Mura-kami gave him the posthumous title of Butsu-ji Zen-ji.

The Ei-hei-ji and Sō-ji-ji are called the two principal monasteries of the Sō-tō sect in Japan.

Afterwards, in the reign of the Emperor Go Kō-myō, 1644-1654 A. D., a Chinese priest named In-gen came to Japan. He was a disciple by descent of the Ō-ryū school, a branch of the Rin-Zai, and established here the Ō-baku sect.

The Rin-Zai, Sō-tō and O-baku are called the three Japanese Contemplative sects or schcools.

(b) The origin of the Southern and Northern sects.

As it has been mentioned, there have long existed two branches of the Contemplative sect in China as the southern and Northern sects. This division took place between the two worthies, E-nō and Jin-shū, disciples of Kō-nin, the fifth patriarch, On a certain occassion, the teacher told all his disciples that the right law of Buddha was difficult to understand, and that they should not merely rely upon the words of their master, but their own views. So they were ordered to compose verses expressing their own opinions, with the condition that he whose verses were correct in meaning should he given the cloaks and the alms-

bowl of Sâkyamuni, transmitted through the Indian and Chinese patriarchs, as the symbols of the rightful successor. Then the venerable Jin-shū, the head of seven hundred disciples, composed the following verses:—

"The body is like the knowledge tree.
The mind is like a mirror on its stand.
It should be constantly and carefully brushed,
Lest dust should be attracted to it."[1]

His teacher recognized it and said: 'If men in future should practise their religion according to this view, they would have an excellent reward.' This is the origin of the Northern sect.

The venerable E-nō was then only a servant, employed to clean rice in a mortar, the pestle of which was worked by the foot. Hearing of Jin-shū's verses secretly, he remarked that it was very beautiful, but not perfectly good. So saying, he wrote verses as follow:—

"There is no such thing as a knowledge tree.
There is no such thing as a mirror stand.
There is nothing that has a real existence.
Then how can dust be attracted?"[1]

On seeing these verses, the teacher Kō-nin at once gave him the symbols of the cloaks and bowl. This is the origin of the Southern sect. The doctrine of this sect is a most sublime one of thought transmitted

---

[1] Dr. Edkins, Chinese Buddhism, p. 162.

ZEN-SHŪ. 121

by thought, being entirely independent of any letters or words. It is in later period called the Patriarch's Contemplation (So-shi-zen), because it contains the key of the thought of the Indian patriarch Bodhidharma. But it is a mistake that some call the doctrine of the Northern sect the Tathâgata's Contemplation (Nyo-rai-zen).

Thus in China there have been the two divisions of the Southern and Northern sects and the former was subdivided into five houses and seven schools as before said. Three schools of the Southern sect exist in Japan at present. But all these are the descendants of Bodhidharma, and the principle of their doctrine is only to show what appears in one's own thought. If one wishes to understand the true meaning of the doctrine, he must study it under the instruction of a right teacher. There are however numerous works containing the instructive words of the teachers of different schools. They are called Goroku, or 'Records of sayings,' which may be serviceable in understanding the doctrine of this sect.

CHAPTER XI.

The Shin-shū, or True sect.
1. A history of the sect.

The full name of the sect is Jō-do-shin-shū, or 'True sect of the Pure Land.' The Pure Land is the term antithetical to that of the Shō-dō or Holy Path. The object of the followers of this sect is to be born in the Pure Land Sukhâvatî of Amitâbha. The third word Shin or 'True' is used to show the antithesis to the Gon-ke-hō-ben, or 'Temporary expedients.' Among those who follow the doctrine of the Pure Land, there are several different systems of teaching, which are as follow: — Some say that we should practise various good works, bring our stock of merits to maturity, and be born in the Pure Land. Others say that we should repeat only the name of Amitâbha Buddha, in order to be born in his Pure Land, by the merit produced from such repetition. These doctrines are all considered as yet the temporary expedients. To rely upon the power of the Original Prayer of Amitâbha Buddha with the whole heart and give up all idea of Ji-riki or 'self power' is called the truth. This truth is the doctrine of this sect. Therefore it is called the Shin-shū, or True sect.

Shin-ran, the founder of the sect, makes in his work a clear distinction of four systems with as

many terms known as the 'two pairs' and 'four folds' or tiers (Ni-sō Shi-jū). They are: 1. The 'lengthwise going-out' (Shu shutsu), that is the attainment of Enlightenment after long practice and perseverance, through many kalpas or periods, in the way of holy men. 2. The 'lengthwise passing-over' (Shu-chō), which refers to Enlightenment in this life, or to the attainment of Buddhahood in the present existence. 3. The 'crosswise going-out' (Ō-shutsu), i. e. the attainment of birth in a region where the state of beings is like that of those in the womb, and a border-land, or species of limbo, adjoining the Pure Land. The imperfection of this birth is the result of carelessness and doubt. 4. The 'crosswise passing-over' (Ō-chō), i. e. birth in the true Land of Amitâbha Buddha according to his Original Prayer.[1] Of these four systems, the fourth is the doctrine of the Shin-shū.

There are three principal sacred books of this sect, all of which contain *S*âkyamuni's teaching on the doctrine of going to be born in Sukhâvatî. These are the same Sûtras as those mentioned in the previous chapter on the Jō-do-shū. The Dai-mu-ryō-ju-kyō,[2] or Larger Sukhâvatîvyûha, the longest of the three Sûtras, is taken as a special text book. This is because in it are spoken the forty-eight Original

---

[1] See note 6 in Mr. James Troup's translation of the Shin-shū-kyō-shi. [2] *No.* 27.

124 SHIN-SHŪ.

Prayers of Amitâbha, the eighteenth of which is the foundation of the doctrine of the 'crosswise passing-over' (Ō-chō).

This doctrine was transmitted at various times and in different places by the so-called 'Seven High Priests' (Shichi-kō-sō), who were the patriarchs of the three countries of India, China and Japan. They were the two Bodhisattvas Nâgârguna (Ryū-ju) and Vasubandhu (Ten-jin) of India, Don-ran, Dō-shaku and Zen-dō of China, and Gen-shin and Gen-kū of Japan. Their works are most minute in explaining the doctrine of the sect, for which reason the authors are reckoned as patriarchs. The seventh patriarch Gen-kū also called Hō-nen was the teacher of Shin-ran, the founder of the sect.

Shin-ran was a scion of the Fuji-wara family (born 1173 and died 1262 A. D.). He was a descendant of Uchi-maro, and son of Ari-nori, who was an official belonging to the palace of the Empress Dowager. As a boy he went to mount Hi-ei, where he studied the doctrine of the Ten-dai sect. In his twenty-ninth year, he became the disciple of Hō-nen, from whom he received the tradition of the doctrine of the Pure Land. Although there were many fellow-disciples, he was especially favoured by his teacher. Afterwards he compiled a book with the title of Kyō-gyō-shin-shō-mon-rui, or 'Collection of Maxims concerning the Doctrine, Practice, Faith

SHIN-SHŪ.

and Enlightenment. In this work he showed the important meaning of the doctrine, as taught by the master. This is therefore the standard book of this sect.

II. The doctrine of the sect.

As has already been stated, the foundation of the doctrine of this sect is the Original Prayer of Amitâbha Buddha. Therefore its faith and practice have for their only object to follow the 'Other Power, of the Original Prayer' (Hon-gwan-ta-riki), and to go to be born in the Pure Land of the Buddha. The Original Prayer is the eighteenth of his forty-eight prayers, which is as follows: — 'If any of living beings of the ten regions, who have believed in me with true thoughts and desire to be born in my country, and have even to ten times repeated the thought (of my name), should not be born there, then may I not obtain the perfect knowledge.'

This Original Prayer sprang from his gerat compassinate desire, which longed to deliver living beings from suffering. With this Original Prayer, he practised good actions during many kalpas, intending to bring his stock of merits to maturity for the sake of other living beings. All his actions, speeches and thoughts were always pure and true, so that he accomplished his great compasionate desire. It is also called the great and wide wisdom of Buddha. This Prayer and Practice excelled those of all other

Buddhas. The state of Buddha which is the fruit of such a cause is called Amida, or Amitâbha and Amitâyus, that is, 'Immeasurable Light' and 'Immeasurable Life. It also means the perfection and unlimitedness of wisdom and compassion. Therefore he can take hold of the faithful beings within his own light and let them go to be born in his Pure Land. This is called the 'Other Power of the Original Prayer.'

The creed of the sect is explained as the believing thought which follows the Original Prayer, and is in correspondence with the wisdom of Buddha. This is the same as the therefold faith enumerated in the Original Prayer, namely, 1. the true thought, 2. the belief, and 3. the desire to be born in the Pure Land. Though these are reckoned as three, the substance is only one, that is called the 'believing thought,' or the 'one thought.' If we examine our own heart, it is far from being pure and true, being bad and despicable, false and hypocritical. How can we cut off all our passions and reach Nirvâna by our own power! How can we also form the threefold faith! Therefore knowing the inability of our own power, we should believe simply in the vicarious Power of the Original Prayer. If we do so, we are in correspondence with the wisdom of Buddha and share his great compassion, just as the water of rivers becomes salt as soon as it enters the sea. For this reason,

SHIN-SHŪ. 127

this is called the faith in the 'Other Power' (Ta-riki).

If we dwell in such a faith, our practice follows spontaneously, as we feel thankful for the favour of Buddha, remember his mercy, and repeat his name. This is the 'repetition of the thought (of Buddha's name) only ten times,' as spoken in the Original Prayer. It does, of course, not limit to the number ten, so that the words Nai-shi, or 'even to' are added. There will be some who may repeat the name of Buddha for the whole life, while walking, dwelling, sitting or lying down. Some may, however, do the Nem-butsu, or 'remembrance of Buddha' only once before they die. Whether often or not, our practice of repeating Buddha's name certainly follows our faith. This is explained as we can constantly practise Buddha's compassion, because we share the great merciful heart of Buddha. Again this Nem-butsu does not only mean to invoke Buddha's name, but the body and thought are also in correspondence with it, and not separated from the Buddha's mercy. This is not the action of the 'self power' of ignorant people. It is therefore called the practice of the 'Other Power' (Ta-riki-no-ki-gyō).

This faith and practice are easy of attainment by any one. Accordingly the general Buddhistic rules of 'becoming homeless, and free from worldly desires, in order to attain to Buddhahood,' are not considered as

essential in this sect. Consequently even the priests of the sect are allowed to marry and eat flesh and fish, while those of all other Buddhist sects are strictly prohibited from doing so.

Those who belong to this sect are recommended to keep to their occupation properly, and to discharge their duty, so as to be able to live in harmony. They should also cultivate their persons and regulate their families. They sould keep order and obey the laws of the government, and do the best for the sake of the country. Buddha says in the Great Sûtra (i. e. the larger Sukhâvatîvyûha): ' You should separate yourselves from all evil, and select and practise what is good, thinking and cansidering well.' The followers of this sect are already in correspondence with the Original Prayer of Amitâbha Buddha, so that they are also in harmony with the instruction of Sâkyamuni, and the general teaching on morality. This is the Samvriti-satya (Zoku-tai), or truth by general consent, a part of the doctrine of this sect, which has reference to the distinction of good and evil in conduct in this world.

Now, as to the Paramârtha-satya (Shin-dai), or 'true truth,' which refers to the distinction of belief and doubt in the mind, what benefits do the believers derive by their putting faith in Buddha? In the present life, they become the members of the Samyaktva-râsi (Shō-jō-ju), or 'mass of absolute truth.'

SHIN-SHŪ.

In the next life they attain to Nirvâṇa (Metsu-do).

In the first place, the mass of absolute truth means the class of beings who will certainly be born in the Pure Land of Amitâbha Buddha, and attain to Nirvâṇa there in the next life. They are taken hold of within the light of Amitâbha Buddha, joyful in heart, practising always the great compassion of Buddha, and suffer transmigration no more. Therefore they are called Avaivartikas (Fu-tai-ten), or 'those who never return again.' They derive this benefit at the moment of their putting faith in Buddha.

In the second place, to attain to Nirvâṇa means to join the state of enlightenment of Amitâbha Buddha, as soon as they are born in his Pure Land. The cause of their going there, is to receive the great mercy and wisdom of Buddha; so that they can most assuredly attain to the state of Buddha (or Nirvâṇa), in which both the mercy and wisdom are full and perfect. The cause and effect are quite natural indeed. Those who belong to several schools of the Holy Path have to practise the three trainings of the higher morality, thought and learning, with their own power, and destroy all human passions, in order to attain to Nirvâṇa. Those of the other schools of the doctrine of the Pure Land are said to attain to Buddhahood, having practised good works for a long time in the Pure Land, where they are born

from here. But in the True sect, the difference is explained by the term Ō-jō-soku-jō-butsu, or 'going to be born (in the Pure Land) is becoming Buddha.' That is to say, when the believers abandon the impure body of the present life (i. e. die) and are born in that Pure Land, they at once accomplish the highest and most excellent fruit of Nirvâna. This is because they simply rely upon the Other Power of the Original Prayer.

In this sect, neither spells nor supplications to Buddhas or other objects worshipped are employed for avoiding misfortunes, because misfortunes are originated either in the far causes of previous exisstences, or in those of the present life. The latter kind of causes should be carefully avoided; so that the believers in this doctrine, following Buddha's instruction, may become free from the present causes of misfortunes. But the far causes, having been originated in previous existences, cannot be stopped. As to the past, reproof is useless; but the future may be provided against. This is the reason why anything like a spell is not at all used in this sect. Moreover the principle of Buddhism is to obtain release from the state of transmigration and enter that of Nirvâna. Then, no happiness or misfortune of this world can desturb the thoughts of the believers. But when they turn their thoughts towards the good of others, the peace of the world should of course be desired by

them. If so, they should do nothing but follow the instruction of Buddha *S*âkyamuni. Then there will follow ultimately such benefits as the world being harmonious, the country prosperous, and the people peaceful.

CHAPTER XII.

The Nichi-ren-shū, or Nichi-ren sect.
I. A history of the sect.
(a) The origin of the establishment of the sect.

Although *S*âkyamuni's manners of teaching are numbered by thousands of myriads, such as the Hînayâna and the Mahâ-yâna, temporary and true, apparent and hidden, subordinate and original, etc., yet his object is nothing but to leâd living beings to the highest state of Nirvâna by the way of gradual teaching. Therefore, in the last period of his life, *S*âkyamuni preached the Saddharma-pun*d*arîka-sûtra (Hoke-kyō),[1] or 'Sûtra of the Lotus of the Good Law.' In this Sûtra, he compared all the Sûtras preached in the three periods past, present and future; and called the Saddharma-pun*d*arîka the best of all. This judgment was made by him according to the rules of preaching of all Buddhas past, present and future; so that even Mañ*g*usrî and Kâsyapa dared not say a word againist it.

As *S*âkyamuni's own preaching was in this order, all the Buddhist teachers in the later periods followed that order, through the Three Periods of the Law, viz., the Period of the Right Law (Shō-bō), of the Image Law (Zō bō), and of the Latter Day Law (Mappō). During the two thousand years of the first

[1] *No.* 134.

NICHI-REN-SHŪ. 133

two periods, therefore, all the great teachers promulgated the Law, either the Hîna or the Mahâ-yâna the temporary or the true, according to *S*âkyamuni's command. Now, the Period of the Latter Day of the Law came, when the original or primitive doctrine of the Saddharma-pu*n*darîka was to be expounded. In 1252 A. D., when all the other sects had already been established, Nichi-ren, founder of the sect, began to promulgate the doctrine of the Saddharma-pu*n*darîka only. He did so, following the rules of *S*âkyamuni's teaching, and explaining the doctrine taught by *S*âkyamuni himself. This excellent doctrine, giving benefits to the people of the present period, had never been known, during two thousand two hundred and twenty years since *S*âkyamuni entered Nirvâ*n*a. For Nichi-ren was most probably an incarnation of the Bodhisattva Vi*s*ish*t*a*k*âritra (Jō-gyō, lit. 'eminent conduct'), who had been a 'primitive convert' (Hon-ke)[2] of *S*âkyamuni, and received special instruction from the latter, in the chapter on the Transcendent Power of the Tathâgata,[3] amidst the so called 'Sky

---

[2] For this Bodhisattva, see the 15th and 21st chapters of the Ho-ke-kyō, i. e. Kumâra*g*îva's Chinese tranlation, and also the 14th and 20th chapters of Kern's English version of the Saddharma-pu*n*darîka, Sacred Books of the East, Vol. XXI.

[3] I. e. the 21st chapter of Kumâra*g*îva's version, and the 20th of Kern's.

Assembly' at Mount Gridhrakûta. This Bodhisattva was born in Japan under the name of Nichi-ren, at the proper time for promulgating the doctrine, which had been transmitted to him from Sâkyamuni. Thus Nichi-ren first established this sect in Japan, expecting to make his doctrine known in the world at large, during the ten thousand years of the Period of the Latter Day of the Law.

The sect is, therefore, either called Hokke-shū or 'Saddharma-pundarîka-sect,' after the title of the principal Sûtra, or Nichi-ren-shū, after the name of the founder. Though this sect adopts the Saddharmapundarîka as the principal Sûtra, like the Ten-dai sect, yet the substance of the doctrine is very different from the latter; so that it is also called Nichi-ren-hokke-shū, or Nichi-ren's Saddharma-pundarîka sect.

The following are the principal Sûtras and commentaries of this sect:

1. Myō-hō-ren-ge-kyō (Saddharma-pundarîka-sûtra),[4] eight volumes, translated by Kumâragîva, under the Shin dynasty of the Yō family, 384–417 A. D.

2. Mu-ryō-gi-gyō (Amitârtha-sûtra),[5] translated by Dharmagâtayasas, under the Northern Sei dynasty, 479–502 A. D.

3. Kwan-fu-gen-kgō (Samantabhadra–dhyâna-sûtra),[6] translated by Dharmamitra, under the Sō

[4] *No.* 134. [5] *No.* 133. [6] *No.* 394.

NICHI-REN-SHŪ.   135

dynasty, 420-479 A. D.

The second and third Sûtras are called the Introduction to and Conclusion of the first sûtra.

4. Chū-ho-ke-kyō, or 'Commentary on the Saddharma-puṇḍarîka-sûtra,' ten volumes, compiled by Nichi-ren.

5. Ku-ketsu, or 'Oral Decisions,' two volumes, containing the teaching of Nichi-ren, as recorded by his chief disciple Nichi-kō.

(b) The Line of Transimission of the Law.

In Nichi-ren's Sadharma-puṇḍarîka-sect, there are two lines of transmission of the Law, viz, internal and external. The external transmission is the line of the teachers in the three countries of India, China and Japan, who expounded the doctrine of the Saddharma-pundarîka, namely: —

Sâkyamuni Buddha. } India.
Bhaishagyarâga (Yaku-ō) Bodhisattva.
Ten-dai Dai-shi (the 'great teacher').   China.
Den-gyō Dai-shi. }
Nichi-ren Dai-bo-satsu (Bodhisattva } Japan.
    Mahâsattva).

The internal transmisson is the line of those who understood the truth of the 'original or primitive doctrine' (Hon-mon), contained within the Stûpa of Prabhûtaratna (Ta-hō-tō), according to the chapters on the Preacher (Hosshi-hon, i. e. the 10th chapter) and the Transcendent Power of the Tathâgata (Jin-

dzū-hon, i. e. Jin-riki-hon, the 20th chapter of the Sanskrit text and the 21st of the Chinese version), namely:—

Sâkyamani Buddha.
Visishtakâritra Bodhisattva (Jō-gyō Bosatsu).
Nichi-ren Dai-bo-satsu.

Though the outer form of the doctrine of this sect depends on that of the Ten-dai sect, the principle is absolutely in harmony with the principal Sûtra; so that the internal transmission is much more correct than the external one.

II. The Doctrine of the sect.

(a) An outline of the Saddharma-pundarîka-sûtra.

The Saddharma-pundarîka-sûtra contains the doctrine which is characterized by the term Gon-jitsu-hon-jaku-kai-e, i. e. 'open comprehension of temporary and true (doctrines), and that of original and subordinate (states of Buddha).' The 'temporary'(Gon) doctrine is that of all the Sûtras spoken by Buddha during the first forty years of his career, before he spoke the Saddharma-pundarîka-sûtra, which alone contains the 'true' (Jitsu) doctrine. The 'original' (Hon) or primitive state of Buddha means the 'original enlightenment' (Hon-gaku) of the very remote time when Buddha was in his primitive stage (Hon-ji). The 'subordinate' (Shaku, lit. footprint) or secondary state of Buddha is the 'first enlightenment' (Shi-kaku) of Buddha's life-time in this world (Sui-

NICHI-REN-SHŪ. 137

shaku). The 'open comprehension' (Kai-e) means to show the final truth, as the object of the appearance of Sâkyamuni in this world.

In the first place we shall explain the 'open comprehension of the temporary and true doctrines'(Gon-jitsu-kai-e). When Sâkyamuni appeared in this world, there were three classes of beings concerning the power of their unederstanding. The lowest class was called Srâvakas (Shō-mon) or 'hearers;' the middle, Pratyekabuddhas (En-gaku) or 'singly enlightened;' and the highest,Bodhisattvas (Bo-satsu) or 'beings of wisdom.' Buddha taught the Srâvakas to destroy passions, separate from transmigration, and attain to the state of Arhat (A-ra-kan). He instructed those who were capable of becoming Pratyekabuddhas, to attain to that state. The Bodhisattvas were taught to make the great vow and prayer to save all beings and bocome Buddhas like Sâkyamuni himself, when their meritorious actions had been completed. These three classes were called Tri-yâna (San-jō) or 'three vehicles,' the first two being the Hîna-yâna (Shō-jō) or 'small vehicle,' and the last, the Mahâ-yâna (Daijō) or 'great vehicle.' One who attained either to the state of Arhat or Pratyekabuddha, according to the Hîna-yâna, did not become Buddha of the Mahâyâna; and vice versâ. One person could not comprehend two ways at once. They were, therefore, taught to practise any of the three vehicles at their

pleasure. So, there were three distinct classes of people, who became the sages of as many vehicles. This is called the doctrine of temporary expedient.

Thus, during the first forty years, Buddha spoke several Sûtras, observing the distinctions of three vehicles. But in the Saddharma-puṇḍarîka, he declared that all his speeches of the first forty years were expedients, and that there was only one vehicle (Eka-yâna) and not three. Farther he said: 'The Śrâvakas and Pratyekabuddhas are also the Mahâyâna and able to become Buddhas. Even the Ikkhantis (Is-sen-dai) or 'unfaithful men' and women are able to attain to Buddhahood. All living beings are possessed of the nature of Buddha; so that there is reason to believe that every one without exception can become enlightened. This is my true doctrine, which should not be doubted. However the temporary doctrine of expedients has been spoken by me for the purpose of leading men to the true path of the Saddharma-puṇḍarîka. Therefore the temporary doctrine itself is true in some respects. The temporary doctrine is like the lotus flower, and the true doctrine is like the fruit or seeds of the lotus. The flower is truly the expedient for the fruit. The expedient and the truth are unseparable. No expedient exists without truth. No truth appears without expedient. They are almost one, though numbered two. This is called the Lotus of the Good Law.'

NICHI-REN-SHŪ. 139

When Buddha spoke these words, the practisers of the three vehicles at once understood the truth of the one vehicle by the merits produced from their previous practice according to the temporary doctrine. So, even Devadatta and the daughter of the king of the Nâgas or serpents immediately ascended the throne of Buddha.

This is the form of preaching of the 'subordinate doctrine' (Shaku-mon) of the Saddharma-puṇḍarîka, in which the 'temporary' doctrine is explained to be expedient for showing the truth, and the three vehicles are looked upon as if they were only one.

In the second place, the 'open comprehension of the original and subordinate states of Buddha' (Honjaku-kai-e) is explained in the following way : —

The state of Buddha to which Śâkyamuni attained in this world through the eight stages of his life (Has-sō-jō-dō), is called Shi-jō-shō-gaku, or the 'first accomplishment of the perfect enlightenment.' The term is shortened into Shi-kaku, or the 'first enlightenment; and this is the subordinate Buddha (Shaku-butsu). The enlightenment of Śâkyamuni here was only to perceive that he himself had been the Buddha of original enlightenment, the lord of the Dharmadhâtu (Hokkai, lit· 'element of law or existence'), since very remote times. All Buddhas of the ten regions of the three times, past, present and future, are in the same way. During the 'tem-

porary' teaching of the first forty years, *Sâkyamuni* spoke of himself as he first attained to Buddhahood in this world as it appeared to be so. But when he spoke the Saddharma-pu*n*darîka, he manifested his real state of 'original enlightenment,' as he was the Buddha of permanency and the lord of the whole universe. But no 'original enlightenment' is manifested unless the 'first enlightenment' has been attained here, just as the flowers and the moon of the former days can be understood only after we see those of to-day. Again we can know the Buddhas of the ten regions by seeing one Buddha only, and recognise that we ourselves are already Buddhas by hearing the state of other Buddhas. All Buddhas of the subordinate state are like the images of the moon reflected upon several waters, and only the Buddha of the original state is like the real moon in the sky. The 'subordinate' state is shown by the 'original' one, and vice versâ. Though they are different from each other, their virtue is one and the same. This is called the Lotus of the Good Law.

When Buddha preached this doctrine, the whole assembly of living beings of ten different worlds, who were present in the Dai-ko-kū-e, or 'Great Sky Assembly,' upon Mount G*r*idhrakûta (Ryō-zen), attained to the state of Buddha. This is the form of preaching of the 'original doctrine' (Hon-mon) of the Saddharma-pu*n*darîka.

NICHI-REN-SHŪ. 141

In short, the character of the 'subordinate doctrine' (Shaku-mon) is to sum up all his speeches, and explain the original intention of his appearance in the world, which is to cause all men and women, whether good or bad, strong or weak in understanding, to join Buddhism. It is also to make the distinctions of several teachings even, and show the wisdom of the one vehicle of Buddha which is just and equal. But the character of the 'original doctrine' (Hon-mon) is to show the origin of all beings, and the real state of enlightenment of the Buddhas of the three times, past, present and future. It also explains that all laws are good and all beings are Buddhas.

The Bhagavat did not teach this excellent law of the original doctrine to the ordinary Bodhisattvas such as Mañgusrî, Bhaishagyarâga (Yaku-ō) and others. How much less did he teach it to the inferior disciples? He carefully instructed in this doctrine the Bodhisattva Visishtakâritra (Jō-gyō) and some others who appeared on the earth. The place in which they were appointed to promulgate the law is this world Sahâ (Sha-ba) or Gambudvîpa; and the time is called either the Period of the Latter Day of the Law, the World of evil and corruption, or the Last 500 years. This is called the Special Instruction in the Original Doctrine of the Soddharma-puṇḍarîka.

142 NICHI-REN-SHŪ.

(b) The Three Great Secret Laws.

The important points of the doctrine of Nichi-ren's sect are called the Three Great Secret Laws or Doctrines, which include all rules of Buddhism. In the chapter on the Duration of the Life of the Tathâgata (Ju-ryō-hon) in the Saddharma-puṇḍarîka, Buddha spoke of the permanency of the three bodies of Buddha, namely, 1. Dharma-kâya (Hosshin) or the 'spiritual body,' 2. Sambhoga-kâya (Hō-shin) or the 'body of compensation,' and 3. Nirmâṇa-kâya (Ō-ge-shin) or the body capable of transformation. This doctrine is the essence of the Sûtra and the object of the appearance of Buddha in the world; so that it is taken to be the substance of the Three Great Secret Laws. In the Sûtra there occurs the term 'the Tathâgata's Secret Supernatural Power'(Nyo-rai-hi-mitsu-jin-dzū-shi-riki), whence the name of the Three Great Secret Laws.

The Three Laws are the Hon-zon, Dai-moku, and Kai-dan of the Hon-mon, i. e. the chief Object of Worship, the Title of the sûtra, and the Place for learning the Sîla or moral precepts, all of which belong to the Original Doctrine. The substance of these is contained in the title of the Sûtra which consists of the five Chinese characters, Myō-hō-ren-ge-kyō (Saddharma-puṇḍarîka-sûtra). We remember in our mind the chief object of worship, recite with our mouth the title of the Sûtra, and keep in our body the place of

NICHI-REN-SHŪ.

Sïla, or simply moral precepts.

First, the chief object of worship (Hon-zon) of the Original Doctrine is the great Mandala of the ten different worlds, which is the body of Buddha, in whom the followers of the sect believe. This Mandala represents the original Buddha of very remote times. This Buddha's 'spiritual body' (Hosshin) consists of the five elements (Faith, Water, Fire, Wind, and Ether) of the Dharmadhâtu of ten regions. The five Skandhas or collections (Form, Perception, Name, Conception, and Knowledge) of the Dharmadhâtu of the ten regions form the nature of the 'body of compensation' (Hō-shin) of this Buddha. The six organs of sense of all beings of ten regions are the form of the 'body capable of transformation' (Ō-ge-shin) of this Buddha. The three actions (of Body, Speech, and thought) and the four dignified postures (of Going, Remaining, sitting, and Lying) of all beings are the actions of this Buddha. The wisdom and virtue of all sages and wise men of every region and the enlightenment of all Buddhas are the supernatural powers of this Buddha. All countries of every region are his dwelling-place. He is free from birth and death, even after passing through immeasurable Kalpas. He is the Buddha of permanency, without beginning and end. This Buddha is called Sâkyamuni who truly accomplished his state of Buddha in very remote times (Ku-on-jitsu-jō), or the 'original

Buddha of three bodies that do nothing' (Mu-sa-sanjin-no-hon-butsu).

The ten worlds from the world of Buddhas down to that of hells, are all transformations of this original Buddha. The chief object of worship (Honzon) is the representation of this Buddha, so that the five characters of Myō-hō-ren-ge-kyō (Saddhamapundarîka-sûtra) are written down in the middle, around which the forms of the ten worlds are added to show the nature of the original Buddha.

Now Sâkyamuni said of himself, in the chapter on the duration of the Tathâgata's life, that he was really this original Buddha. But not only was Sâkyamuni so, but even we ourselves are the same. This is the way of meditating on the chief object of worship.

Secondly, the five characters Myō-hō-ren-ge-kyō form the title of the Sûtra, so that the name of Daimoku or 'title' is given to them. To these five characters, two more viz No-mu (Namas, or 'adoration') are added. Thus we repeat Na-mu-myō-hō-ren-ge-kyō (Namah Saddharmapundarîkâya Sûtrâya), or 'adoration to the Sûtra of the Lotus of the Good Law.' This is to believe in the Good Law of the heart with the heart of the Good Law. The title of the Sûtra which consists of five characters, is the essence of the whole Sûtra as well as of the holy teaching of Buddha's whole life, the principle of all

NICHI-REN-SHŪ.

things, the truth of eternity, and the secret importance of Buddha's original state and of the virtue of his enlightenment. It is quite beyond the reach of explanation and reasoning, except in so far as one may say that it is inexplicable and inconceivable. It is not understood even by the subordinate Buddhas and the highest Bodhisattvas. How much less can it be known by the inferior beings? It is simply to be believed in, and not to be understood at all. This is the title of the original doctrine.

Thirdly, the Kai-dan, or 'place for receiving instruction in *S*îla or moral precepts,' of the original doctrine is explained as follows: To keep the *S*îla is the most important matter of all the divisions of Buddha's doctrine, whether of the great or small vehicle of the true or of the temporary. Therefore there is in the original doctrine the first true *S*îla which is held by Buddha permanently. The Kai-dan is the Bodhi-ma*n*da (Dō-jō) or 'place for the way,' where the ceremony to receive instruction in the *S*îla is to be accomplished. The place is now mentioned instead of the law which is to be observed there.

The substance of this *S*îla is the title of the five characters Myō-hō-ren-ge-kyō. One who believes in this title and observes it, is said to be the holder of the excellent *S*îla of the original doctrine. The place where he keeps and holds it, is the Pure Land

of the Calm Light (Jak-kō-jō-do), i. e. the Kaidan.

In short one should remember that his own body is the Original Buddha (Hon-zon), thought is the Good Law (Dai-moku), and the dwelling-place is the Pure Land of Constantly Calm Light (Kai-dan). Thus he should dwell in the Dharmadhâtu, or 'spiritual state,' of his own thought.

Though the rules of practice of Buddhism are various, the three trainings (San-gaku) of the higher morality (Kai), thought (Jō) and learning (E) are the most important. By the higher morality one keeps off the bad conduct of his body; by the higher thought, he tranquilizes his mind; and by the higher learning, he becomes free from confusion and attains to enlightenment. There is no Buddhist sect which does not take these three trainings as the principle of their practice, though each sect possesses its own peculiar excellence.

So this sect is the same. The Three Great Secret Laws are the three trainings of the sect. The Kaidan is of course the morality (Kai). The meditation or thought (Jō) is to believe in the chief object of worship (Hon-zon) and to meditate on the Good Law. The learning (E) is to repeat the title of the Sûtra (Dai-moku), which contains the wisdom of all Buddhas, and to show the excellence of the wisdom.

If one keeps these Three Secret Laws, the three

NICHI-REN-SHŪ. 147

trainings are quickly accomplished, and immeasurable Samâdhis (San-mai) or meditations and Pâramitâs (Ha-ra-mitsu) or perfections of practice are spontaneously completed. Therefore even a being of weak understanding can enter on the precions rank of the enlightened in his present life. Thus the doctrine of this sect is very deep and wonderful indeed.

Sanskrit-Chinese Index.

Akusala-mahâbhûmika-dharma, 8	大不善地法
Akshobhya, 92	阿閦
Aṅguttara-nikâya (Pâli), 35	增一阿含
Agâtasatru, 105	阿闍世
Agita, 73	阿逸多
Atata, IX	頞哳陀
Advesha, 7	無瞋
Adhi*k*itta, 109	定(三學之１)
Adhipra*gñ*â, 109	慧(同)
Adhimoksha, 7	勝解
Adhisîla, 109	戒(三學之１)
Anapatrapâ, 8	無愧
Anavatapta, 52	阿耨達(池)
Anâgâmin, 109	阿那含
Anâthapi*n*da*d*a, XVII	給孤獨
Anityatâ, 10	滅
Aniyata-bhûmika-dharma, 9	不定地法
Apatrapâ, 7	愧
Apapa, IX	臛々婆
Apratisa*m*khyâ-nirodha, 10	非擇滅
Apramâda, 7	不放逸
Aprâpti, 9	非得
Abhidharma, 16	阿毗達磨
Abhidharma-kosa-sâstra, 1	阿毗達磨俱舍論
Abhidharma-pi*t*aka, 2	阿毗達磨藏

150

Abhinishkramana-sûtra XV　本起經
Abhisheka, 75　灌頂
Amitâbha, 93　阿彌陀(無量光)
Amitâyur-dhyâna-sûtra, 105　觀無量壽經
Amitâyus, 126　阿彌陀(無量壽)
Amitâyus-sûtra, 104　阿彌陀經
Amitârtha-sûtra, 134　無量義經
Amoghavagra, 75, 79, 81　不空金剛
Amoghasiddhi, 93　不空成就
Ayodhya, 32　阿踰闍
Arûpa, 37　無色
Arbuda, IX　頞部陀
Arhat, 3, 26, 110, 137　阿羅漢
Alobha, 7　無貪
Avatamsaka, 52, 71　華嚴
Avatamsaka-sûtra, 22, 32　華嚴經
Avalokitesvara, 90, 97　觀世音(觀自在)
Avalokitesvara-vriti, 96, 98　觀音院
Avigñapti-rûpa, 5　無表色
Avidyâ, 85　無明
Avîki, IX　阿鼻(無間)
Avaivartika, 129　不退轉
Asrâddhya, 8　不信
Asvaghosha, 52, 53, 59, 106, 115　馬鳴
Ashtapattra-vriti, 97　八葉院
Asamkhya, 11, 42, 62, 57　阿僧祇耶(無數)
Asamga, 32　無著
Asamgñika, 9　無想果

Asam*gñi*-samâpatti, 9　無想定
Asamskrita, 4,87　無為
Asamskrit*v*-dharma, 10,33,40　無為法
Astika, 47,48,49　有見有執
Asura, 61　阿修羅
Ahimsâ, 7　不害
Ahrîkatâ, 8　無慚

Âkâsa, 10,11　虛空
Âkâsagarbha-v*ri*ti,96,98　虛空藏院
Âgama, 35,71　阿含
Âkârya, 75,77　阿闍梨
Âtman, 12,14,15,16,35　我
Âdar*s*ana-*g*ñâna, 100　大圓鏡智
Ânanda, 26,115　阿難陀
Âyatana, 4　處
Âlaya-vi*g*ñâna, 39　阿頼耶識

I*kkh*anti, 138　一闡提
Indriya, 5　根

Îrshyâ, 8　嫉

Utpala, IX　嗢鉢羅
Upaklesa-bhûmika-dharma, 8　小煩惱地法
Upagupta, 26, 53, 115　優婆毱多
Upanâha, 8　恨
Upâdhyâya, 28, 73　和上

152

Upâli, 21, 26　　　　　　　優波離
Upekshâ, 7　　　　　　　　優捨
Uruvilvâ-kâsyapa, XIV　　優樓頻螺迦葉

Eka-mudrâ-parshad, 91, 95.　一印會
Ekayâna, 66, 138　　　　　一乘
Ekavyavahârika, 52　　　　一說部
Ekottarâgama, 35　　　　　增一阿含

Auddhatya, 8　　　　　　　掉擧

Kapimala, 116　　　　　　　迦毗摩羅
Kapilavastu, XII, XV　　　迦毗羅衞
Karma, 11, 90, 91　　　　　羯磨(業)
Karman, 21, 25, 28　　　　 羯磨
Karma-parshad, 91, 96　　　羯磨會
Karma-mandala, 90, 94　　　羯磨曼荼羅
Karma-vakana, 25　　　　　 羯磨文
Karma-vagra, 93　　　　　　羯磨波羅蜜
Karmânubhâva, 90　　　　　 羯磨部
Kalpa, 11, 62, 67, 104　　 劫波
Kânadeva, 116　　　　　　　迦那提婆
Kâtyâyana, 2　　　　　　　 迦旃延
Kâma, 36　　　　　　　　　 欲
Kâya, 5　　　　　　　　　　身
Kâya-vignâna, 6, 38　　　　身識
Kâlayasas, 105　　　　　　 畺良耶舍
Kâlasûtra, IX　　　　　　　黑繩

Kâlya, XIV 迦陵迦
Kâsyapa, 115 迦葉
Kâsyapîya, 27 迦葉毘部
Kâshi, 116 香至
Kinnara, X 緊那羅
Kinnara-râga Druma, XV 純真陀羅王
Kumâragîva, 14, 17, 45, 73, 104 鳩摩羅什
Kumârata, 116 鳩摩羅多
Kumârila-bhatta, 13 俱摩羅陀
Kusala-mahâbhûmika-dharma, 7 大善地法
Kusalasamgrâha-sîla, 70 攝善法戒
Kushi, XVIII 拘尸(那城)
Krityânushthâna-gñâna, 100 成所作智
Kaukritya, 9 惡作
Kaundinya, XIV 憍陳如
Kausîdya, 8 懈怠
Krodha, 8 忿
Klishtamano-vigñâna, 38 染汚意識
Klesa-mahâbhûmika-dharma, 7 大煩惱地法
Klesâvarana, 43 煩惱障
Kshana, 15 刹那
Kshatriya, 50 刹帝利
Kshânti, 12 羼提(忍辱)
Kshitigarbha-vriti, 96, 98 地藏院

Gagasîrsha, XIV 象頭

154

Gandha, 5 香
Gandharva, X 乾闥婆
Garu*d*a, X 迦樓羅
Garbha-dhâtu, 78,79,88,89,- 胎藏界
　90,96,99,102
Gr*i*dhrakûta, 74,114,140 耆闍崛(山)
Godhanya, XV 瞿耶尼
Gomukha, 53 牛口
Grantha, 32 頌本

Ghrâna, 4 鼻
Ghrâna-vi*gñ*âna, 6,38 鼻識

*K*akshur-vi*gñ*âna, 6,38 眼識
*K*akshus, 4 眼
*K*atur-mudrâ-parshad, 81,94 四印會
*K*andâla, 50 旃陀羅
*K*itta, 5,38 心
*K*itta-râ*g*a, 38,40 心王
*K*itta viprayukta-dharma, 33, 心不相應法
　40
*K*itta-viprayukta-samskâra, 9 心不相應行
*K*intâmani, XIX 如意寶珠(摩尼)
*K*etanâ, 7 思
*K*aitta-dharma, 5,38,40 心所有法

*Kh*anda, 7 欲

Gambu-dvîpa, 57,141 閻浮提
Gayata, 116 羯闍夜多
Garâ, 10 生異
Gâti, 10 生
Gihvâ, 4 舌
Gihvâ-vignâna, 6,38 舌識
Gîvita, 10 命根
Geta, XIV,XV 祇陀
Geta-vana Anâthapindada-
    ârâma, XIV 祇樹給孤獨園
Geta-vana-vihâra, 29 祇園精舎
Gnânaprabha, 46 智光
Gnânaprasthâna-sâstra, 2 發智論
Gneyâvara*n*a, 43 所知障

Tathâgata, 13,23,26,32,35, 如来
    49,53,65,78,80,87,89,104,142
Tathâgata-garbha, 65 如来藏
Tathâgatânubhâva, 89 佛部
Tapana, IX 焦熱
Tiryag-yoni-gata, VIII 畜生道(傍生趣)
Tiryag-yoni-sattva, 83 傍生有情
Tushita, 32 兜率(天)
Tegodhara-vriti, 96 持明院
Trayastrimsa, XVIII 忉利(天)
Tripi*t*aka, 2,13,14,20,26,49,51,
    52,80,85,104,108 三藏
Triyâna, 137 三乘

Trividha-sîla, 69 　三聚浄戒
Trailokya-viǵaya-parshad, 91, 95 　降三世羯磨會
Trailokya-viǵaya-samaya-parshad, 91,95 　降三世三昧耶會

Dasabhûmi, XIII 　十地
Dasabhûmi-vibhâshâ-sâstra, 59 　十住毘婆沙論
Dâna-pâramitâ, 12 　檀那波羅蜜多(施度)
Divâkara, 46 　日照
Divyadundubhimeghanirghosha, 97 　天鼓雷音
Digha-nikâya (Pâli), 35 　長阿含經
Dîrghâgama, 35 　同前
Deva, 25,45,47,54,55 　天
Devadatta, 139 　提婆達多
Devapâla, XIV 　提謂波利
Devasarman, 3 　提婆設摩
Devî, XII 　王后(夫人)
Dvâdasa-nikâya (or mukha)-sâstra, 44,48 　十二門論

Dharma, 4,10,14,15,16,21,23, 32,35,36,38,40,41,65,70 　法
Dharma-kâya, 63,69,78,82, 110,142 　法身
Dharmakâla, 27 　法時
Dharmagupta, 13,20,21,26,27 　曇無德

Dharmagupta-vinaya, 22,23 四分律
Dharmagâtayasas, 134, 曇摩伽陀耶舍
Dharmadhâtu, 22,30,101,143 法界
Dharmadhâtu-prakriti-gñâna, 99 法界體性會
Dharmadhâtu-mandala, 83 法界曼荼羅
Dharmadhâtvavatâra, 58 入法界
Dharmapâla, 33 護法
Dharma-mandala, 90,94 法曼荼羅
Dharmamitra, 134 曇摩蜜多
Dharmalakshana, 32 法相
Dharmavagra, 93 法波羅蜜
Dharma-skandha-pâda, 2 法蘊足論
Dhâtu, 4,88 界
Dhâtu-kâya-pâda, 3 界身足論
Dhâranî, 57,62 陀羅尼
Dhritaka, 115 提多迦
Dhyâna, 12,20,114 禪那
Dhyâna-gokara, X 四禪天

Namas, 144 南無
Namah Saddharmapundarî-kâya Sûtrâya, 144 南無妙法蓮華經
Namo 'mitâbhâya Buddhâya, 106 南無阿彌陀佛
Nâga, 139 龍
Nâgabodhi, 79,81 龍智
Nâgarâga, XIV 龍王

Nâgârguna, 45,47,48,49,52,53,54,57,
　59,74,79,80,81,106,116,124　龍樹(龍猛)
Nâmakâya, 10　　　　　　　名身
Nâraka, 83　　　　　　　　捺羅迦(地獄之有情)
Nâlanda, 33　　　　　　　　那爛陀(寺)
Nâstika, 47,48,49　　　　　　無見(空執)
Nirarbuda, IX　　　　　　　尼剌部陀
Nirodha, 11,16　　　　　　　滅
Nirodha-samâpatti, 10　　　　滅盡定
Nirmâna-kâya, 70,142　　　　化身
Nirvâna, 11,12,21,2ff,47,49,51,
　52,71,80,93,115,126,129　　涅槃(滅度)
Nirvâna-sûtra, XVIII,XX　　　涅槃經
Nîlanetra, 45,46　　　　　　青目
Nîlapadmanetra, 53　　　　　青蓮華眼
Nyâyânusâra-sâstra, XXI　　　順正理論

Padakâya, 10　　　　　　　　句身
Padma, IX,89,90　　　　　　鉢特摩(蓮華)
Padmânubhâva, 89　　　　　　蓮華部
Paratantra-lakshana, 36　　　　依他起性
Paranirmita-vasa-vartin, XVII　他化自在天
Paramârtha, 3　　　　　　　真諦
Paramârtha-satya, 128　　　　勝義諦
Parikalpita-lakshana, 36　　　　遍計所執性
Parinirvâna, 43　　　　　　　般涅槃
Parinishpanna-lakshana, 36　　圓成實性
Pâramitâ, 11,70,105,147　　　波羅蜜多

Pârsva, 115 澁栗濕縛
Pindola, 25 賓頭盧
Punyamitra, 116 不如蜜多
Punyayasas, 115 富那夜奢
Pushya, XV 弗迦沙
Pûgâ-parshad, 91 供養會
Prakarana-pâda, 3 品類足論
Pragña, 58 般若(三藏)
Pragñapti-pâda, 3 施設足論
Pragñâ, 12,42,110 般若
Pragñâtara, 116 般若多羅
Pragñâ-pâramitâ, 52,71 般若波羅蜜多
Pragñâ pâramitâ-sûtra, XVI 般若波羅蜜多經
Pragñâ-sûtra, 65 般若經
Pratâpana, IX 大焦熱
Pratigha, 9 瞋
Pratisamkhyâ-nirodha, 10 擇滅
Pratîtyasamutpâda, 4 緣起
Pratyutpanna-buddha-sammu-
    khâvasthita-sûtra, XV 般舟經
Pradâsa, 8 惱
Prabhûtaratna, 29,135 多寶
Pramâda, 8 放逸
Pramuditâ-bhûmi, 49 歡喜地
Pratyavekshana-gñâna, 100 妙觀察智
Pratyekabuddha, 11,51,85,137 緣覺(獨覺)
Prasrabdhi, 7 輕安
Prâpta, 9 得

Preta, 51,83　　　　　　　餓鬼

Bahusrutika, 1352　　　　多聞部
Bahusrutika-vibhagya, 52　多聞分別部
Bimbisâra, 105　　　　　　頻婆娑羅
Buddha, 1, etc.　　　　　佛陀(覺者)
Buddha-dhyâna-samâdhi-sâgara-
　sûtra, XV　　　　　　　観佛三昧海經
Buddhanandi, 115　　　　　佛陀難提
Buddhabhadra, 57　　　　　覺賢
Buddhamitra, 115　　　　　伏駄蜜多
Buddhayasas, 27　　　　　佛陀耶舎
Buddhâvatamsaka-mahâvaipul-
　ya-sûtra, 62,87　　　　大方廣佛華嚴經
Buddhigati-parshad, 91,95　覺趣會
Bodhi, 42　　　　　　　　菩提
Bodhidharma, 115,116,117　菩提達磨
Bodhimanda, 145　　　　　道場
Bodhisattva, 11,etc.　　　菩薩(像有情)
Bodhyaṅga, 91　　　　　　菩提分(覺支)
Brahmagâla-sûtra, 25　　梵網經
Brahman, 115　　　　　　梵天
Brâhmana, 50,117　　　　婆羅門
Bhagavat, 80,114　　　　世尊(具福智者)
Bhavaviveka, 46　　　　　清辯
Bhikshu, 25,49,53　　　　比丘
Bhikshunî, XV　　　　　　比丘尼
Bhûtatathatâ, 65　　　　真如

Bhaishagyarâga, 135,141　　藥王

Magadha, 33,51,105　　摩掲陀
Makilinda, XIV　　文麟
Magghima-nikâya (Pâli), 35　　中阿含
Mañgusrî, 51,63,97,107,132,
　　141　　文殊師利
Mañgusrî-vriti, 96,98　　文殊院利
Mandala, 78,88,90,91,94,96,
　　102,103,143　　曼荼羅
Mati, 7　　慧
Mada, 9　　憍
Madhyamaka-sâstra, 44,47,48　　中論
Madhyamâgama, 35　　中阿含
Madhyamika, 44　　中論派
Madhyântika, 26　　末田地
Madhyânta-vibhâga-sâstra, 32　　辯中邊論
Manas, 5　　意
Manaskara, 7　　作意
Manu, 50　　摩拏(法住者)
Manura, 116　　摩拏羅
Mano-râga, 6　　心王
Mano-vigñâna, 6,38　　意識
Mantra, 79,90　　眞言
Marîki, X　　摩利支
Mahâkâsyapa, 26,49,52,115　　摩訶迦葉
Mahâkrodhakâya, 95　　大忿怒身
Mahâkintya-sâstra, 59　　大不思議論

Mahâpadma, IX 摩訶鉢特摩
Mahâparinirvâna, 22 大般涅槃
Mahâparinirvâna-sûtra, 22 涅槃經
Mahâpûgâ-parshad, 94 大供養會
Mahâpragâpatî, XV 摩訶波闍波提
Mahâpragñâ-pâramitâ-sâstra, 21 大智度論
Mahâpragñâ-pâramitâ-sûtra, 36 大般若經
Mahâbrahman, 114 大梵天
Mahâbrahmarâga-pariprikkhâ-sûtra, XX 大梵王問佛決疑經
Mahâbhûta, 99 大大
Mahâbhûmika-dharma, 6 大地法
Mahâmandala, 90 大曼荼羅
Mahâmati, 49 大慧
Mahâmaudgalyâyana, 2,62,64 大目犍連
Mahâyâna, 14, etc. 大乘
Mahâyâna-vinaya, 25 大乘律
Mahâyâna-sraddhotpâda-sâstra, 56,66 大乘起信論
Mahâyâna-sûtra, 49,51,105 大乘經
Mahâyânâlamkâra-sâstra, 32 大乘莊嚴論
Mhârâga, XII 大王
Mahâraurava, IX 大叫喚
Mahâvibhâshâ-sâstra, 3 大毘婆沙論
Mahâ-vriti, 96 大院
Mahâvaipulya, 63 大方等
Mahâvaipulya-mahâsamnipâta-

sûtra, XIV 大方等大集經
Mahâvairokana, 78,80,81,79,92,
 94,95,97 大日
Mahâvairokanâbhisambodhi-
 sûtra, 78 大日經
Mahâsamghika, 27,51 大衆部
Mahâsamghika-vinaya, 27 摩訶僧祗律
Mahâsattva, 135 摩訶薩(大士)
Mahîsâsaka, 13,27 彌沙塞部
Mahesvara, X 大自在天
Mahoraga, X 摩睺羅伽
Mâtsarya, 8 慳
Mâna, 9 慢
Mâyâ, 9 諂
Mâyâ-sûtra, 53 摩耶經
Mikkhaka, 115 彌遮迦
Middha, 9 睡眠
Muktapushpa, 97 開敷華
Mudrâ, 92,94,101 印
Mrigadâva, XVI 鹿苑
Maitreya, 32,31,73,97 彌勒(慈氏)
Moksha, 110 解脱
Moha, 8 無明
Mraksha, 8 覆

Yaksha, X,XIV 夜叉
Yasas, XIV 耶舍
Yasodharâ, XII 耶輸陀羅

Yâna, 11,16,22,49,54,72 乘
Yoga, 32,33,72,76,77,79,86,100, 101,102 瑜伽
Yoga-sâstra, 41 瑜伽師地論
Yogâkârya-bhûmi-sâstra, 32, 65 瑜伽論
Yogana, 64 由句

Ratna, 90 寶
Ratnadeva, 53 寶天
Ratnadhvaga, 97 寶幢
Ratnavagra, 53 寶波羅蜜
Ratnasambhava, 52 寶生
Ratnânubhâva, 90 寶部
Rasa, 5 味
Râkshasa, X 羅刹
Râgagriha, 9,51 王舍(城)
Râhu, X 羅喉
Râhula, 45 羅喉羅
Râhulata, 116 羅喉羅多
Rûpa, 4,5,21,36,85 色
Rûpadharma, 38,40 色法
Raurava, IX 叫喚

Lakshana, 37 性
Laṅkâ, XVI 楞伽
Laṅkâvatâra, 49 入楞伽
Laṅkâvatâra-sûtra, 48,66 入楞伽經

165

Lokottaravâda, 52   說出世部

Vagra, 79,88,89,102   金剛
Vagrakarma, 93   金剛業
Vagraketu, 93   金剛幢
Vagragandhi, 93   金剛塗香
Vagragîti, 93   金剛歌
Vagraghantâ, 94   金剛鈴
Vagrakkhedikâ-pragñâpâramitâ-
  sâstra, 32   金剛般若論
Vagratikshna, 93   金剛利
Vagrategas, 98   金剛光
Vagradharma, 93   金剛法
Vagra-dhâtu, 18,88,89,90,91,
  96,99,102   金剛界
Vagradhûpa, 93   金剛香
Vagranriti, 93   金剛舞
Vagrapâni-vriti, 96,98   金剛手院
Vagrapushpa, 93   金剛華
Vagrabandha, 92   金剛索
Vagrabodhi, 75,79,81   金剛智(三藏)
Vagramâli, 93   金剛鬘
Vagrayaksha, 93   金剛牙
Vagraraksha, 93   金剛護
Vagraratna, 93   金剛寶
Vagrarâga, 93   金剛愛
Vagrarâga, 93   金剛王
Vagralâsa, 93   金剛嬉

166

Vagravâk, 93 　　金剛語
Vagrasekhara-sûtra, 93 　　金剛頂經
Vagrasattva, 75,78,79,80,81,
　89,93,99 　　金剛薩埵
Vagrasandhi, 93 　　金剛拳
Vagrasâdhu, 93 　　金剛善
Vagrasphota, 94 　　金剛頻
Vagrahâsa, 93 　　金剛咲
Vagrahetu, 93 　　金剛因
Vagrânkusa, 93 　　金剛鈎
Vagrânubhâya, 89 　　金剛部
Vagrânubhâva-vriti, 96,98 　　金剛院
Vagrâloka, 93 　　金剛燈
Vasasuta, 116 　　婆舍斯多
Vasubandhu, 32,33,106,116,
　124 　　天親(世親)
Vasumitra, 3,119 　　世友
Vârânasî, XIV 　　波羅奈
Vâstîputrîya, 27 　　婆蹉富羅
Vikâra, 9 　　思
Vikikitsâ, 9 　　疑
Vignâna, 5,37,65,85,99 　　識
Vignâna-kâya-pâda, 3 　　識身足論
Vitarka, 9 　　尋
Vidyâmâtra, 32,33 　　唯識
Vidyâmâtra-siddhi-sâstra, 38,
　41 　　成唯識論
Vidyâmatra-siddhi-sâstra-

kârikâ, 38 　唯識三十頌
Vinaya, 14,20, etc. 　毘奈耶(律)
Vinaya-piṭaka, 26 　毘奈耶藏
Vibhaga-yoga-sâstra, 32 　分別瑜伽論
Vimalakîrtti-nirdesa, 18,52 　維摩經
Vîmalakîrtti-nirdesa-sûtra,
　XVI 　同
Visishṭakâritra, 133,136,141 　上行
Viseshakinta-brahma-paripṛikkhâ-
　sûtra, XVI 　思益梵天所問經
Visvakarman, X 　毘首羯磨
Vishaya, 5 　境
Vihimsa, 8 　害
Vîga, 90 　稲芋
Vîrya, 7,12 　勤(精進)
Venuvana, XIV,XVII 　竹林
Vedanâ, 6,85 　受
Vaidehî, 105 　韋提希
Vaipulya, 71 　方等
Vairokana, 29,63,69,72,73,75 　毘盧遮那(大日)
Vaisâli, XIV,XVI,XVIII 　毘舎離
Vaisya, 50 　吠舎
Vaisramana, 25 　毘沙門(多聞)
Vyañganakâya, 10 　文身

Sakra Devânâm Indra, X 　釋提桓因
Sanavâsa, 26,115 　商那和修
Satasâstra, 44,54,5â 　百論

Śabda, 5 聲
Śabda-vidyâ, 33 聲明
Śâkya, 45 釋迦
Śâkyamuni, 21, etc. 釋迦牟尼
Śâkya-vriti, 96,98 釋迦院
Śâthya, 9 諂
Śâriputra, 2,62,64 舍利弗
Śâla, XVIII 婆娑
Śâstra, 1,12, etc. 論
Śikshâ, 109 學
Śikshânanda, 58 實叉難陀
Śîla, 12,21,24, etc. 尸尸羅(戒)
Śîlananda, 53 尸羅難陀
Śîla-pâramitâ, 21,29 尸羅波羅蜜多(戒度)
Śîlabhadra, 33 戒賢
Śuddhodana, XII,XV 淨飯
Śubhakarasimha, 75,81 善無畏
Śûdra, 50 首陀羅
Śûramgama-samâdhi-sûtra, XVI 首楞嚴三昧經
Śraddhâ, 7 信
Śramana, 52 沙門
Śrâvaka, 11,16,51,62,64,85, 137 聲聞
Śrâvastî, XIV,XVII 舍衛
Śrîmâlâ, 18 勝鬘
Śrîmâlâ-devî-simhanâda, 52 勝鬘經
Śrîmâlâ-devî-simhanâda-sûtra,

XVI

Srîmâlâ-sûtra, 21,42 　勝鬘經
Sreshthin, XIV 　長者
Srotra, 4 　耳
Srotra-vignâna, 6,28 　耳識

Shat-pâda, 2 　六足
Shan-mahâbhûta, 99 　六大

Samyuktâgama, 35 　雜阿含
Samyutta-nikâya (Pâli), 35 　同
Samvriti-satya, 128 　世俗諦
Samskâra, 85 　行
Samskrita, 4 　有爲
Samskrita-dharma, 40 　有爲法
Sakridâgâmin, 109 　斯陀含(一來)
Samgîti-paryâya-pâda, 2 　集異門足論
Samgha, 21,55 　僧伽
Samghâta, IX 　僧伽
Samghanandi, 116 　僧伽難提
Samghabhadra, XXI 　衆賢
Samghayasas, 116 　僧伽耶舍
Samghavarman, 404 　僧鎧
Samgîva, IX 　僧活
Samgñâ, 6,85 　想
Sattvavagra, 93 　金剛
Sattvârthakriyâ-sîla, 70 　饒益衆生戒
Satya, 4,16,105 　諦

Satya-siddhi-sâstra, 13,14,15, 17 成實論
Saddharma-puṇḍarîka, 18,22, 71,74 妙法蓮華經
Saddharma-puṇḍarîka-sûtra, 22,44,67,122, etc. 同
Saṃdhinirmoḵana-sûtra, 32, 35,36,37,65 解深密經
Saptaparṇa, 49 七葉
Sabhâgatâ, 9 同分
Samatâ-gñâna, 100 平等性智
Samaya, 84,95 三昧耶
Samaya-parṣhad, 91,94 三昧耶會
Samaya-maṇḍala, 90,94 三昧耶曼荼羅
Samantabhadra, 63,97 普賢
Samantabhadra-dhyâna-sûtra, 134 觀普賢經
Samantabhadra-bodhisattva-ḵaryâ-dharma-sûtra, XVIII 普賢菩薩行法經
Samâdhi, 7,20,147 三摩地
Samyaktva-râśi, 128 正定聚
Sambhâra-sîla, 69,70 攝律儀戒
Sambhoga-kâya, 70,142 報身
Sarvagña-vṛiti, 96,98 遍知院
Sarvanivâraṇa-vishkambhi-vṛiti, 96,98 除蓋障院
Sarvâstivâda, 13,15,21,27 一切有部、
Sarvâstivâdin, 1,12 同

Sahâ, 105,112,113,141 娑婆
Sâgaramudrâ-samâdhi, 61 海印三昧
Siddha, 76 悉曇(成就)
Siddhi, 72,77 悉地
Simha, 116 師子
Sukhâvatî, 49,104,105,106,113, 122,123 蘇訶提(極樂)
Sukhâvatîvyûha, 123,128 無量壽經阿彌陀經
Sukhûvatîvyûha-sûtra, XVIII 同
Sudatta, XIV 須達(長者)
Sumeru, XV 須彌(山)
Suvarna-prabhâsa, 52 金光明經
Suvarna-prabhâsa-sûtra, XVI 同
Susiddhi-vriti, 96,98 蘇悉地院
Sûkshma-parshad, 91,94 微細會
Sûtra, 18,22,32, etc. 修多羅(經)
Sûtrâlamkâra-sâstra, 32 大莊嚴論
Sûrya, X 蘇利耶
Sûryasoma, 45 須利耶蘇摩
Soma, X 蘇摩
Sautrântika, 2,13 經部
Skandha, 4,10,16,85,143 蘊
Stûpa, 135 塔
Styâna, 8 昏沈
Sthavira, 51 上座
Sthiti, 10 住
Sparsa, 57 觸
Smriti, 7 念

172

Srota-âpanna, 109 須陀洹(預流)

Haklenayasas, 116 鶴勒那
Harivarman, 13 訶梨跋摩
Hâhâdhara, IX 虎虎溪
Himâlaya, 52 雪山
Hînayâna, 1,13, etc. 小乘
Hînayâna-vinaya, 25 小乘律
Hînayâna-sûtra, 53 小乘經
Hridaya, 97 心
Hetu-vidyâ, 33 因明
Hrî, 7 慚

CORRECTIONS.

Page	Line	
2	25	for ' sâstra ' read ' pâda.'
10	8	for ' deat a ' read ' death '
13	18	for ' ohers ' read ' others '
18	7	for ' Ho-ssō read ' Hossō
21	15	for ' Gō-sho ' read ' Gossho '
27	13	for ' Mahâsamghika read ' Mahasamghika '
28	6	for ' Dō-kō ' read ' Dō-gō '
"	20	for ' Gō-shū read ' Yō-shū '
30	21	' the Sîla-at ' to be left out.
37	9	for ' systems ' read ' manners '
43	2	for ' Klesa-' read ' Klesa-'
45	2	for ' system...is ' read ' manners...are
46	6	for the second ' Sō-rō ' read ' Sō-sen '
"	26	for ' Af ter ' read ' After '
52	11	for ' Ekavyahârika ' read ' Ekavyavahârika '
55	8	for ' Swore ' read ' swore '
65	26	for ' Suddhas ' read ' Buddhas '
72	24	for ' Fina-lly ' read ' Final-ly '
86	14	for ' chin ' read ' shin '
94	15	for ' Dai-ku-jō-e ' read ' Dai-ku-yō-e '
105	6	for ' Amitâyus-' read ' Amitâyur-'

發兌元　佛教書英譯出版舍
　　　　東京々橋區南佐柄木町五番地

出版人　佐野正道
　　　　全京橋區南佐柄木町
　　　　五番地
　　　　大坂府平民

著譯者　南條文雄
　　　　東京淺草永住町
　　　　四十七番地
　　　　福井縣平民

明治十九年九月廿五日版權免許
同　年十二月　出版

所　捌　賣

全　日本橋通壹丁目　北畠茂兵衞

全　本所外手町三十九番地　新報社

全　麻布日ヶ窪町　鴻盟社

全　三十間堀一丁目　明教社

全　京橋銀坐四丁目　博聞社

全　日本橋通リ三丁目　九善書店

全　本町四丁目　岡島眞七

大坂備後町四丁目　博聞分社

全　西六條花屋町　永田調兵衞

西京東六條中珠數屋　西村七郎兵衞

'TRUE SECT' OF BUDDHISTS

ON THE
TENETS OF THE SHINSHIU
OR
'TRUE SECT' OF BUDDHISTS.

(Paper read before the Asiatic Society of Japan, October 21st, 1885, — reprinted, by permission, with emendations, from the Transactions of the Society.)

By

James Troup.

英文眞宗教旨 和文付

英國領事ゼームス、ツループ君著
英國文學士 南條文雄師 同校
日本本願寺司教赤松連城師

Kobe:—
Kobundo Motomachi-dori, go-chome.

ON THE TENETS OF THE SHINSHIU OR 'TRUE SECT' OF BUDDHISTS.

By James Troup.

[*Read October 21st, 1885.*]

An account of the development in Japan of the doctrine of the Pure Land, or Paradise of Amitâbha Buddha,—the central doctrine of the Shinshiu,—ought properly to commence with an enquiry into this doctrine as held by priests of the Tendai Sect, and others, who were the first to follow it in this country, and who in their turn derived it from the Chinese schools. Thereafter, the foundation, in the latter part of the twelfth century, by Genku, otherwise known as Hōnen Shōnin, of the Jōdo Sect, would come to be treated of; and, finally, the establishment, by the well-known Shinran Shōnin, in the earlier part of the thirteenth century, of the Jōdo Shinshiu, now known simply as the Shinshiu, or 'True Sect.' As a fragment, however, giving a limited view of this doctrine and the others that hinge on it, as at present held by the last-mentioned Sect, the following, it is hoped, may not be devoid of interest.

A pamphlet entitled *Shin Shiu Kio Shi* (真宗教旨), or, A Synopsis of the Doctrines of the 'True Sect,' issued in December, 1876, by the Department of Instruction of the Eastern Hongwanji, and, as is stated on the first page, drawn up by the Compilation Department of that

Temple, may, coming from that source, doubtless be taken as fairly representing what this important and active Sect wish to be considered their tenets. The following paper is an attempt at a summary, and, partly, a translation of the portions of this pamphlet which would appear to be the most interesting, and the purport of which the present writer conceives he has apprehended.

In the First Section of the pamphlet are enumerated the Seven who are reckoned Patriarchs by this Sect. They are Riujiu Bosatsu (*Nāgārjuna*), Tenjin Bosatsu (*Vasubandhu*), Donran Daishi (*Than-luan*), Dōjaku Zenshi (*Tao-ch'o*), Zendo Daishi (*Shan-tao*), Genshin Oshō (also called Ye-shin), and Genku Daishi (Hōnen). The reasons why these are reckoned as the Patriarchs are set out, severally, under each. Their claims to this rank are, for the most part, based on their writings,—those parts only of their writings being held in the highest estimation, by the Sect, which refer to the doctrine of the Pure Land and the worship of Amida (*Amitābha*) Buddha. As the details of this section are generally coincident with, although not so full as the sketch of the history of this Sect, from the pen of Mr. Bunyiu Nanjio, given in the *Anecdota Oxoniensia*, Aryan Series, Vol. I, Part II, edited by Max Müller, they need not be repeated here. The Section concludes :—" Now the substance of the doctrine of the " Seven Patriarchs consists in the calling of Buddha to " remembrance. As far as they treat, by the way, of " other matters, they then have reference to the means of " salvation by one's own power,—the method of the Holy

"Path," The distinction between the method of salvation of the Holy Path,—by one's own power,—and that of the Pure Land,—by the Power of Another,—will be brought out more clearly further on. The opportuneness, in these Latter Days, of the teaching of the Patriarchs relative to the method of the salvation of the Pure Land, by the Power of Another, would appear to be what is indicated in the last sentence :—" Kukai (i.e. Kōbō Daishi) " has said : The wise man keeps silent ; he who awaits " his opportunity, who awaits his audience, is such."

The Second Section is entitled, The Transmission (or Dissemination) of the Law (Light), and proceeds :—
"There are fourteen sects in Japan, viz.:—the Ku sha|
" shiu, Jō-jitsu-shiu (Jisshiu), Risshiu, Hossō-shiu, San-
" ron-shiu, Ke-gon-shiu, Ten-dai-shiu, Shin-gon-shiu, Zen-
" shiu, Dai-nem-butsu-shiu, Jō-do-shiu, Ji-shiu, and Nichiren-
" shiu. Our sect is called the Jōdo Shinshiu. This name
" is derived from the expression ' Nem-Butsu jō-Butsu ji
" ' Shinshiu' (calling Buddha to remembrance and attaining
" Buddhahood constitute the true sect [or doctrine]). Shin-
" ran Shōnin is considered the Founder of the Sect. The
" Shōnin was a descendant of the Tai-shoku-kwan (Minister)
" Prince Kamataru, and son of Prince Fujiwara no Arinori.
" The lady, his wife, Tama-hi, was the daughter of the
" Sessho Kwambaku (Regent) Prince Kanezane. First,
" Genku Daishi established the Jō-do Sect. It spread
" abroad within the seas. The number of his disciples
" exceeded three hundred. The Shōnin truly became his
" most distinguished pupil. The Regent turned to the

"Daishi. He became his great benefactor. One day he said:—'[You] Daishi observe the Prohibitions while calling Buddha to remembrance. Your disciple eats (i.e. I eat) flesh and lives with a wife. Is there no distinction of excellent and base in this?' The Daishi replied:—'All equally call Buddha to remembrance. What fault is there in this?' The other said:—'Your disciple has (i.e. I have) a daughter; let your chief follower condescend to become my son-in-law, and thus remove all doubt for future ages in the Empire.' The Daishi proposed this to the Shōnin; the Shōnin declined; the other would not listen [to his refusal]. This was the circumstance which brought about the founding of the Sect.

Section Third is entitled "The Divisions of Doctrine", and may be rendered thus:—"The Doctrine of the Life [of *Sákya*] is divided according to two bodies, (or orders,) the Shōdō-mon and the Jōdo-mon (they of the Holy Path and they of the Pure Land). [The distinctions of] the Greater Vehicle and the Lesser Vehicle,[1] the 'partial' and the 'complete,' the 'temporary' and the 'true',[2]

---

[1] The *Maháyána* and *Hinayána*.

[2] The 'partial' and the 'complete,' the 'temporary' and the 'true.' These expressions are explained as referring back to subdivisions of the Maháyána school or doctrine, and doubtless were terms in use from the earlier centuries of Buddhism; but the writer has been unable to find that they, and those referred to under the next note, have all been identified. The expressions 'partial' (半) and 'complete' (滿), abridgments of 半字教 and 滿字教, the 二字教, or 'two doctrines' taught by Bōdhi Ruchi (A. D. 503-535), are explained as signifying 'unfinished meaning,' or

" the 'apparent' and the 'hidden'³ appertain to the Shōdō-mon. These relate to the doctrine of entering on the Holy Path in this world. The *Dai-mu-riō-jiu-kiō* (*Amitâyus Sûtra*, Larger *Sukhâvatî Vyûha*) *Kwam-mu-riō-jiu-kiō* (Sûtra of Meditation) and *Amida-kiō*, appertain to the Jōdo-mon. These relate to the doctrine of the

imperfectly developed doctrine, and 'clear meaning,' or complete doctrine (*ardha akshara* and *pûrna akshara*).

The term 'temporary,' (權) is explained by 'means,' or devices used towards an end, as opposed to the 'true' (實) or real. The 'temporary' includes the doctrines of the Hossō and Sanron Sects, which are therefore called the 'Temporary' Greater Vehicle; the 'true,' including the doctrines of the Kegon, Tendai, Shingon, and Zen Sects, which are known therefore as the 'True' Greater Vehicle. The doctrine which Sâkya Buddha is represented as having taught, previous to his fiftieth year, is termed the 'partial,' or imperfectly developed, and is contained in the four Sutras the 般若 (*Pradjñâ Pâramitâ Sûtra*,) the 華嚴, the 阿含 (*Agama*,) and the 方等; that which he is represented as having taught from his fiftieth year, the 'complete' doctrine, which is contained in the 法華 (*Saddharma Pundarika Sûtra*,—the 'Lotus of the Good Law,') and the 涅槃 (*Nirvâna Sûtra*).

Most of the information contained in this and the following note the writer has received from high Japanese authority on this subject.

³Explained as 'apparent doctrine' and 'hidden doctrine,'—the former including all the doctrines of the Mahâyâna school except that of the Shingon Sect, which alone is called the 'hidden' doctrine. According to another authority, however, there is reckoned a third doctrine, coming between the above two, viz., a traditional doctrine, of which the Zen Sect is the present representative in this country; and, by the same, the Kegon and Tendai Sects are reckoned the special representatives of the 'apparent' doctrine.

The above four pairs of terms,—Greater and Lesser Vehicle, 'partial' and 'complete,' 'temporary' and 'true', 'apparent' and 'hidden', are used not only by the Shinshiu, but by all the other schools also.

"salvation of (i.e. Birth into) the Pure Land.

The three Sûtras here mentioned, which together are known as the *Sam-bu-kiō*, constitute the Scriptures of this Sect. They are known shortly as the *Dai-kiō*, (Greater Sûtra,) *Kwan-giō*, (Sûtra of Meditation,) and *Sho-kiō*, (Lesser Sûtra).

"Again, within the Shōdō-mon there are the methods (schools) of 'lengthwise going-out' and 'lengthwise passing-over.' The Hossō and San-ron Sects belong to the school of 'lengthwise going-out;' the Ke-gon, Tendai. Shingon and Zen Sects belong to that of the 'lengthwise passing-over.' In the Jōdo-mon there are the methods of 'crosswise going-out,' and 'crosswise passing-over.' Salvation by various actions constitutes 'crosswise going-out.' This depends on the power of one's self. Salvation by remembrance of the Name of Buddha constitutes 'crosswise passing-over.' This depends on the Power of Another."

The expressions 'lengthwise' and 'crosswise,' 'going-out' and 'passing-over'[4] are to be explained with

---

[4] For further explanation of these terms the writer is indebted to high Japanese authority on this subject, already referred to. It is to the following effect:—

These four terms are known as the 'two pairs' (二雙) and 'four folds' or tiers (四重) and are used and explained by Shinran is his work called 愚禿鈔, as follows:—The 'lengthwise going-out' ('going-out along') is the attainment of Enlightenment after long practice, and perseverance, through many kalpas, in the way of holy men. The 'lengthwise passing-over' ('stepping-over along') refers to Enlightenment in this life,—the attainment of Buddhahood in the present existence. The 'crosswise going-out'

reference to the methods employed to attain salvation, or deliverance from the Cycle of Birth and Death,—in other words, to reach Nirvâna,—and appear to be meant to indicate the comparative slowness or quickness of the methods used. The former methods are slow and laborious, the latter more speedy,—the last being direct and complete. The first two may be taken to indicate ways of salvation by good works,— by the practice of the *Páramitás* or 'cardinal virtues,' the observance of moral and religious precepts and prohibitions. The third, without doubt, indicates the system of salvation by 'Faith by one's 'own power,' alluded to further on, under the ninth section,—a faith excited and kept alive by means of religious observances. The fourth, the surest and speediest method, is the way of salvation by dependence on the power of *Amitábha Buddha*,—a salvation by faith only.[5]

The Fourth Section is entitled "The Three Times," or Periods, which term is explained as follows:—"There

---

('going-out across') is the attainment of birth in a region where the state of beings is like that of those in the womb,—a borderland, or species of limbo, adjoining the Pure Land (*Sukhâvati*),—the imperfection of this birth being the result of carelessness and doubt. This, as will be seen in the next note, refers to the method of the Jōdo Sect. The 'crosswise 'passing-over' ('stepping-over across') is to go to be born in the true Land of *Amitábha* according to his Original Vow. (See Note 12, p.10)

[5] The third method or school refers to the Jōdo-shiu, from which the Shinshiu sprung, and which,—although coming under the classification of the Jōdo-mon, since it also holds the doctrine of the Pure Land,—is still reckoned, from the Shin-shiu point of view, as holding the doctrine of salvation by one's own power.

"are Three Periods of the Law. For the space of five
"hundred years from the death of [Sâkya] Buddha is the
"Period of the Right (lit. upright) Law. There then exist
"the Doctrine, the Practice (lit. Action) and Realization
"(Salvation). After those five hundred years, for the space
"of a thousand years, is the Period of the Image Law.[6]
"There then exist the Doctrine and the Practice (Action),
"but there is no Realization.

"After those fifteen hundred years, for the space of
"ten thousand years, is the Latter Day Law (Period of
"the Latter Days of the Law). The Doctrine exists, but
"without the Practice and Realization. At present it is
"2,825 years since the death of Buddha.[7] The inferior
"capacities of men are dark; they cannot tread the Holy
"Path and rise to perfection. This is the reason why the
"Shōdō-mon does not prosper. It is forcing a law which
"cannot be practised upon men who cannot practice it,—like

---

[6] The conservation of religion by means of the use of images,—the
'Period of Image Worship.' See Beal, *Catena of Buddhist Scriptures*, p.
141, note, where reference is made to the passage in the '*Lotus*,' on
which this doctrine of the Three Periods is founded. Eitel (*Hand-book*)
explains the term as the Period of 'fanciful religion.' The passage in the
present pamphlet seems to suggest that the expression may mean the
'Period of the *simulacrum* of religion,'—when the Right or True Law no
longer existed, although the Doctrine and Practice which existed under the
Period of the Right Law were still followed.

[7] This would place the date of the death of Sâkya-muni Buddha as
early as 949 B. C. The usual date according to Singalese authors is 543
B. C. Rhys Davids arrives at 412 B. C. as the most probable date; and
Max Muller's calculations bring it to 477 B. C. See the latter's *Hibbert
Lectures*, pp. 134-5, notes.

"urging fowls to go into the water. How can this be
"reasonable? But the Original Vow[8] of Amida (*Amitábha*)
"Buddha, passing through the three periods, includes the
"five Classes-of-beings-capable-of-hearing-the-Law.[9] There
"is thus no time when the Law cannot be practised, no
"men who cannot practice it. It is said in the Sûtra
"(in the Greater Sûtra):— There still remains this Sûtra.
"It endures for a hundred years (*i.e.* for long time). Even
"after the ten thousand years of the Latter Days of the
"Law, it endures for a hundred years. Ten thousand
"years! and much more! The Doctrine, enduring through
"time, presents the means of Practice (lit. Action) and
"thus the true Realization of the Jōdo-mon (*i.e.* of them
"of the Pure Land) even now flourishes. Having entered
"on the period of the Latter Days of the Law, now to
"desire the Holy Path (Shōdō) is like wearing fur garments
"in summer and linen in winter. How can this be reason-
"able?"

It does not follow from this that the Shin-shiu condemns the methods of salvation by means of moral and religious actions, followed by the other sects, as being in themselves at variance with true Buddhistic teaching; but merely that this sect holds such methods to be inopportune and impossible in the present age of the world.

The Fifth Section proceeds to sum this up by stating the "Four Laws," or the "Fourfold Law," according to which salvation is now attainable. It says:—" The *Dai-*

[8] The Original Vow. See note 12, under page 10, *post*.
[9] That is, Men, Gods, S'*rávakas*, P*ratyêka* B*uddhas* and *Bodhisattvas*.

"*mu-riō-jiu-kiō* (Greater Sûtra) contains the true Doctrine;
" calling to remembrance the Name is the true Practice
" (= Means). This is from the seventeenth Vow.[10] The
" Threefold Heart (*i.e.* the Heart of sincerity, of believing
" joy, and having a longing for birth in the Pure Land)
" is the true Belief. This is from the eighteenth Vow.[11]
" Surely the attainment of Nirvâna is the true Realization
" (Salvation). This is from the eleventh Vow.[12] A great

---

[10] The 17th Vow:—" If, when I attain Buddhahood, the innumerable
" Buddhas of the worlds of the ten regions (universe) do not, with sighs
" on every side, chant-and-praise My Name, then may I not attain Enlight-
" enment.—(Bôdhi)"

[11] The 18th Vow:—" If, when I attain Buddhahood, any of the living
" beings of the ten regions who, with sincerity, having faith and joy,
" and an ardent desire to be born into My Country, call (My Name) to
" remembrance ten times, should not (then) be born there, may I not
" attain Enlightenment —(Bôdhi) But from this the five classes of
" reprobates,1 and revilers of the Right Law are excluded."

1 The five classes of reprobates are:—Parricides, matricides, they who incite the priesthood to quarrel, they who shed the blood of a Buddha, they who put to death an Arhat.

[12] The 11th Vow:—" If, when I attain Buddhahood, the men and
" Devas of My Country who dwell together do not reach Nirvâna, then
" may I not attain Enlightenment.—(Bôdhi)"

The Three Vows here quoted are from the Greater Sûtra (Dai-mu riō-jiu-kiō), and are respectively the 17th, 18th and 11th of the forty-eight vows made by the being called *Amitâbha* in a previous state of existence in respect of his determination to attain the rank of Buddha. These vows are frequently termed "*Hon-gwan*" (本願), " original vows," and the expression " original vow of Amida," at page 9, refers to this,—or rather to the eighteenth of those " originals vows." The same expression, "Hon-gwan," gives the name to the principal temples at Kiōto of the

"leader Teaches by Means of the Name; which all living
"beings, hearing, Believe in, and thus attain Salvation.
"This is what is termed the Fourfold Law.[13]

In Sections Sixth and Seventh, which treat of the
"Three vows"[14] and the "hidden" and "apparent", further developments of the subject are briefly alluded to, but as these involve references which cannot at present be followed up, they are here omitted.

Section Eighth is entitled the "Vow Name",—that is, the Name referred to in the Vow,—the Name of Him who made the Vow,—and proceeds:—" For us unenlight-
"ened, if we desire to be born into the Pure Land it is
"necessary to have Faith (lit. to put forth the Believing
"Heart) by the Power of Another. If we desire to have
"Faith by the Power of Another, we must hear the Vow
"Name. If we desire to hear the Vow Name we must
"look to the good and wise. If we already have looked
"to the good and wise, heard the Vow Name and have

---

two main branches of the Shinshiu, and, after them, to many temples throughout the country.

The eighteenth Vow is distinguished from the others as expressing the condition under which the salvation of the Pure Land should be attainable,—namely by calling to remembrance the name of Amitâbha. The other vows, generally, express the nature of which this Paradise was to be. The eighteenth vow being thus the one affecting men seeking this salvation, is sometimes called, *par excellence*, the Original Vow,—an expression which in this paper has sometimes been rendered simply 'the Vow.'

[13] The Fourfold Law:—the Doctrine, the Means, Belief, Salvation.
[14] The three vows. See note 12, *supra*.

"a mind taking refuge in the behest[15] [of *Amitâbha*], "this is Faith by the Power of Another.

"At present are the Latter Days of the Law; it "is difficult to keep in the Holy Path (*Shōdō*). They[16] "live in great temples; they style themselves abbots. "Externally they exhibit worth and goodness; internally "they are full of covetousness and sordidness. They wear "silks and satins; they sit on hair rugs luxuriously. "Proudly they cultivate outward forms (lit. appearances); "they delude men, they deceive themselves. How can such "be called superior persons? They who forsake the family "(i.e. enter the priesthood) are like this; how much more "they who remain in the family (i.e. the laity). Alas! "They drink wine, they eat flesh. How can they be said "to keep the Prohibitions[17] (*i.e.* the Buddhist Moral "Precepts)? They love their wives, they love their child- "ren. What family affections do they forego? Being thus, "they increase covetousness. How can they say they prac- "tice Almsgiving?[18] If they are not employed at one thing, "they are at another. How can they have leisure for "Meditation?[19] Of inordinate lust, greedy for gain, "what Zeal[20] in the performance of religious duty do they "possess? They envy the worthy, they revile the good.

---

[15] "Taking refuge in the behest of,"—relying on the help,—invoking the assistance of (*Amitâbha.*)

[16] *I.e.*, they who in these days profess to follow the Holy Path, the priesthood of other sects.

[17] *I.e.*, practice Morality (*Sila*).   [18] Almsgiving (*Dàna*).

[19] Meditation (*Dhyâna*).   [20] Zeal (*Virya*),

"What Patience[21] do they possess? Certainly they have
"no Knowledge[22] They cannot regulate their conduct
"according to the truth. Thus at one time they are
"courageous in the performance of religious duty; impetu-
"ously they set about practising the Six *Páramitás*[23] [but]
"they cannot continue. If they have not ability to prac-
"tice the Six *Páramitás*, it is certain they cannot attain
"deliverance.

"Zendo has said :—'We are truly like this: unenlight-
"'ened we are subject to the evil of Birth and Death;
"'for long kalpas we revolve, sinking and floating [in
"'the sea of existence]; there seems no cause of escape.'
"How should we not think of it! But He, Amida Buddha,
"long kalpas ago putting forth a heart of great compas-
"sion, planning through five kalpas, having accomplished
"the long kalpas, perfected his Vow. He said :[24] 'If
"'any living beings of the ten regions who, with sin-
"'cerity, having faith and joy and an ardent desire to
"'be born into My Country, call My Name to rememb-
"'rance ten times,[25] should not [then] be born there, May
"'I not attain Enlightenment.—(Bôdhi).' 'If there are
"'any of the living beings of the ten regions',—be they
"householders or houseless (i.e. laity, or mendicants who
"have left their homes), breakers of the Prohibitions or

---

[21] Patience (*Kshânti*).   [22] Knowledge (*Prajnâ*).

[23] The six *Páramitás*, or cardinal virtues, the practice of which leads to the "other shore,"—all referred to in the previous sentences.

[24] 18th Vow.

[25] Or, say, 'concentrate their mind on Me.'

"without (i.e. not having taken vows to observe) the
"Prohibitions,—having wives or not having wives, having
"children or not having children, whether or not drinking
"wine or eating flesh, whether they be husbandmen or
"merchants,—if only they put forth the Believing Heart
"and take refuge in the behest of (invoke) Amida Buddha,
"then will Buddha throw out a radiance and receive (favor)
"such. At the end of life they will be born in Heaven, they
"will reach the great Nirvâna. Is it not a boundless great
"compassion? If you desire to acknowledge this mercy,
"you must chant-and-praise the name of Buddha."

Section Ninth is entitled:—"The Believing Heart
"(Faith) by the Power of Another,"[26] and continues:—
"But although you fail in no wise to chant-and-praise the
"name of Buddha, [yet] you cannot be born into the true
"Land-of-reward.[27] You must without fail put forth the
"Believing Heart (i.e. have Faith), and thereafter can you
"first attain so to be born. [And] although you put forth
"the Believing Heart, [yet] by the Faith which is by
"one's own power, you cannot be born into the true Land-
"of-reward. You must without fail put forth the Believing
"Heart which is by the Power of Another, and thereafter
"can you first attain so to be born (attain this salvation).
"The putting forth of the Believing Heart by means of the

---

[26] The expression, "Power of Another" (他力), would appear to have been used first by Donran. Previously the expression used to denote a similar idea was, "The Power of the Vow" (願力).

[27] The Land which Amitâbha attained to have as the recompense or result of his Vows.

"Power of Another is called the Believing Heart (Faith) by the Power of Another. The Power of Buddha is the 'Power of Another.' Clearly to believe in the knowledge (wisdom) of Buddha is the Believing Heart. The heart which believes clearly in the knowledge of Buddha is produced by the Power of Buddha: it is not put forth by one's self. For one's own heart to excite this is called the 'Believing Heart by one's own power.' That heart is not strong; speedily it changes. It is like a picture drawn on water. But the Believing Heart by the Power of Another,—this recedes not from its strength: it is like the diamond."

"The expression 'Believing Heart' is in the Vow of Mida.[28] He said:—'With sincerity, faith and joy, and ardent desire to be born into My Country.' The union of these three[29] Shiaka (Sâkya) calls the 'Believing Heart.' Tenjin (Vasubandhu) calls it the 'United (steadfast) Heart.' Buddha confers this Heart; He bestows it on all living beings. This is the Believing Heart by the power of Another. The Believing Heart is in the Name of Mida. Zendo says:—'The expression Namu[30] "is a taking refuge in His behest" (or, "an invocation of Him"). Our Founder said:—'To take refuge in His behest' (or 'to invoke Him') is the Mandate enounced

---

[28] Mida, a common contracted form of Amida.

[29] These Three:—Sincerity (至心), Faith and Joy (or, Believing Joy) (信樂), and Ardent Desire for Birth (欲生) in the Pure Land.

[30] 'Namu Amida,'—the expression chanted in calling to remembrance the name of Amitâbha Buddha.

"'by the Vow.' The Heart which takes refuge in His behest (or, which invokes Him,) is not produced by one's self; it is produced by the command of Buddha. Hence it is called the 'Believing Heart by the Power of Another.'"

* * * * *

"It is said in the Sûtra:—'To hear the Name [and] rejoice with the Believing Heart.' For the Name .... to enter the heart of living beings,—this constitutes the Believing Heart. The Name and the Believing Heart must be known to be one. As an illustration:—The unenlightened heart is like unclean water; the Heart of Buddha is like a pure Mani pearl.[31] If the Mani pearl is put into the unclean water, the water changes and becomes pure. If the Heart of Buddha enters the unenlightened heart, the heart changes and becomes believing"

The Section goes on to indicate that, where this believing heart, or Faith, exists, its existence will be declared by the Action of calling to remembrance, with the living voice, the name of Amida,—" as where there is fire there will certainly be smoke." The two together are termed the " Union of Faith and Action " (Practice). It further continues:—" Faith by one's own power cannot afford rest to the heart. It is said:—'Shall I surely attain salvation, or shall I not?' and thus what is called

---

[31] *Mani* pearl,—one of the *Sapta Ratna*, or Seven Precious things,—a round pearl which is said to keep always clean and bright, etc.—See Eitel. *Handbook of Buddhism*, p. 72.

"faith is in reality doubt. Riujiu (*Nâgârjuna*) has said:—
"'Where there is doubt the flower will not open.' Faith
"by the Power of Another affords rest to the heart. It
"is said:—'I am borne by the power of that Vow; I
"'shall certainly attain salvation.' There is not the smallest
"doubt in the heart.

"Those who follow the method of 'self-power,' repea-
"ting the name of Buddha with a view to reward, act
"with the object of attaining salvation. Those who
"follow the method of 'Another's power,' show their
"gratitude by calling to remembrance the name of Buddha."

* * * * *

"Those who follow the method of 'self-power' believe
"in other (many) Buddhas; those who follow the method
"of 'Another's-power' believe only in [the] One[32] Buddha,—
"as a faithful servant does not serve two masters. The
"'self-power' belief is of nine sorts; the lands (regions)
"of birth [under it] are also nine. In the Sûtra this
"is called birth in embryo. The 'Other's-power' belief
"is of one kind and no other; the land of birth under
"it is also One Boundless Bright Land. In the Sûtra
"this is called the birth of Transformation."

The Tenth Section is termed "The Popular System,"
in contradistinction to the "True System." The "Popular
System" has reference to the distinction of good and evil
in conduct, in this world; the "True System" to that
of belief and doubt in the mind, on which depends the

---

[32] From the fact of this sect believing only in *One* Buddha, they are sometimes called the "Ik-kō Shiu" (一向宗).

salvation of the other world. This Section shows the practical application of the doctrines of the Sect in the various circumstances and relations of human life. It commences:—" The appellations 'true' and 'popular' are "an important matter. Our Sect terms the attaining of "the rest of the heart the True System; the observation "of the relations of life the Popular System. Our Sect "has granted the permission to marry. Hence the five "relations of life[33] necessarily exist. Where the five "relations of life exist, the duties involved in them must "be observed. This is termed the Popular System. It "is said in the Sûtra:— ' The living beings of the ten "' regions,—be they householders or houseless ' (i.e. laity "or *religieux*). Thus the Sovereign, who installs his "Consort, and partakes of his royal viands, attains salvation. "The commoner, who possesses a wife and eats flesh, "[also] attains salvation. Shall the Holy Path be different "for them? Although the sins of the unenlightened be "many, if these are contrasted with the Power of the Vow "they are not as a millet seed to the ocean. The eating "of flesh, the having of wives are nothing to speak of. "A stone is by nature heavy; if you precipitate it into "the water, it inevitably sinks, [but] if you place it upon "a ship, it assuredly floats. The sins of the unenlightened

---

[33] The Five relationships of human life, viz.:—Husband and wife, father and son, brethren, prince and subject, friends,—according to the Chinese philosophy.

"are heavy; if you precipitate them on the Three worlds,[34]
"they inevitably sink; [but] if you place them on the
"ship of the Vow, they assuredly become light The merit
"of living beings is full of leaks. Mida's Land-of-reward
"has no leaks. With the merit which is full of leaks, you
"cannot be born into the Land where there are no leaks."

"Although our Sect does not set up Prohibitions and
"Rules, yet it certainly regulates conduct according to
"the relations of life. Hence, in it, faithful servants,
"filial children, dutiful wives and true friends are numer-
"ous. The foundation of the relations of life is set forth
"in the Greater Sûtra. It is said:—'For a servant to
"'betray his lord, for a child to deceive his father, for
"'brothers and sisters, husbands and wives, wise or unwise
"'(priesthood or laity), to fail in their duty to each other,—
"'these are the actions violating the relations of life
"'which the venerated Shiaka (*Sákya*) has denounced.'

"Going out to battle and dying by arrow or stone,—
"this is fidelity. Dying, to be born into the realm of
"Bliss,—this is faith. One meritorious action, two
"advantages. When the Nations are not silent about
"[their] armies, we cannot ensure our safety without
"fighting. If one attains faith now, then in the time of
"battle also will it be well. In battle, for a man of faith
"to face death is like being born. If we do not make
"the voyage to foreign countries, we do not know their

---

[34] The Three Worlds of the Buddhist Universe, viz.:—the World of Desire (*Kama-loka*), the World of Forms (*Rupa-loka*), and the world of Abstraction, or, World without Forms (*Arupa-loka*)

"characteristics; if we do not know their characteristics, "for protection in war we are at a disadvantage. If on the "ocean tempests arise, or one's life is endangered, if he has "already attained faith, then to die will it still be well.

"The land which holds Buddha in remembrance "assuredly the all-seeing Gods and the spells of Buddha "will protect. It is said in the Sûtra:—'The Empire "'in tranquility, the Sun and Moon clear and bright; the "'wind and the rain observe their seasons, scourges and "'pestilences do not arise; the country fruitful, the people "'in peace; the arms of the soldier are unused.' Is this "not good reason for gratitude towards one's country?"[35]

"Men who hold Buddha in remembrance are assuredly "numerous in showing returns of gratitude to their Prince. "It is said:—'He nourishes us in peace; calling Buddha "'to remembrance, he satisfies our wants; living or dying, "'we receive the favors of our Prince.'

"Our sect especially abhors dereliction of filial duty. "It is said:—'To meet with hatred, with angry eyes, "'the admonitions of father and mother,'—and again:— "'To be without a child is better than this.' Ren-shī "(Ren-nio Shōnin) has said:—'Unfilialness is the head of "'all wickedness.'

"The nations render themselves illustrious by means "of learning. By assiduous devotion to learning becoming "one's self illustrious, to make others illustrious, this is

---

[35] "One's country" is synonymous with "the Governing Powers," "the Ruler."

"what constitutes a dutiful son. Becoming learned and "not caring for one's parents—to be without learning is "better than this."

"[As to] the way of the husbandman, the artisan "and the merchant, [each] tries to emulate the other in "skill; [he says] shall I only be behind in good fortune? "[Yet] while they press to the uttermost the strength of "the soil, [or] examine into the nature of things, [and thus] "even impose commands upon Nature, still must returns "of gratitude be shown to parents."

Personal excesses are rebuked, as involving unfilial conduct, and the other family relations are then adverted to.

" Love between husband and wife arises naturally; but "if it is not possessed along with the remembrance of the "name of Buddha, that love is not complete. Those who "call Buddha to remembrance are humbled (lit. ashamed) "before Heaven, are humbled before the Gods; they do "not diverge from the maintenance of fixed principles."

"It is said in the greater Sûtra:—'Sun and Moon "'shining behold, the all-seeing Gods take note; for what "'is done in the open light there is shame before Sun "'and Moon, for what is done in the shade there is shame "'before the Gods. How may we offend against pro- "'priety?'

"A husband loves his wife, therefore he causes his "wife to call Buddha to remembrance. The wife also "likewise [the husband]. [Thus] living they are good son "and daughter; dying they accompany each other into the

"Land of Bliss. Is it not well?"

"An elder brother loves a younger brother, a younger brother respects an elder brother,—still in accordance with the law of Heaven. But if they do not do so along with the remembrance of the name of Buddha, differences between [the same] flesh and bone may be the result. Quarrels between brethren arise from selfishness. It is said :—' The good is for me, the bad can go to the 'other.' He who calls Buddha to remembrance considers himself about to become a Buddha or Bodhisattva, and thus, exerting his strength, he uproots selfishness; his splendor is complete. It is said in the Sûtra of Meditation:— ' The Bright all-shining One receives (lit. comprehends) and rejects not [all] the living beings of the ten regions who call Buddha to remembrance.' If [therefore] you are already among those whom the Bright One receives (comprehends) and rejects not, shall you endanger an elder brother, shall you cause evil to a younger brother?"

"Our Founder said :—' Brothers within the four seas.' Faith by the power of Another proceeds from Mida. Thus Mida is Father and Mother; [all] within the four seas are brothers. The Chinese call foreigners barbarians; foreigners call China uncivilized. Both, we consider, are wrong.[36] Those who do not observe the relations of life are the barbarians, without distinction of home and foreign.

---

[36] There is internal evidence in the pamphlet of its having been written with a view to a Chinese audience; about the time of its appearance there was a movement by the Shin-shiu leaders in the direction of propagandism in China.

"Throughout all that the heaven covers, wherever sun and moon shine, what is there that we shall call barbarian or uncivilized? When the heart (mind) is [wide as] heaven and earth, the discourse [clear as] sun and moon, then first is attained the equitable and the just. Between heaven and earth there is no one to be disassociated, no spot not to be reached. The kindly relations of intercourse make the friend. Two persons, the same mind; their spirit is [as] disseparated gold. One country, the same mind; [as] a golden bowl without defect. All countries, the same mind; then first is attained the perfect equitability. The foundation of the same mind is the calling to remembrance of the One Buddha."

The section continues for a few sentences more in a similar strain, and the pamphlet concludes with the next section, which does no more than enumerate a number of "forms" for the performance of various duties, which, the writer states, will be enlarged upon verbally in the assembly.

It is felt that some apology is due to the writer of the pamphlet for the imperfect manner in which his production has been presented here in an English dress.

Much of this section bears reference to the Chinese, or Confucian, system of morals, and forms no necessary part of the teaching of the Shin-shiu. The specific points of moral conduct which a Shin-Shiu teacher would inculcate would vary with the requirements of time and place.

Reprinted, with emendations, from the Transactions of the Asiatic Society of Japan.

日本佛教徒ニ告ク

這回印度神智協會ヨリ左ノ書柬ヲ以テ贈品ノ義ヲ依嘱シ來レリ是レ寔ニ我邦佛家交義ニシテ將來一致結合ヲ以テ歐米各洲ニ佛日ノ光赫ナラシムルノ好機ナリ故ニ余輩ニ於テレカ媒タランコトヲ欲ス乞フ佛門有志ノ諸兄翼贊愛護シ多少ノ贈品アラハ甚タ幸甚ナリ、諸君ハ下名ヨリ轉送スル且手續問合給ハ拜答チナス可シ

神戸元町通五丁目廿三番地
船井弘文堂敬白

錫蘭コロンボ神智協會書記局ニ於テ一千八百八十七年十二月十四日於テ神智協會々長コロネル、オルコット氏ノ雄心奮氣ヲ以テ國家ト宗教トニ盡スヘキノ記ヲ設立シ我々人民ニ喚起シテレヲ日夜從事セシメ我輩ハ既ニ感謝ニ堪ヘサルナリ我輩ハ此會ノ事業ヲ進捗セシムルノ刷局ヲ置キ又ハ新聞ノ翻譯出版センメ一週間両回發兌セリ又同地ニ一ノ堂宇ヲ印セル佛教學校ヲ建設シテ佛教徒ヨリ淨財ヲ募リ實ニ我輩ハ此會ノ事ヲ翼贊シ且毎年佛ノ寺院トヲ建立シルハ其収入金ヲ以テ同會ノ經費ニ充ツルナリ希クハ貴下ノ佛教問答シテ實ニ我輩ニ於テ多達セリ但シ此慈善會ノ舉行ヲ贊助シ暹羅東塞新嘉坡愛慈善會ヲ開設シ且廣ク貴國人民ニ慈福ヲ與ヘラレ實ニ我輩ニ於テ一千百ルビー（五百五十圓）ニ達セリ但シ此慈善會ノ舉行ヲ贊助シ暹羅東塞新嘉坡ノ物品及書籍等ヲ贈セラレ何卒貴下ノ厚意ヲ以テ日本佛教徒兄弟ニ懇請シテ此義ハ遅々アラン欣喜ノ至ナリ又昨年慈善會ノ收入金ノ一千百ルビーニ達セリ但シ此慈善會ノ舉行ヲ贊助シ暹羅東塞新嘉坡愛護慈善會ヲ開設シ日本語ノ翻譯出版セシムルノ業務ヲ進捗セシムルノ

大日本西京 水谷涼然君貴下

等ノ物品及書籍等ヲ贈セラレ何卒貴下ノ厚意ヲ以テ日本佛教徒兄弟ニ偏ニ懇請シテ此義ハ遅々アラン欣喜ノ至ナリ又時々貴下ノ所望スル時ハ貴下ノ爲メ佛教徒ノ事情ヲ報道シクマハンコトヲ希フ倘貴下爲メ佛世尊ノ冥助ヲ祈ル頓首

書記 エッチ、ドン、ダビッド

○魔教論目次　●魔神ノ論。如來ノ論。佛書ノ論。●魔神三位ノ建立論。佛ノ三身建立論　●魔敎ノ原罪論。佛敎ノ原罪論　●耶蘇ノ總論。釋迦ノ總論　●魔敎ノ天堂地獄論。佛敎ノ極樂地獄論　●耶馬敎ノ大意　●希臘敎ノ大意　●新敎派ノ大意等ノ十五箇條ヲ論及ス

一タビ辨斥魔敎論ノ世ニ出シヨリ爾來魔敎信者之佛敎ニ化スルモノ數百人ノ多キニ及ヒ且該書ノ發賣高既ニ數千部ノ多ニ至リ發行者ノ欣喜何ヲ以テカ之ニ加ヘンシテ數千部ノ發賣高ハ多ニ似タレトモ未ダ發行者ノ意ニ滿タス。ラバ如何トナレバ魔敎ノコンパチルレハ續々我國人ノ腦理ニ穿入シタリ我國中ニ蔓延シ一大茶毒流サントセリ此時ニ當リ使用スル救治ニ必要タル辨斥魔敎論ノ撲滅藥ノ丸劑アレトモ未ダ此丸劑當之ガ其人ニ乏シキハ抑衛生當路者卽チ僧侶諸君敎ヲ誤認スル食饌ヲ佛前ニ供スルチ是事トシ破邪顯正ノ事業ニ跛ナル旨敎テラン此ルモ最モ恐ルベキ尤モ忌ムベキ彼ノ魔敎コンパチルレハ撲滅シテ發行者ノ因メテ發行シ得敎論ヲ甘心スルモノアレバ有益ナル可カラザル。シテ眞理是於テカ該書購求ノ便益者ハ一層價値チ低廉ニシ汎ク諸君ニ頒タントシ右ニ供ヘ破邪ノ鐵槌トナシ魔敎撲滅ノ効チ奏セシメンフチ發行者ノ切ニ望ム所ナリ

坐ニ

乙

○殺活自在弁　大僧都芦津實全師著　全壹冊　定價拾五錢　近刻

○日本宗教未來記　大僧都芦津實全師著　全壹冊　近刻　定價廿錢

○道理ノ問答　小原正雄著　全壹冊　定價拾四錢　郵稅四錢

○十善法語和解　目賀田護法居士編　前後　實價拾錢

○辨斥魔教論　陸軍中將從四位勳二等子爵鳥尾公序文　藤澤南岳先生序文　目賀田護法居士著　全貳冊　從來正價四拾五錢ノ處今般改正實價貳拾五錢　郵稅金拾四錢

●郵券代用ハ一割増之事

○船井弘文堂佛書發兌書目

○英文眞宗教旨　和文付　全壹冊　定價　金廿錢
　　　　　　　　　　　　　郵税金四錢　○郵券代用承諾
英國領事ゼームス、ツルーブ君著ニシテ眞宗ノ綱
英國梵學士　南條文雄師
日本本願寺司教　赤松連城師　同校
右ハ佛教ノ外護者タル英國領事ゼームス、ツルーブ君ノ著ニシテ眞宗ノ
要ヲ知ルノ捷徑ナリ且ツ和文ヲ附シ讀者ノ便ニ供ス

○印度東洋圖書館祈福圖　寫眞板壹葉　○郵税自弁
　　　　　　　　　　　　　　定價　金六拾錢
右ハ現今印度國ニ流布セル佛教●婆羅門教●韋紐派●大自在天派●拜火宗
等之首領及神智協會々長ヘンリ、エス、オルヂット氏、幷ニ印度大學士之肖像
ヲ鮮明ニ撮影シ紙幅長大尤モ閲覧ニ便ナリ苟モ社會ニ立チ宗教ニ志アルノ
士ハ參考トスベキ頁材ナリ

○梵英阿彌陀教　和文付　全壹冊　近刻
本庄堅宏師編纂

○佛教脩身讀本　全貳冊　近刻

三府大賣捌所

東京橋區三十間堀壹丁目
　明　教　社
同　麻布區北日ヶ窪
　鴻　盟　社
同　日本橋通三丁目
　丸　善　書　店
同　日本橋區久松町
　博　文　堂
同　東六條中珠敷屋町
　永　田　調　兵　衞
西京花屋町通西洞院
　西　村　七　郎　兵　衞
大坂備後町四丁目
　吉　岡　平　助
同　北久太郎町四丁目
　柳　原　喜　兵　衞
同　南久寶寺町四丁目
　前　川　善　兵　衞

明治二十一年五月五日印刷
同　　年五月七日出版

版權所有

定價金二十錢

著作者　神戸駐劄英國領事
　　　　ゼームス、ツループ

發行者　攝津國神戸區神戸元町通五丁目
　　　　廿三番邸
　　　　船井政太郎

印刷者　大阪府下北久太郎町貳丁目四十番地
　　　　大阪活版製造所
　　　　辻田榮助

或ハ適合セサルノ條項アルヲ免レス故ニ今玆ニ原文中ヨリ抜萃抄出シテ其要領ヲ記シヌ讀者幸ニ其意ヲ了セヨ